Understanding Practical Unix

RAYMOND GREENLAW

Armstrong Atlantic State University
Savannah, Georgia

Franklin, Beedle & Associates, Inc. • 8536 SW St. Helens Drive, Suite D • Wilsonville, OR 97070 • 503/682-7668

President and Publisher	Jim Leisy (jimleisy@fbeedle.com)
Manuscript Editor	Tom Sumner
Production	Tom Sumner
	Stephanie Welch
Proofreader	Stephanie Welch
Cover	Ian Shadburne
Marketing	Chris Collier
Order Processing	Lois Allison
	Krista Hall

Printed in the U.S.A.

Names of all products herein are used for identification purposes only and are trademarks and/or registered trademarks of their respective owners. Franklin, Beedle & Associates, Inc., makes no claim of ownership or corporate association with the products or companies that own them.

Rights and Permissions
Franklin, Beedle & Associates, Incorporated
8536 SW St. Helens Drive, Suite D
Wilsonville, Oregon 97070

Library of Congress Cataloging-in-Publication Data
Greenlaw, Raymond.
    Understanding Practical Unix / by Raymond Greenlaw.
       p. cm.
    Includes bibliographical references and index.
    ISBN 1-887902-53-8
      1. UNIX (Computer file) 2. Operating systems (Computers) I. Title.

QA 76.76.O63 G7294 2001
005.4'32--dc21

                                   2001023983

In loving memory of my father
Robert Wilson Greenlaw

Remembering Dad

A ripple in a pond on a clear summer day,
You often talked about the big one that got away.
A brisk walk on a path at 4mph,
You loved to visit us from Georgia to NH.
I'll see you in nature, in the mountains and streams,
You will be there in the glowing sunbeams.
Memories of a lifetime that me feel glad,
That I was fortunate to call a man like you Dad.
You are here with me, you are here in me.
I will think of you in whatever I do.
I will remember you Dad. I love you dearly.
I will remember and love you Dad! Most sincerely.

CONTENTS

PART TWO: COMMUNICATION

CHAPTER 21   HTML and Web Pages   323

CHAPTER 22   Internet File Transfers   339

PART EIGHT: PROGRAMMING

LIST OF TABLES

LIST OF FIGURES

PREFACE

Use of the Unix operating system and its derivatives has grown tremendously over the last few years. Unix always had a strong hold in academic circles and in companies doing certain types of development, for example, companies involved with data communications and networking. Now its domain is expanding to many other groups of users. Developers working on a wide range of problems currently use a Unix environment. Many recreational users are now running Linux on their personal computers. This book suits an introductory, 1–3-credit Unix course. It also can be used to supplement any programming course that uses a Unix development environment. This includes courses in disciplines other than computer science too. The only prerequisite is a machine running a version of Unix, and maybe some keyboarding experience.

In this introductory book we provide you with up-to-date information on the Unix operating system. Nearly all of the concepts we discuss in this book apply to all Unix-based systems. (The Linux operating system is a free version of Unix.) All Unix systems share the core commands. We focus on the most important Unix commands and the Unix culture of computing.

Our goal is to help you learn to be a proficient user of Unix in a relatively short period of time. This book covers all of the material that you will need to become a functional and efficient Unix user. It provides you with a foundation and pointers to other resources so you will be capable of becoming a Unix guru. The phrase "Unix guru" denotes a person who knows an enormous amount about Unix and is capable of answering almost any question about Unix.

We will assist you in learning about many aspects of Unix including the following:

❑ the most important Unix commands.
❑ fundamental concepts about the Unix operating system.
❑ the Unix culture.
❑ how to communicate online with other Unix users.
❑ electronic mail, including the pine mailer.
❑ Unix command syntax.
❑ the Unix file system.
❑ file and directory creation, manipulation, and management.
❑ setting file and directory permissions.
❑ a standard Unix shell.

- ❏ redirection, pipes, and filters.
- ❏ process and job control.
- ❏ text editing using the standard Unix editors pico, emacs, and vi.
- ❏ basic Unix applications.
- ❏ the Internet and the World Wide Web.
- ❏ the history of the Internet.
- ❏ HTML and installing Web pages on a Unix Web server.
- ❏ Internet file transfers.
- ❏ program development under Unix.
- ❏ the LaTeX document preparation system.

Who Should Read This Book?

Anyone with an interest in learning the Unix operating system or a derivative of it, such as Linux, will benefit from this book. In this book you will learn about fundamental concepts and the most important commands, rather than lots of specific details and less commonly used features of the operating system. Our goal is not to cover every single option for every single command but rather to focus on what every Unix user should know. This book is not intended to be a comprehensive reference manual for a proficient Unix user. It is an introductory book for a beginning Unix user.

More specifically, who should read this book? This book is a good starting point for

- ❏ anyone interested in learning the popular Unix operating system.
- ❏ a user who is familiar with DOS and wants to learn Unix.
- ❏ anyone interested in program development on a Unix operating system.
- ❏ a person who wants a straightforward approach to learning Unix fundamentals.

Organization of the Text

The material is organized for a one-semester college course. We present the subject matter in an order appropriate for an inexperienced computer user. Those with more experience may decide to skim over some of the early sections. The book contains exercises at the end of appropriate sections. The exercises are designed to help you practice what you have learned and in some cases to extend the material in the section. This text can also be used as a self-study guide for anyone with an interest in teaching themselves the Unix operating system. The only real prerequisite is that you have a computer running some version of a Unix operating system.

The book contains chapters dealing with the following topics:

❑ introduction to the Unix operating system.
❑ logging into a computer using Unix.
❑ the Unix online help facility.
❑ the top ten Unix commands.
❑ communicating online with other users.
❑ electronic mail.
❑ the **pine** mail program.
❑ Unix command syntax.
❑ other fundamental Unix commands.
❑ an overview of the Unix file system.
❑ file and directory permissions.
❑ file manipulation.
❑ managing directories.
❑ text editing.
❑ the **emacs** editor.
❑ the **vi** editor.
❑ the basics of the C-shell.
❑ redirection, pipes, and filters.
❑ process and job control.
❑ the history of the Internet.
❑ HTML and installing Web pages on a Unix-based Web server.
❑ Internet file transfers.
❑ program development using Unix.

We provide several appendices that consolidate important sets of information for easy reference. There is a Unix command summary, a mapping from Unix to DOS commands, a mapping from DOS to Unix commands, a summary of **pico** commands, a summary of **pine** commands, a summary of **emacs** commands, a summary of **vi** commands, and an introduction to the LATEX document preparation system. In addition, we provide a list of references, a glossary, a list of all the acronyms used in the book, and a comprehensive index.

Accompanying Web Presentation

We have developed a Web presentation that accompanies the book. It includes several helpful elements. The online presentations can be accessed through Franklin, Beedle & Associates' Web site, **www.fbeedle.com**, or by visiting Ray Greenlaw's Web page at **www.cs.armstrong.edu/greenlaw**.

About the Author

Dr. Raymond Greenlaw grew up in Rhode Island. He received a BA in Mathematics from Pomona College in 1983, an MS in Computer Science in 1986 from the University of Washington, and a PhD in Computer Science in 1988 from the University of Washington. Ray has won a number of international awards including two Senior Fulbright Scholarship Research Awards, a Humboldt Fellowship, a Spanish Fellowship for Scientific and Technical Investigations, and a Japan Society for the Promotion of Science Invitation Fellowship. Ray has written 10 books and three invited book chapters in the areas of complexity theory, graph theory, the Internet, parallel computation, theoretical computer science, and the World Wide Web. His books are used in over 75 computer science programs in the United States as well as internationally and have been translated into other languages. Ray's numerous technical papers have appeared in over 30 different journals and conference proceedings. He has received research funding from 10 different agencies and groups, including the National Science Foundation. His research has been supported by the governments of Germany, Hong Kong, Iceland, Italy, Japan, and Spain as well as the United States.

Ray has been using the Unix operating system for almost 20 years.

Ray is Head of the Department of Computer Science at Armstrong Atlantic State University and Regional Coordinator of the State of Georgia's Yamacraw Project. He resides in Savannah, Georgia, with his wife Laurel.

Suggestions and Corrections

The text may still contain some errors and may have omitted certain topics that readers feel are especially relevant for inclusion. In anticipation of possible future printings, we would like to correct any mistakes and incorporate as many suggestions as possible. Please send comments via email to **greenlaw@armstrong.edu**.

Acknowledgments

A warm thanks to my colleague and friend Ellen Hepp of the University of New Hampshire for many discussions about Unix, email, ftp, the Internet, and the World Wide Web. She greatly influenced the direction of this book and made a number of significant contributions to it.

A special thanks to Laurel for her support, and for a careful and timely reading of this technical book. Her comments helped to improve this work.

Thanks to Killface the cat, who sat on my lap while I wrote this book. Her refusal to get up greatly accelerated this project. Her companionship will be sorely missed on future writing projects.

Thanks to Greg Geller at Armstrong Atlantic State University for his comments, suggestions, and insights on the first draft of this work.

Thanks to Steve Jodis at Armstrong Atlantic State University for his careful reading of a number of chapters of this book. His suggestions helped to improve it.

Thanks to my collegues in the Department of Computer Science and the Department of Mathematics at Armstrong Atlantic State University. Thanks to Mirna Morrison for her support during this project.

Thanks to the book's reviewers for valuable suggestions. We appreciate your interest in this book.

Thanks to Jim Leisy at Franklin, Beedle & Associates, Inc., for working with me on this project, for suggesting this book, and for his strong support during all phases of the project. Also to Tom Sumner, Stephanie Welch, Ian Shadburne, Sue Page, Chris Collier, Lois Allison, and Krista Brown for their good work. It has been fun working with you.

—Raymond Greenlaw
Department of Computer Science
Armstrong Atlantic State University
11935 Abercorn Street
Savannah, Georgia 31419-1997
email address: **greenlaw@armstrong.edu**
web page: **www.cs.armstrong.edu/greenlaw**

INTRODUCTION—
UNIX BASICS

chapter 1

INTRODUCTION

The goal of this book is to teach you how to use the Unix[1] operating system. We often refer to "the Unix operating system" simply as Unix. We describe concepts from the point of view of a beginning user who wants to learn the basics of Unix. The only prerequisite for this book is that you have access to a computer that is running some form of the Unix operating system; this will allow you to try out the commands and features of Unix we describe.

In this chapter we will

❑ provide some background about operating systems.
❑ overview the history of Unix.
❑ discuss the various forms of the Unix operating system.
❑ explain the conventions we use.
❑ outline the book's contents.

1.1 Operating Systems Overview

An *operating system* is a complex computer program that serves as an interface between a computer's hardware and a computer user. A schematic diagram of this is shown in Figure 1.1. You can think of an operating system as managing the resources of your computer. The goal of an operating system developer is to create a computing environment that

❑ is convenient for you to use.
❑ makes efficient use of your computing hardware.

---

1. Sometimes you will see Unix written in all capitals as UNIX, perhaps because its original name was an acronym (see page 6). We prefer to write it as Unix in this book since it appears frequently on each page and the capital letters become a little too dominant. Unix is pronounced "u nicks."

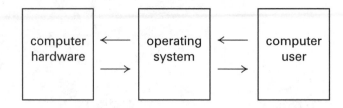

Figure 1.1—Simplified View of an Operating System

Several of the most popular operating systems are Unix, Mac OS, and Windows. Typically, there are many versions of each operating system, since they are often improved and bug fixes are incorporated. In Section 1.3 we will discuss several variants of the Unix operating system. You have probably heard of some of the different versions of Windows such as Windows 95, Windows 98, Windows 2000, and Windows NT. The Windows systems were all developed by one company, Microsoft. Many different companies and groups have developed Unix-like operating systems, and because all of the various efforts have gone in somewhat different directions, Unix is considerably more complicated.

When you enter commands into your computer, the operating system interprets those commands and takes care of executing them for you. For example, when you type a password into your computer to log in initially, the operating system takes care of the details of verifying that the password goes with the account name you entered. If the password is not correct, you will not be permitted access to the account. If you decide to send a file to the printer, the operating system schedules your print job in the print queue and sends the file you specified to the printer. The operating system is very important for interpreting the commands you enter and providing your computing environment.

Computer systems can be single-user or multiuser systems. On a single-user system you will not be competing for resources with other users. For example, on a single-user system such as a personal computer (PC) running Windows 98, the processor of the computer will be dedicated entirely to your work. You will not have to share the processor's computing power with other users.

Many Unix systems are *time-sharing* systems. The idea behind such a system is the same as for time-shared condos. With a time-shared condo, for example, each owner is allowed to use the condo for one week per year. Thus, the cost to each owner is reduced—no one has to pay the full cost of the condo; only about $1/52$ and some fees. A time-shared computer works the same way. A group of users can share the resources of an expensive computer. Rather than sharing on the time scale of a week, a powerful computer will share its processor on the order of tiny fractions of a second. Your requests will appear to be serviced continuously although other user requests will be interleaved as well. That is, each user will get a tiny fraction of processing time then wait a tiny fraction of time while other users are being processed, then get a tiny fraction of processing time, then wait, and so on until the user's job is finished.

If the processor is fast enough, a user may not even realize the system is being shared with others. In contrast, on a heavily loaded system you may begin to wonder why your requests are being serviced so slowly. On a time-sharing system, the operating system takes care of scheduling and handling different user's requests. The details of how an operating system does this are very interesting but somewhat complex. The interested reader can learn more about these details by pursuing the references at the end of this book.

In a time-sharing system the users are referred to as *clients* and the computer that provides the users with resources and meets their requests is called the *server*. The whole arrangement is called the *client-server model*. Figure 1.2 depicts a schematic diagram of the general situation, where many clients' requests are met by the same server. It is helpful to think of clients as customers at a restaurant and the server as a wait-person. One wait-person can take the food orders from several tables of customers; the wait-person "time shares" by visiting each table in turn. The customers place their orders and when the food has been prepared by the cook, the wait-person serves it to the appropriate customer. As with a crowded restaurant, the service degrades on a heavily loaded computer.

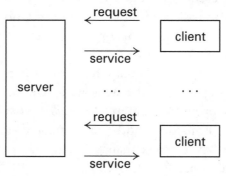

Figure 1.2—Client-Server Model

The client-server model has many applications in computer science, particularly in the area of computer networking.

In summary, think of an operating system as a user interface, the interface between you and the computer, that is designed for convenience and also designed to take advantage of the underlying computer hardware. Therefore, an operating system provides you with commands

❑ to carry out the computing functions you would like.

❑ that execute efficiently.

❑ that are easy to use.

The Unix operating system meets the first two conditions very well. However, it is not as easy to use and learn as some operating systems. Unix is well worth learning because it provides an excellent development environment, has a strong tradition, and is widely used. A vast majority of users who learn to use Unix prefer it to all other operating systems. Our goal in this book is to help you learn to use the system well.

1.2   History of Unix

Unix was developed in 1969 by Ken Thompson, Dennis Ritchie, and several others at Bell Laboratories (known as Bell Labs), a division of American Telephone and Telegraph (AT&T). Brian Kernighan suggested the original name of "Unics," standing for *UNiplexed Information and Computing System*, a pun on Multics, one of the large operating systems being developed during this time. Later the name of the system was changed to Unix.

The history of Unix is complicated because the operating system evolved in many different locations and directions. We present an overview of Unix history here. The references included at the back of the book contain a great deal of additional information about the history of Unix. A query to any Internet search engine of the form "Unix history" will turn up many interesting Web presentations about Unix.

We begin with some computer terminology. An *algorithm* is a well-defined sequence of steps. When the steps are followed, the algorithm typically will solve some specific problem of interest. A *high-level programming language* is one that is algorithmic in nature, can be implemented on a variety of different computer systems, and has a syntax that is intuitive and mathematical. Examples of such languages are Ada, APL, BASIC, C, C++, FORTRAN, Java, Lisp, and Pascal. An *assembly language* is one whose instructions are specific to a given type of computer hardware and are difficult for non-expert programmers to understand. Fortunately, most programming is done using high-level languages.

We say a computer system or program is *portable* if it can be implemented on a range of computers. A computer system or program is *user portable* if a computer user can move easily from one computer installation to a different one running the same system and have little or no trouble adjusting to the new system.

Clearly, it is desirable to design operating systems that are both portable and user portable.

The original version of Unix was written at Bell Labs in assembly language, as were all early versions of Unix. Assembly language made operating systems larger, more difficult for a programmer to work on, and nonportable. In 1973 the Unix operating system was almost entirely rewritten in the C programming language. A small portion of assembly-language code remained. The inner core of the Unix operating system code is referred to as the Unix *kernel*. In most of today's variants of Unix the kernel is written in C.

In the mid 1970s Unix was distributed outside of AT&T for the first time. The C *source code* for Unix was made available at little cost to several universities. Source code refers to the high-level programming language code, as opposed to the *executable code*. The executable code is the code that a computer actually runs; it is expressed in a low-level language (binary) that is very difficult for people to understand. AT&T continued its development on Unix, and the computer scientists at the University of California at Berkeley (UCB) did a lot of independent development on the system.

In the 1980s Berkeley released several versions of the Unix operating system. Their releases are known as BSD Unix, where BSD is an acronym for Berkeley Software Distribution. BSD Unix included facilities for remote login (covered in Chapter 8), file transfer (covered in Chapter 22), TCP/IP (the protocols that hold the Internet together), and many other important pieces of software. AT&T's version of Unix became known as the System V release. BSD Unix and System V were the two most popular versions of Unix until the late 1990s.

In 1984 Richard Stallman, working at the Massachusetts Institute of Technology (MIT), began developing a free version of Unix that he called GNU, standing for "GNU's not Unix." By the early 1990s Stallman's project had completed much of the development of this Unix system except for the kernel.

In the early 1990s Linus Torvalds, a student at the University of Helsinki in Finland, programmed a small Unix kernel from scratch. This Unix kernel and the GNU system were combined to create the variant of Unix that is now popularly called Linux (pronunciation varies, including "Lynn nicks" and "Lie nicks"). The Linux system was completely free of charge as it involved only newly developed code by noncommercial programmers. A number of different versions of the Linux system have been developed and some are commercially supported. The most popular one as of this writing is known as Red Hat Linux. Among other things, what is attractive about Linux is that it is free, it is a small operating system in terms of storage requirements, and it provides an excellent development environment. Linux works well on personal computers and is portable.

In summary, Unix was developed by Bell Labs at AT&T in the late 1960s. In the mid 1970s the C source code was sold at very little cost to several universities. The University of California at Berkeley developed and released BSD Unix, which became extremely popular in academic and research settings. In parallel, AT&T continued its development of Unix and their system became known as System V Unix. From these two versions of Unix many other variants evolved in the 1980s, as discussed in the next section. In the early 1990s the Unix kernel developed by Linus Torvalds and the GNU system started and developed by Richard Stallman were combined to create a compact and free version of Unix known as Linux. Linux gained enormous popularity in the late 1990s and was commercially supported.

1.3 Unix Derivatives

As described in Section 1.2, Unix was developed at Bell Labs. AT&T sold the C source code for Unix at little cost, and this made it possible for other groups to modify the operating system and improve it. Until recently, there were two dominant Unix versions:

❑ System V Unix.
❑ BSD Unix.

Now Linux, the version of Unix developed independently from System V Unix and BSD Unix by combining the works of Stallman and Torvalds, appears to be the most popular version of Unix.

In the evolutionary tree of Unix there have been many other mutations and derivatives. Fortunately, all versions of Unix have a core set of commands. These are the commands that we will focus on in this book. Thus, the knowledge you gain from reading this book will be portable to most Unix systems.

Some other versions of Unix that you might encounter are as follows: Chorus, SCO Unix, XENIX, Solaris, SUN OS, Free BSD, and Net BSD. Of course, there are a multitude of others as well.

Each version of Unix consists of essentially the same three parts:

❑ the Unix kernel.
❑ a hierarchical file system.
❑ a collection of programs, most of which implement the Unix commands.

The *shell* is the most important program that comes with Unix. The shell is an interactive program that executes your commands as you enter them. The shell also has its own interpreted programming language as described in Chapter 17. There are many different shells in use, and Table 1.1 provides a list of some of the more popular shells.

Shell Name	Program Name	Brief Description
Bourne shell	**sh**	original Unix shell developed by Steven Bourne at Bell Labs
Bash	**bash**	extended version of the Bourne shell developed as part of the GNU project; Bash stands for "*Bourne again sh*ell"
C-shell	**csh**	shell developed by William Joy for BSD Unix
Korn shell	**ksh**	extended version of the Bourne shell developed by David Korn
Tcsh	**tcsh**	extended version of the C-shell developed by Ken Greer and others

Table 1.1—Popular Unix Shells

The two most popular shells are the *C-shell* and the *Bourne shell*. The default *prompt* (defined in Section 1.4) used by the C-shell is the **%** symbol, whereas the default prompt used by the Bourne shell is the **$** sign. The word *default* refers to the initial value of a computer setting before it has been changed, that is, the preset value. This is the value that the developers expect most users will want to use. If you are using a Unix shell that responds with **%**, you know you are using the C-shell. Similarly, if your system responds with **$**, you know you are using the Bourne shell. Fortunately, all of the shells have a common set of commands and a similar theme. In this book we will focus on the C-shell (covered in Chapter 17). Once you learn to use the C-shell, your knowledge will transfer over to the other shells easily.

1.4 Conventions in This Book

1.4.1 Linux Versus Unix

In this book we refer to any hybrid of the Unix operating system as Unix unless we are distinguishing between features of two separate Unix systems. In general, all of the basic Unix commands work on all Unix systems. On your system, you may find a few differences between the commands we describe in this book and those available on your computer. This is to be expected and should not trouble you.

1.4.2 Technical Words and Commands

We place technical words in italics on their first usage, and in most cases define them immediately following. In some cases it is more appropriate to define the technical phrase later in the book. All technical words used in the text are indexed so the curious reader may decide to look up the definition immediately in such cases. Most technical words are also included in the glossary.

We write Unix commands using the following style:

```
%command
```

where "command" denotes a Unix command. At the beginning of each chapter, we provide a table that lists the Unix commands covered in the chapter. In the table we also provide a brief intuitive description of the command and, where appropriate, give the equivalent Disk Operating System (DOS) command. Some commands may be listed in more than one chapter, as it may be appropriate to discuss various aspects of a command at different parts in the text. The book contains appendices mapping from Unix to DOS commands and vice versa, as well as an appendix listing all Unix commands covered in the book.

We also distinguish special words that are input to the computer or have a special computer meaning by putting them in boldface. For example, a computer password would be written in boldface.

1.4.3 Unix Prompt

We use the % symbol to represent the Unix prompt. A prompt is the symbol a computer displays to a user to indicate the computer is ready for input. The > sign is also commonly used as a prompt and the $ sign is used by the Bourne shell as its prompt. In general, a user can define any symbol or sequence of symbols to be the prompt. For example, a user who wants the computer to act as its servant might define the machine's prompt to be

```
yes%
```

In this case the prompt consists of four characters. A user named Ellen might define her prompt to be

```
next command Ellen>
```

Some users have the prompt specify the *current working directory* that is in use; that is, the work area currently being used. Other users set the prompt to be the name of the machine being worked on. For example, on the machine named cervino, the prompt might be set to

```
cervino%
```

In Chapter 17 we will explain how to set the value of the prompt.

1.4.4 Graphical User Interfaces

Unix commands are often two-character sequences such as **cd**, **ls**, and **rm**. To some people these commands are elegant because they are concise; to others the process of typing in short command sequences to the Unix prompt (this line is called the *command line*) is something far less than elegant—it can be frustrating and nonintuitive. In fact, to some, the greatest weaknesses of the Unix operating system is its user interface. The original interfaces were all keyboard driven. The advantage is that once you learn to use such an interface, you can work very efficiently (if you are a touch-key typist) because you never have to take your hands off the keyboard to use the mouse. Learning how to do things from the command line will help you gain a deeper understanding of the Unix system. The disadvantage of the command line interface is that the system is nonintuitive and is designed more for programmers than nontechnical users.

Over the years, a large number of *graphical user interfaces* (GUIs, pronounced "gooeys") have been developed for Unix. A graphical user interface is a mouse-driven and graphically-oriented computer interface. This is in contrast to a keyboard-driven interface. In this book we focus on the standard keyboard interface to Unix. Such an interface through the shell is available on all Unix systems. Ultimately, you may decide that you want to use Unix through a GUI, however. Most of the GUIs are intuitive and easy-to-learn windowing systems.

For completeness we mention a few of the GUIs that have been developed for Unix: Common Desktop Environment (CDE), Motif, Open Windows, X Window System, and Unix Desktop Environment (UDE). Keep in mind there are many other GUIs as well. To find out more about these and other GUIs, you can enter a query of "Unix GUIs" to your favorite Internet search engine.

1.4.5 Unix's Influence

Unix has been and continues to be one of the most important computer operating systems. It has had a tremendous influence on computing. A number of operating systems have incorporated Unix-like features and commands into them. For example, DOS has incorporated many Unix-like commands and sometimes even uses the same specification for the commands. In this book we provide tables showing DOS commands that are equivalent to the Unix commands we describe. On the other side of the coin, various operating systems have had an impact on Unix. If you use Unix with a GUI, you will find it has a flavor similar to other graphical-based operating systems.

1.4.6 Exercises

At the end of many sections of the book, we include exercises. The exercises will teach you additional features of Unix and also provide you with an opportunity to try out the concepts you have learned. It is a good idea to be logged on to the computer while reading this book.

1.4.7 Friendly Advice

You probably have already been warned that Unix is a difficult operating system to learn. As you work your way through this book, it would be helpful if you had a local *Unix guru* who could answer your very specialized questions or who could help you out if you ran into trouble online. As we noted in the preface, the phrase "Unix guru" is accepted terminology for a person who knows an enormous amount about Unix and is capable of answering almost any question about Unix.

There are worldwide newsgroups dealing with Unix issues as well as lots of online help facilities for learning more about Unix. You will be able to find information about these resources by querying your favorite search engine.

We should point out that *before* asking someone for help on a Unix system it is expected (as part of the Unix culture) that you will have read all available documentation pertaining to your question. We cover the **man** command in Chapter 3 for accessing the online documentation.

A word of caution is in order. We cover a large number of important Unix commands in this book. With all the different variants of Unix, it is possible that your particular system does not have all the commands discussed here. In some cases your system may have a similar command, perhaps with a different name. In other cases the person in charge of your system may be able to install the command for you or tell you the equivalent command on your system.

1.5 Overview of Contents

This book contains chapters dealing with the following topics:
- ❑ introduction to the Unix operating system.
- ❑ logging into a computer using Unix.
- ❑ the Unix online help facility.
- ❑ the top ten Unix commands.
- ❑ communicating online with other users.
- ❑ electronic mail.
- ❑ the **pine** mail program.

- ❑ Unix command syntax.
- ❑ other fundamental Unix commands.
- ❑ file structure and directories.
- ❑ overview of the Unix file system.
- ❑ file and directory protections.
- ❑ the Unix directory system.
- ❑ file manipulation.
- ❑ managing directories.
- ❑ text editing.
- ❑ the **emacs** editor.
- ❑ the **vi** editor.
- ❑ Unix shells, pipes, and jobs.
- ❑ basics of the C-shell.
- ❑ redirection and pipes.
- ❑ process and job control.
- ❑ history of the Internet.
- ❑ HTML and installing Web pages on a Unix-based Web server.
- ❑ Internet file transfers.
- ❑ program development using Unix.

The book is intended to be read sequentially; however, experienced users may skip over sections or chapters they are familiar with. Many of the chapters can be read independently; for example, the chapters on editing, the **emacs** editor, the **vi** editor, the Unix shell, installing Web pages on a Unix-based Web server, important application programs, and the LaTeX document preparation system.

We also provide several appendices that group together important sets of information for easy reference. There is a Unix command summary, a mapping from DOS to Unix commands, a mapping from Unix to DOS commands, a summary of **pine** commands, a summary of **emacs** commands, a summary of **vi** commands, and an introduction to the LaTeX document preparation system. In addition, we provide a list of references, a glossary, a list of all the acronyms used in the book, and a comprehensive index.

LOGGING IN TO THE COMPUTER

chapter 2

In this chapter we discuss the following commands:

Unix Command	DOS Command	Description
exit	EXIT	close your current session on your computer account
fg	—	activate the most recently stopped job
last	—	display a record of the logins and logouts to a computer or a computer account
lock	—	temporarily suspend your terminal
login	LOGIN	start work on your computer account
logout	EXIT	close your current session on your computer account
more	MORE	display a file one screenful at a time
passwd	—	change the password of your computer account
telnet	—	log in to a remote computer

2.1 Introduction

Since Unix is a time-sharing operating system, many users can have computer accounts on the same machine. It is important that the users and the computer be able to keep track of the accounts and keep them separate. The Unix operating system manages computer accounts using *userids* and *passwords*. A userid, which is short for "user identification," is simply an account name on a Unix system. A password is the key that is used to gain access to an account.

Before starting to use Unix, you need to have an account set up on a computer that you have access to. If you are a student, the Computer and Information Services (CIS) Department at your school will likely set up an account for you. If you are working at a company, the *system administrator* will set up an account for you. A system administrator is a person who manages and takes care of a computer system, including its operating system. For example, this person sets up new accounts, deletes expired accounts, installs bug fixes, monitors the system, and so on. Once your account is in place, the person who set up the account will give you your userid and password. You are now ready to log in to the system.

Before discussing how to log in to the computer, it is worth delving further into the important concepts of userids and passwords.

2.2 Account Names

On some systems a userid is referred to as a *user name* or simply an *account name*. Your userid identifies you to the computer.

In many settings you will have a choice in selecting your userid. In such cases it is a good idea to choose a userid that in some way identifies you or is linked to you. There are a number of reasons for doing this—one is that your email address (email is discussed in Chapter 6) begins with your userid. In selecting a userid that is somehow related to your name, your friends and others who send you email will find it easier to remember your email address.

One convention adopted by many people for choosing a userid is to use their last name as their userid. For example, Howard Jones might have a userid of **jones** or perhaps **hjones**. If there already were two users on the system using these names (say Mary Jones and Harvey Jones, respectively), another userid such as **howardjones** might be chosen. Notice that userids are always written in lowercase letters. Unix is a case-sensitive operating system, so you *cannot* use lower- and uppercase letters interchangeably. For example, all Unix commands should be entered in lowercase letters.

Suppose your system has five Steve Smiths on it. Their userids might be **smith**, **smith1**, **stevesmith**, **ssmith**, and **smith2**. It will be difficult for users to always direct email to the correct Steve. In such a case one of the Steves might decide to use his widely known nickname, such as **stevie**, as a userid.

On some systems you will not have any say in choosing your userid. For example, your userid may be generated randomly by a computer program. In this case your userid has no mnemonic meaning and is not linked to you. This makes it difficult for other people to remember your email address. For example, suppose Sally Tomas's userid were computer-generated as **bbb2baabb3a**. It would be very difficult to remember her email address. If you have a choice in selecting your userid, pick a descriptive name but one that is also easy to type. Table 2.1 depicts some good and poor choices[1] of userids for a couple of different names. It is a very good idea to avoid using dashes (-) and underscores (_) in userids. A lowercase "l" (ell) is also known to look just like a "1" (one) in some fonts. These two symbols should never be used in combination. On some computer monitors it is almost impossible to distinguish them. Thus, dash and underscore confuse many users. Be careful transcribing email addresses or Web page addresses that contain these symbols.

Person's Name	Userid	Classification
Stacy Lewis	slewis	good
	stacy	good
	lewis	good
	bob	poor
	s_l-stay	poor
	coolwoman	poor
Celeste Noble	celeste	good
	buffy	poor
	c	okay
	godnoble	good and funny
Dino Flintstone	dino	good
	dflintstone	good
	dinof	good
	d49.12	poor
	fred	poor
	wilma	poor

Table 2.1—Userid Selection

Internet service providers (ISPs) sometimes assign their customers the "next available" letter or number combination as a userid. The userid is not associated with the actual user's name. For example, suppose Felix Hughes signed up for an account with his ISP and was assigned a userid of **gtyusil23**. Further, suppose

1. Good and poor as used here are relative to identifying the user based on the name alone.

you were the very next person to sign up with the same ISP. In this case you might be assigned a userid of **gtyusil24**. It may happen that you often receive Felix's email (and vice-versa) since it would be easy for someone to type your userid instead of his.

Exercises

1. Give five sensible userids for a user named Robert Wiley Melon.
2. What is your userid? Were you able to select it? If so, why did you choose this userid? If not, what userid would you have chosen and why?
3. What are the shortest and longest lengths of userids your Unix system allows? (If you are unable to determine this at present, hazard guesses and explain why your answers make intuitive sense.)

2.3   Protecting Your Account—Passwords

Your password is a secret key that unlocks your account by authenticating you to the computer. This is done simply to prevent unauthorized access to your account. If you have an ATM (automatic teller machine) card for a bank machine, you are familiar with this process. Think of your ATM card as your userid. Once you place the card in an ATM, it prompts you to enter your PIN (personal identification number). Your PIN is like your computer password. Without the PIN you cannot access your bank account; similarly, without your password you cannot access your computer account.

When the computer specialist at your installation gives you your initial password, it will likely be randomly generated and hard to remember. For example, it may be **7\#@bnp-43iekd=88**. You will probably want to change this to something that is easier for you to remember. However, you should not change it to something that will compromise the security of your account. We consider password selection below and explain how to change your password online.

On most computer systems, your password will have to meet several criteria in order to be allowed. Passwords not conforming to such restrictions would be a security risk. For example, if your password is a word in the dictionary, a programmer might be able to write a program that tries to break into your account by simply testing every word in the dictionary as a password. Since dictionaries are easily accessible online, this is not a difficult task for some programmers. (*Note:* On some systems, a user who types in an incorrect password to an account three times in a row is "locked out" of the account.)

A good password should meet the following requirements:

❑ be at least six characters long.

❑ have at least one nonalphabetical symbol such as %, $, &, and so on.

❑ contain at least one digit.

❑ possess a mixture of lower- and uppercase letters.

Case is significant in passwords, just as it is in Unix operating system commands. Some examples of hard-to-crack passwords are **DyDy12-dyza**, **44444**Ff!**, and **MoUSeKE!te43**. It is very unlikely someone would be able to guess your password if you chose one of these. However, these passwords are difficult to remember. In fact, they are so difficult to remember that if you chose one of them, you would probably have to write it down. It would be easy for someone to find a post-it attached to the front of your computer or placed on your desk with this password on it. Such a person could then access your account. Thus, it is a good idea to choose a password that you do not need to write down and which you can accurately type. Some examples of good passwords would be strings such as **8787@FF!**, **abcABC67***, and **igo10LAPS**. These are passwords unlikely to be guessed but easy to remember.

One school of thought in password selection is if you are logging into a multiuser system, pick fairly easy-to-remember passwords and change them regularly. In fact, some Unix systems are set up so that you must change your password every month. If you try to change your password to its previous value, the system will complain since it stores a copy of your old password. How much history is stored depends on the system and system administrator.

Another alternative in password selection is to set a good password and stick with it. This way you do not have to write the password down. If you have multiple computer accounts, ATM PINs, credit card PINs, and so on to remember *and* you have to change the passwords on the computer accounts every month, you will probably find that it is necessary to write the passwords down. Of course, this defeats the purpose of changing the passwords frequently since security is likely to be compromised if you have to write the passwords down.

You should change your password immediately if you think someone has discovered it.

Exercises

1. Which of the following passwords meet the criteria outlined above: **4the**, **&&&&&&**, **blondie**, **5starFilm**, **Micemouse**, **T5n5T**, and **ThisDoes**? Explain your answers.

2. If **tommie** were a legal password, would it be a good choice for Thomas Bartson? Explain your answer.

2.4   Logging In and Out of a Computer

Suppose that you have obtained your computer account and now have a userid and an initial password. You are ready to log in to Unix. When you sit down at a Unix terminal, you will see a login message that looks similar to the one depicted in Figure 2.1. It is a good idea to read the login message, as it often contains important information. In this case there is some information about acceptable uses of the system and monitoring of the system.

```
        Armstrong Atlantic State University, Savannah, GA
             Computer and Information Services
               Academic Computing Resource
     THIS SYSTEM IS FOR THE USE OF AUTHORIZED USERS ONLY.


Individuals using this computer system without authority,
or in excess of their authority, are subject to having all
of their activities on this system monitored and recorded
by system personnel.

In the course of monitoring individuals improperly using
this system, or in the course of system maintenance, the
activities of authorized users may also be monitored.

Anyone using this system expressly consents to such moni-
toring and is advised that if such monitoring reveals pos-
sible evidence of criminal activity, system personnel may
provide the evidence of such monitoring to law enforcement
officials.

login:
```

Figure 2.1—Typical Login Screen

At the **login:** prompt you can type in your userid. Suppose your userid is **laurel**. After you type your userid, press the **Return** or **Enter** key. This is the key that tells the computer you are ready to have the information you just typed processed. From now on we will refer to this key on your keyboard as the **Enter** key. Your screen will appear as follows:

```
login: laurel
Password:
```

Notice the computer responded by displaying **Password:**.

You can now type your password in. The password is not *echoed* on the screen. In Unix the word "echo" is a synonym for "display." If text is echoed on the screen, this means it appears on the screen. If something is not echoed, this means it is not displayed. In fact, on many Unix systems you will not see anything new displayed on the screen while you type your password in. This is in contrast with DOS, where you will see a * displayed for each character you type. Once you have typed in your password, press the **Enter** key. If you type in the password corresponding to the userid correctly, you will get a welcome message such as

```
Last login: Fri Jan 14 05:12:57 from hop.ims.u-tokyo.
Sun Microsystems Inc.     SunOS 5.6     Generic August 1997
You have mail.
%
```

If this is your first login, you will not have a "last login" message. Notice the system responds by telling you what type of Unix is running. In this case there is also an indication about email. Finally, the system displays **%**. This prompt indicates the C-shell is running.

If you type in your password incorrectly and press **Enter**, you will see a message like

```
Login incorrect
```

You may get another system message, and this will be followed by the **login:** prompt again. On most Unix systems you get three tries to log in correctly. If you fail on the third time, the system will lock you out. This is analogous to trying three different PINs at an ATM, after which time the machine keeps your card. To use your ATM card again you need to speak with a bank teller; similarly, to log into your Unix account again you may need to speak with the system administrator.

Some beginning users, in a rush to type in their password, type it in prematurely in response to **login:**. Anything typed into the **login:** command *is* echoed on the screen. If this happens to you and someone is looking over your shoulder, it is probably a good idea to change your password.

Go ahead and try to log in now. Once you log in, one of the first things you will want to do is change your password. The reasons for this are twofold:

❑ initial passwords are usually transmitted by the system administrator in writing (having a password written down compromises security).

❑ initial passwords are typically computer-generated and hard to remember (this means you cannot destroy the written record of the password).

We explain how to change your password in the next section. Before jumping ahead to this, though, we need to explain how to log out. That is, how to end your Unix session.

The easiest way to log out is simply to use the logout command

```
%logout
```

After pressing **Enter**, you will normally be logged off the system as shown below.

```
%logout
Connection closed

login:
```

Notice a new **login:** prompt appears. You may see a message that is different than **Connection closed**. For example, you may see something like **Logged off**. In any case, if the **login:** prompt appears, you can be sure you logged out.

On some systems, you may need to use the **exit** command. This is used similarly to the **logout** command.

There are occasions in which after typing **logout** and pressing **Enter** you will not be logged off the system. For example, you may get a message such as

```
There are stopped jobs.
```

As an aside, we include a brief note here in case you find yourself in this situation. By using the **fg** command (**fg** stands for foreground) you can activate jobs and then stop them. After doing this, you will be able to log out as usual. We discuss job control in detail in Chapter 19.

Remember, it is a good idea to log off the system if you are going to leave your terminal unattended. This frees up the terminal for another user to log into and prevents people from playing any practical jokes using your account.

Exercises

1. Why can't another person watching your computer screen simply write down your password as you type it?
2. Does the welcome message on your Unix system display any important information? If so, summarize it.
3. Log in to your account. What version of Unix is running on your system? Is there email waiting for you? If there is, who could have sent you the email already?

4. Go to the **login:** prompt. Enter your userid. Type in a bogus password and press **Enter**. Did you get a different message than the original welcome message? If so, summarize it.

5. Press the **Enter** key a few times after you have logged in. What happens? Type in the command **man login**. Summarize your findings.

2.5   Changing Your Password

In Section 2.4 we mentioned several occasions on which you would want to change your password. For example, after obtaining your initial password, if you feel the security of your password has been compromised, or after your password becomes several months old. Suppose you decide to change your password. Using the selection criteria discussed in Section 2.3, select an appropriate password, then log in to your account. For this discussion we suppose the account you logged into was **maples**. Once at the Unix prompt, type the command

```
%passwd
```

Many Unix commands are two-letter abbreviations. In this case only two letters are removed from the word "password." After typing **passwd**, press **Enter**. Your screen will look like this once the computer responds:

```
%passwd
passwd: Changing login passwd for maples
Enter login password:
```

At this point you need to type in your old (unchanged) password; that is, the one you logged in with. The password will not be echoed on the screen. This is a security measure. If Unix did not ask you for your old password, then a malicious user could change your password "for you" if you left your terminal logged in while heading off to the bathroom. Mysteriously, the next time you tried to log in, your password would fail.

The **lock** command may come in handy if you want to leave your terminal logged in while you step away from it for a moment. This command "freezes" your account until any key is pressed. At this point your password needs to be entered before the terminal can be used. (Some Unix GUIs provide a similar screen-locking mechanism with fancy screensavers.)

After you have entered your old password, Unix will prompt you with

```
New password:
```

To this you type in the new password you have decided on. What you type will not be echoed on the screen. Unix will then ask you to confirm your selection by typing it in again. You will see

```
Re-enter new password:
```

If what you respond with matches your choice for your new password, then your password on the system will be changed. If you are unsuccessful, simply walk through these three steps again very carefully. If you mistype something, you will see a message such as

```
They don't match; try again.
```

Combining all steps with correct entries, your display will look like the following:

```
%passwd
passwd:  Changing login passwd for maples
Enter login password:
New password:
Re-enter new password:
NIS+ password information changed for maples
%
```

Note: You may see a different response from the system, such as

```
Password successfully changed for maples
```

One problem many novices make is that they type in their new password too soon. Remember, first you need to authenticate yourself to the machine by typing in your old password.

It is worth noting that some systems only allow you to change your password every two weeks. If this is the case, you may see a message like

```
(SYSTEM): Sorry: less than 14 days since the last change.
Permission denied
```

if you try to change it more frequently. If the security of your account has been compromised, you will need to speak with the system administrator.

Unix provides a command that is helpful in monitoring accesses to your account. The Unix **last** command displays a record of logins and logouts to a machine or an account. For example, the command

```
%last
```

displays a record of all logins and logouts to the system in reverse chronological order, that is, the most recent entries will be shown first. The command

```
%last phillips
```

displays a record of all the logins and logouts by userid **phillips**. The information about logins and logouts is stored in a special file by the Unix system. The file may contain lots of information, perhaps more than will fit on your screen. In this case if you type in the command

```
%last phillips
```

the information may scroll by too quickly for you to see. The Unix paging program **more** (discussed in additional detail in Chapter 4) can be used to keep the information from scrolling by too quickly for you to see. The **more** command displays the contents of a file one screenful at a time. Thus, if there is more than one screenful of information, you can view it at your own pace.

The command

```
%last phillips | more
```

displays a record of all the logins and logouts by **phillips** one screenful at a time. To exit the **more** program, you can type **q** or simply page to the end of the file by repeatedly press the **spacebar**.

If in using the **last** command you notice a login to your account using your userid that was not due to you, it may mean that the security of your account has been compromised. In this case you should immediately change your password. If your account has been tampered with, it is a good idea to notify the system administrator.

Keep in mind the advice given in Section 2.3 and change your password as appropriate.

Exercises

1. What is the shortest password your system allows? How did you figure your answer out?
2. Does your system allow you to "change" your password to its current value or is there a history mechanism?
3. Enter the command **man passwd**. What are two new facts you learned from reading the **passwd** documentation?
4. (Requires algebra.) Suppose a password can be made up from 100 different symbols. How many different passwords are there of each of the following lengths: 5, 10, 15, and 20?

2.6 Logging In to a Remote System—telnet Command

There will be many times when you are working on one computer and find it necessary to log in to another remote one. For example, you may need to run a program on the other machine or you may want to look up some information that is stored on a remote machine. The second computer is usually at a different physical location, and hence we refer to it as the "remote" machine. **Telnet** is a program that allows you to log in to another remote computer from a machine you are already logged into. Via **telnet** you can use and interact with software on the remote machine. In order to use **telnet** you will need to have a second computer account that is accessible to you.

We use Figure 2.2 to illustrate the basic idea of **telnet**. In the figure we show two computers, A and B, that are on the same network. Suppose a user named Vincent is logged into computer A and that Vincent also has an account on machine B. If he now needs to access computer B, he can use the **telnet** command to log in to it. Once Vincent is logged into machine B, all of the commands that he executes will be carried out on machine B, not his original machine. In terms of functionality, it will appear as if he were locally logged into machine B. Having completed his work on computer B, Vincent can log out in the usual way and then he will be back working on computer A.

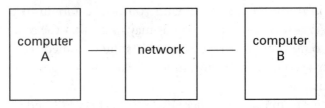

Figure 2.2—Computers A and B Used to Illustrate **telnet**

We now get into the details of the **telnet** command. To invoke **telnet**, simply enter the command

```
%telnet
```

You will see the system respond with the prompt

```
telnet>
```

This indicates that **telnet** is running and waiting for your input. *Note*: This type of prompt is informative in the sense that it reminds you that you are executing the **telnet** command. Unix follows a similar prompting convention for other commands. For example, the same convention is used for the **ftp** command that we will study in Chapter 22; the prompt for the **ftp** command is **ftp>**. Once you see the **telnet** prompt, you are in a position to begin entering commands to the system. The first thing to do is type **help** or **?** to receive information about what commands are available. In Figure 2.3 we display the results of entering

```
telnet>help
```

on our system. Interestingly, the **help** command itself is not listed, only the equivalent **?**. However, rest assured that **help** does work. The most important command on the list is the **open** command. By typing

```
telnet>open plaque.giro.org
```

for example, you can open a connection to the machine **plaque.giro.org**. After entering this **open** command, you will see a message such as

```
Trying 132.179.137.45...
Connected to plaque.giro.org
Escape character is '^]'.

Digital UNIX (plaque.giro.org) (ttyq0)

login:
```

if you are successful in connecting to the remote machine. At this point, you are ready to log in. You simply enter your userid and password, and you can start working on the remote machine. One important thing to notice about the original **telnet** connection message is the line

```
Escape character is '^]'.
```

On occasion you may run into a problem on the remote computer; for example, it might hang or freeze up. The "escape sequence" you need to type in to "bail out" from the machine is specified in this message. On this system, you need to type ^]. That is, you need to hold the **Control** key down while pressing the right bracket key (the] key). This will close your connection to the remote machine and return you to your local computer. It is a good idea to make a mental note of the escape sequence when you first connect using **telnet**. In most cases it is ^], so if you forget to look, you should try this sequence if you run into trouble.

```
telnet>help
Commands may be abbreviated.  Commands are:
close      close current connection
logout     forcibly logout remote user and close the connection
display    display operating parameters
mode       try to enter line or character mode ('mode ?' for more)
open       connect to a site
quit       exit telnet
send       transmit special characters ('send ?' for more)
set        set operating parameters ('set ?' for more)
unset      unset operating parameters ('unset ?' for more)
```

status	print status information
toggle	toggle operating parameters ('toggle ?' for more)
slc	change state of special characters ('slc ?' for more)
z	suspend telnet
!	invoke a subshell
environ	change environment variables ('environ ?' for more)
?	print help information

Figure 2.3—**telnet** Commands

Most of the other **telnet** commands listed in Figure 2.3 are self-explanatory. To learn more about any particular command, you can enter

```
telnet>help command
```

where **command** is the name of the command that you want more information about.

Two important commands are the **quit** command, which allows you to exit **telnet** after you have logged out of the remote machine, and the **status** command, which is useful for printing information about your current **telnet** session.

We should point out that **telnet** is the program you would use to connect to a machine hosting a *multiuser dungeon game* (or *MUD* for short). These are interesting games where you play against other people who are located throughout the world. For more information about MUDs, you can pose a query of "MUD" to any of the popular search engines.

To learn more about **telnet**, you should enter the command

```
%man telnet
```

Exercises

1. Describe two practical situations in which you would want to use **telnet**.
2. Use **telnet** to connect to another system. (There are systems on the Web you can locate that allow users to **telnet** to them freely.) Print out the connection screen demonstrating that you successfully telnetted to the remote system.
3. Print out the **help** screen for your version of **telnet** and explain each of the different command options that are available.
4. Does the **telnet** command have any flags? If so, report on three of them.

UNIX DOCUMENTATION

chapter 3

In this chapter we discuss the following commands:

Unix Command	DOS Command	Description
apropos	HELP	search the online manual for a keyword
man	HELP	access the online help facility
whatis	HELP	display a brief description of a command

3.1 Introduction

Learning to use complex software is not an easy task and may take a great deal of time. While you are learning a new system, you will not always have an expert by your side to answer questions, so it is important to be able to obtain answers to your questions from the computer itself.

Most complex software packages include online documentation. This documentation is often referred to as a *help facility*. In Unix, the online help facility is accessed by using the **man** command (short for manual). In this chapter we explain how to use the **man** command.

After reading this chapter, you will be able to obtain online help via the **man** command and understand how to effectively use the *Unix Reference Manual*.

Exercises

1. What are two advantages of online documentation over printed manuals? What are two disadvantages?
2. Do you prefer reading printed manuals or online documentation? Elaborate on your answer.

3.2 Unix Reference Manual

On any computer system, it is crucial to be able to find documentation online. Once you have mastered the online help facility, it is very easy to acquire new knowledge on your own. If you do not know how to use a command, you can simply look it up.

The Unix help facility is designed more as a reference manual than a basic set of "step-by-step" documentation. It is called the online Unix Reference Manual. Unix online documentation is also commonly referred to as **man pages**. The **man pages** are not particularly easy to understand at first. However, with some practice, you will get the hang of them and benefit from using them.

To invoke the online help facility, you use the **man** command. The **man** command displays information from the Unix Reference Manual. In this book we are concerned only with Volume I of the Unix Reference Manual, which is the most important volume for users of Unix. We'll use the classic Unix Reference Manual from Bell Labs. Other manuals have a very similar flavor.

The manual has nine sections. Table 3.1 displays the name of each section. The descriptive section headings are largely self-explanatory. The most important section of the manual for beginning users is Section 1, where user commands are described. Much of the information contained in the remainder of the manual is more specific and intended for programmers or for people who administer Unix systems.

Section Heading	Section Number
Introduction	0
Commands	1
System Calls	2
Libraries	3
Devices	4
File Formats	5
Games	6
Macros and Language Conventions	7
Administration	8

Table 3.1—Sections in the Unix Reference Manual

If you type in

```
%man
```

you will obtain a response like the following:

```
usage: man  [-]  [-adFlrt]  [-M path]  [-T macro-package ]
            [ -s section ] name ...
        man  [-M path]  -k keyword ...
        man  [-M path]  -f file ...
%
```

As you can see, this information is rather cryptic and is not very helpful to a beginner. The response displays the *usage* of the **man** command. The usage of a command is just an explanation of how the command works and is used in practice. We discuss the concept of usage further in the next section. Later in this chapter we explain the use of the **man** command.

3.3   Unix Commands—Arguments and Usage

In general, when you type in a Unix command[1] without any *arguments*, the system responds by indicating what the usage for the command is. "Argument" derives its meaning from its mathematical use. You can think of arguments as parameters to a command. We elaborate on the concept of argument below.

Suppose we define a function f, which simply adds one to a number, that is, $f(x) = x+1$. The value x is called the argument of f. So, an argument is simply the value(s) that a function is applied to. For example, when $x = 2$, we have $f(2) = 2 + 1 = 3$.

We can think of almost every Unix command as a function. Typing a command without any arguments displays the usage of that command.

We can also define a function with two arguments. For example, we can think of the addition function (+) as taking two arguments and summing them. If g represents the addition function, then $g(x,y) = x + y$. In this example, we say g has two arguments, x and y. For example, when $x = 3$ and $y = 76$, we have $g(x, y) = g(3, 76) = 3 + 76 = 79$. Most Unix commands have zero, one, or two arguments. Some commands may take an arbitrary number of arguments. We consider a couple of examples below.

The command line

```
%more story.txt
```

illustrates the use of the **more** command with one argument, namely **story.txt**.

---

1. A command that normally takes an argument.

The result of this command line is to display the file **story.txt** one screenful at a time.

The command line

```
%ls -l story.txt
```

illustrates the use of the **ls** command with two arguments, namely **–l** and **story.txt**. The result of this command line is to list in the long form information about the file **story.txt**.

In order to use a command effectively and syntactically correctly, you need to know what type of arguments it can take. Throughout the book we cover the most important arguments to each command.

Exercises

1. We cover the Unix commands **lpr**, **mv**, and **rm** in the next chapter. How many arguments are there to each of these commands in the command lines shown below?
   - ❑ **%rm foo.tex**
   - ❑ **%lpr –dhp main.ps**
   - ❑ **%main.tex main.old**
   - ❑ **%rm a b c d**
   - ❑ **%clear**
2. Suppose $g(x,y,z) = (x + y) + z$ and $h(x1, ..., xn) = xn$. How many arguments does function g have? How about h?

3.4   Help—man pages

The display of the **man** command's use on page 31 was admittedly not too helpful. Instead of typing **man** with no arguments, let's try

```
%man man
```

Figures 3.1 and 3.2 display an abbreviated version of the system's response. You should enter the command on your system, as **man pages** do differ some from system to system. While the **man page** is being retrieved, you will see a message such as

```
Reformatting page. Wait...
```

This means the **man page** you were looking for was found and Unix is busy preparing it for display on your screen.

We describe the most important parts of the **man page** below.

```
Reformatting page. Wait... done
User Commands                                                man(1)
NAME
     man - find and display reference manual pages
SYNOPSIS
     man [ - ] [ -adFlrt ] [ -M path ] [ -T macro-package ]
         [-s section ] name ...
     man [ -M path ] -k keyword ...
     man [ -M path ] -f file ...
DESCRIPTION
     The man command displays information from the reference
     manuals. It displays complete manual pages that you
     select by name, or one-line summaries selected either
     by keyword (-k), or by the name of an associated file
     (-f). If no manual page is located, man prints an
     error message.
  Source Format
     Reference Manual pages are marked up with nroff(1).
  Location of Manual Pages
     The online Reference Manual page directories are
     conventionally located in /usr/share/man. The nroff
     sources are
     . . .
     man pipes its output through more(1) to handle paging
     and underlining on the screen.
OPTIONS
     The following options are supported:
     -a Show all manual pages matching name within the
     MANPATH search path. Manual pages are displayed in the
     order found.
     . . .
```

Figure 3.1—First Part of Help for the **man** Command

```
        . . .
USAGE
  Manual Page Sections
    Entries in the reference manuals are organized into
    sections. A section name consists of a major section
    name, typically a single digit, optionally followed by
    a subsection name, typically one or more letters. An
    unadorned major section name acts as an abbreviation
    for the section of the same name along with all of its
    subsections. Each section contains descriptions apropos
    to a particular refer-
        . . .
SEE ALSO
    apropos(1), cat(1), col(1), eqn(1), more(1), nroff(1),
    refer(1), tbl(1), troff(1), vgrind(1), whatis(1),
    catman(1M), attributes(5), environ(5), eqnchar(5),
        . . .
BUGS
    The manual is supposed to be reproducible either on a
    phototypesetter or on an ASCII terminal. However, on a
    terminal some information (indicated by font changes,
    for instance) is lost.
        . . .
```

Figure 3.2—Second Part of Help for the **man** Command

The first thing to notice about the **man page** shown in Figure 3.1 is that there is a brief description of the **man** command itself. This description explains the *semantics* of the **man** command. The semantics of a command is just its meaning. Each **man page** for a user command contains a similar entry under the heading of **NAME**.

The **NAME** entry is followed by the *syntax* of the command. The syntax of a command specifies the exact details about how a command needs to be entered. It is worth seeing a number of examples of Unix commands before being given a general description of Unix command syntax. Thus, we defer such a discussion of command syntax until Chapter 8. At that point, you will have developed a solid context from which to understand the general concepts of command syntax. Until then, we include only concepts that are necessary for the current presentation.

The syntax of a command is described under the **SYNOPSIS** heading. Notice the syntax and usage (as displayed earlier by entering **man**) are the same. Syntax and usage are synonyms in this context. The syntax specifies the arguments that the command may take. For example, the **man** command may take **–T, –s, section, –k,** or **keyword** as arguments, among other possibilities. The explanation of what these arguments mean is given in the **OPTIONS** part of the **man page**.

The **DESCRIPTION** section provides an expanded discussion of the semantics of the command. It is followed by the **OPTIONS** section. Sometimes the **OPTIONS** section includes a number of sample uses of the command. These can be very helpful. Often it is a good idea to try some of the examples out as test cases.

The **OPTIONS** section is followed by **OPERANDS, USAGE, EXIT STATUS,** and **FILES** sections. These in turn are followed by a **SEE ALSO** section. The **SEE ALSO** section lists other related commands. In many cases you may decide to explore some of these as well—either to help clarify a point you are unsure of or because one of these commands may be what you were actually looking for initially.

The **SEE ALSO** section is followed by a **NOTES** and a **BUGS** section. These include any special information about the command and any known problems with the command, respectively. It is a good idea to at least skim these parts over when viewing a **man page**.

You will primarily be interested in the **NAME, SYNOPSIS, DESCRIPTION, OPTIONS,** and **SEE ALSO** paragraphs.

Notice in the top right-hand corner of Figure 3.1, **man(1)** is displayed. The number in parenthesis indicates that this information comes from Section 1 of the Unix Reference Manual.

We see from the **DESCRIPTION** of the **man** command that by typing

```
%man name
```

we can obtain documentation about the command called **name**. The word "**name**" here represents a command; we are not talking about a command called **name**. More specifically, we know this from the sentence "It displays complete manual pages that you select by name" from the **DESCRIPTION** section. This means that all **man pages** matching the argument **name** are displayed. For example,

```
%man login
```

provides help about the **login** command and

```
%man passwd
```

provides help about the **passwd** command. It is a good idea to try these examples to begin familiarizing yourself with **man pages**. It requires a lot of practice before you can make effective use of the **man pages**. However, the time you invest is well spent.

Table 3.2 provides a summary of the sections of a **man page**. These sections will vary slightly from system to system. However, all Unix Reference Manuals have the same basic flavor.

Heading	Description
NAME	one-line summary
SYNOPSIS	terse description of the syntax
DESCRIPTION	expanded explanation
OPTIONS	explanation of the arguments available
OPERANDS	explanation of additional arguments
USAGE	more details about how the command is used
EXIT STATUS	describes values returned after execution
FILES	lists relevant files
SEE ALSO	provides references to other related parts of the Unix Reference Manual
NOTES	summary of any special information
BUGS	list of known problems

Table 3.2—Important Parts of a **man page** for a User Command

Notice that the information displayed by the **man** command is displayed using the **more** program. To get another screenful of information, you simply press the **spacebar**, and to quit the help information you press **q**.

You can get help on more than one command at a time by typing the **man** command with more than one argument. For example,

```
%man logout passwd man
```

provides help about the **logout, passwd**, and **man** commands. Notice that you separate these arguments by a blank space rather than a comma. A similar result can be obtained by using the **man** command three times—once on each individual command.

If you scroll all the way to the bottom of the display for **man passwd**, you will see

```
SEE ALSO
     finger(1), login(1), nispasswd(1), nistbladm(1),
     yppasswd(1), domainname(1M), eeprom(1M), id(1M),
     passmgmt(1M), pwconv(1M), su(1M), useradd(1M),
     userdel(1M), usermod(1M), crypt (3C), getpwnam(3C),
     getspnam(3C), nis_local_directory(3N), pam(3),
     loginlog(4), nsswitch.conf(4),  pam.conf(4), passwd(4),
     shadow(4), attributes(5), environ(5), pam_unix(5)
%
```

The items in parentheses denote the section of the manual that the related information comes from. For example, **finger(1)** indicates there is information about the **finger** command in Section 1 of the Unix Reference Manual and **passwd(4)** indicates there is related information about passwords in Section 4 of the manual. The command

```
%man -s 4 passwd
```

displays the information in Section 4 of the manual about the *password file*. The password file is the place on Unix systems where information is stored about local user accounts. The –s following the **man** command is called a *flag* or an *option*. You can think of a flag as an argument to a command that changes the semantics of the command. The –s option to the **man** command followed by a number **x** tells the **man** command to display information from Section x of the manual.

The **man** command displays all the information about a command in the Unix Reference Manual. Sometimes you will want to see only a brief description of the command. By entering

```
%man -f argument
```

you will be given only the semantic description of the command **argument**. For example,

```
%man -f find
```

displays the following:

```
find     find(1)   - search for files in a directory hierarchy
```

This is a handy way to get an idea of what a command does.

In executing the command **man –f find** we change the semantics of the **man** command from displaying an entire **man page** to displaying just a brief command description of the **man page**. So, the –**f** flag is for brief.

The **whatis** command is available on some systems and it has the same meaning as **man –f**. So, **whatis find** and **man –f find** produce the same information. Naturally, you can replace **find** with any command name you are interested in.

There will be times you are not sure of the Unix command you need to use to perform some function. The **–k** flag to the **man** command lets you search the Unix Reference Manual for a keyword. For example,

```
%man -k login
```

searches the brief semantic descriptions (in the **NAME** section of a **man page**) of each command in the Unix Reference Manual and displays those lines that include the pattern **login**. The results of this command are shown below:

```
idled      idled (8)      - Idle terminal and multiple login
                                 monitor daemon.
logname    logname (1)    - print user's login name
```

Notice that two commands were found that had the word **login** in their **NAME** sections: The **idled** command from Section 8 of the manual and the **logname** command from Section 1.

Of course, you may replace the word **login** with any keyword you want. If you try a query and do not turn up any useful information, you may need to rephrase your query. The **apropos** command may be used in lieu of **man –k**. So,

```
%apropos login
```

yields the same results as **man –k login**.

Exercises

1. How many options are there to the **man** command on your system?
2. Does your system support the **apropos** and **whatis** commands mentioned in this section? Try to use them and also find them in the Unix Reference Manual.
3. On your system how many options are there to the **login**, **logout**, and **passwd** commands?
4. What are the results of the **man –k manual** command on your system? How many of the results are actually related to documentation?

TOP TEN MOST USEFUL UNIX COMMANDS

chapter 4

In this chapter we discuss the following commands:

Unix Command	DOS Command	Description
cd	CD	change to another directory
clear	CLS	clear the screen
cp	COPY	copy a file
grep	FIND	search for a pattern in a file
lpr	PRINT	print a file
ls	DIR	list the files in a directory
mkdir	MKDIR	create a directory
more	MORE	display a file one screenful at a time
mv	RENAME	rename a file
pwd	CHDIR	print the name of the current working directory
rm	DEL	delete a file
rmdir	RMDIR	delete a directory

4.1 Introduction

There are a number of fundamental commands in Unix that every user needs to learn right away. In Chapter 2 we covered the most important commands relating to accounts: **login**, **logout**, and **passwd**; in Chapter 3 we covered the most important commands relating to the Unix Reference Manual: **apropos**, **man**, and **whatis**.

In this chapter we cover a number of very important commands relating to files and directories. These commands handle many of the routine functions that a typical user performs on a daily basis. We describe the most common features of each of these commands here. Later in the book, we will delve into more specialized uses of the commands. Having mastered these ten[1] commands, you will be able to work on a Unix system and perform essential functions such as

❑ list the files in a directory.
❑ display command output one screenful at a time.
❑ change to another directory.
❑ search for a pattern in a file.
❑ print a file.
❑ create a directory to store files in.
❑ copy a file.
❑ rename a file.
❑ delete a file.
❑ delete a directory.
❑ clear the screen.

We cover the "top ten" commands in the order you will probably encounter them.

4.2 Listing Your Files—ls Command

The **ls** command name is an abbreviation for "list." It is used to list your directories and files. Suppose that you have just logged onto a Unix system. You are now in a position to do some useful work. Initially, you will encounter the Unix prompt

```
%
```

When you log into your account, the system by default places you in an area known as your *home directory*. This initial file space contains some very important files and is your home base from which you will begin working. (On some operating systems, directories are called *folders*.)

In the Unix operating system, directories and files are organized into a tree-like hierarchy. Figure 4.1 depicts such a sample structure graphically. It is worth going over some basic definitions about *trees* since the terminology associated with them has been adopted by Unix, and we make use of it throughout this book.

In Figure 4.1 the circles represent *nodes* and the lines between the nodes represent *edges*. The tree is oriented so the part highest up on the page is referred to as the *top*; the other end of the tree is referred to as the *bottom*. The node at the top of the tree, in this case A, is called the *root*. If there is an edge between two

---

1. All right, twelve.

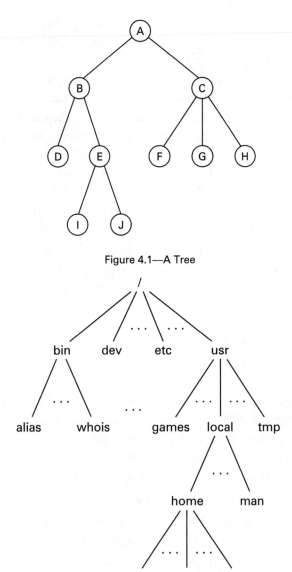

Figure 4.1—A Tree

Figure 4.2—A Simplified Representation of the Unix File System

nodes, we say the nodes are *adjacent*. For example, nodes C and F are adjacent whereas nodes F and G are not. The *children* of a node are the nodes adjacent to it and also below it in the picture. For example, D and E are the two children of B. A *parent* of a node is the node that is above it and adjacent to it. For example,

C is the parent of F, G, and H. A *path* is a sequence of adjacent nodes in the tree. For example, A-C-F is a path, whereas D-A-C-H is not. We are usually interested in paths that go down the tree.

In Figure 4.2 we depict a sample Unix file space in the form of a tree. We do not include circles for nodes in the tree, but instead just write in a directory or file name to represent a node. In the figure only **alias** and **whois** represent files; the other nodes represent directories. The directory at the top of the tree is known as the *root directory* and is represented by the **/** (forward slash) character.

Suppose A and B are directories in a file space represented by a tree T. We say B is a *subdirectory* of A, if there is a path from A to B going down T. So, if all the nodes in Figure 4.1 represent directories, then B and C would be subdirectories of A. In addition, F, G, and H are subdirectories of C.

Some standard subdirectories under[2] the root directory on a large Unix system are **bin**, **dev**, **etc**, and **usr**. Unix users rely on the words "up" and "down" to indicate relative positions in a directory hierarchy. For example, **shelly** is down one from **home** and **home** is up one from **shelly**. That is, **home** is the parent directory of **shelly**. You will hear expressions such as "move down two directories" or "go to the parent directory."

When you initially log in to your account, by default you are placed in your home directory.

Starting from the root directory and proceeding through the tree until you reach your home directory results in a path to your home directory. For example, **usr-local-home-groves** is a path to Brian Groves' home directory. When the directory names you pass through are concatenated together, the result is a *pathname*. The pathname for Brian's home directory is

```
/usr/local/home/groves
```

Pathnames can be *full* or *relative*. A full pathname specifies a complete path through the directory structure starting at the root directory, whereas a relative pathname specifies a path relative to some starting position. For example, we have **/bin/whois** as a full pathname and **local/home/tarvares** as a relative pathname. We will explore the Unix file and directory structure further in Chapters 10–11.

The first forward slash in a pathname represents the root directory. Additional forward slashes in a pathname separate the names of subdirectories. Figure 4.3 shows John Tarvares' directory structure. We will use his account as a model to describe concepts throughout this chapter.

---

2. The word "under" is used because of the physical relationship shown in Figure 4.2.

ABBOTT, **classes**, **HTML**, and **misc** are child subdirectories of **tarvares**. The file **bud** is contained in the directory **ABBOTT**. There are three files in the directory **HTML**.

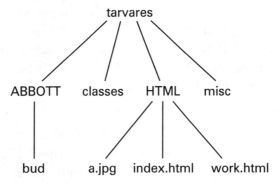

Figure 4.3—John Tarvares' Directory and File Structure

If John enters the command line

```
%ls
```

the directories in his home directory will be listed as shown below.

```
ABBOTT       classes
HTML         misc
```

The **ls** command lists files and directories contained in the directory where the **ls** command is executed from. When you first log in, this will be from your home directory. Later in this chapter we describe how to change directories. If you change to another directory, say a directory called **HTML**, and enter the **ls** command, the files in the directory **HTML** will be listed. In John's case this results in a listing of the files **a.jpg**, **index**.**html**, and **work**.**html**.

The *current working directory,* sometimes called the *working directory* for short, refers to the directory you are in. Unix provides the **pwd** command to display the full pathname of the current working directory, allowing you to find out which directory you are in. After moving up and down the directory tree a large number of times, it is easy to lose track of where you are.

If John enters the command

```
%pwd
```

from his home directory the result is

```
/usr/local/home/tarvares
```

43

assuming he is the same Tarvares as shown in Figure 4.2.

Next we describe two important flags to the **ls** command. As you have seen from the examples of **ls** presented above, by executing the **ls** command we learn only about what files and directories are in the current working directory. We do not actually get any details about the files themselves, such as when they were created or how many bytes they are. To obtain detailed information about the files, the –l flag may be used. The –l (the letter l, not the number 1) stands for "long" form. A sample output for the command

      `%ls -l`

is shown in Figure 4.4. Notice that a lot of information about a file is displayed. We explain all this information in detail in Chapter 11. For now, remember that column 1 pertains to file permissions, column 5 to file size in number of bytes, and columns 6–8 to the last modification date of the file.

```
total 7060
drwx------   2   tweed   faculty        512   Aug  18    1998    SONGS
-rw-------   1   tweed   faculty       5204   Apr  28    1995    atrail.tex
-rw-------   1   tweed   faculty       4048   Jun  28    1996    comrades
-rw-------   1   tweed   faculty       1638   Aug   5    1994    ep15.tex
-rw-------   1   tweed   faculty       3292   Jul  19    1994    highs.tex
-rw-------   1   tweed   faculty       2557   Oct  29   13:43    iron.txt
-rw-------   1   tweed   faculty        299   Oct   1   13:08    labels.tex
-rw-------   1   tweed   faculty        312   Oct   1   13:10    labels2.tex
-rw-------   1   tweed   faculty        518   Feb   1   16:32    loop.aasu
-rw-------   1   tweed   faculty    3579380   Feb  24   18:46    bullalgs
drwx------   2   tweed   faculty       1024   Dec   6   21:11    recs
-rw-------   1   tweed   faculty       1869   Jun   8    1998    rent.sav
```

Figure 4.4—Sample Output from an **ls –l** Command

To list *all* of the files and directories contained in a directory, you use the –a flag to the **ls** command. That is,

      `%ls -a`

lists all files in the current working directory. Unix directories contain special *hidden files*. By using the –a flag to the **ls** command, you are able to view these files as well. We cover hidden files in Section 10.3. A sample output of the **ls –a** command is shown in Figure 4.5. Notice several hidden files are displayed, among others, **.**, **..**, **.cshrc**, **.login**, and **.netscape**. Every directory always contains the **.** and **..** hidden files. These refer to the current working directory (the directory itself) and the directory's parent directory.

```
.                         africa
..                        albany
.addressbook              february
.cshrc                    fish
.history                  fritos
.hotjava                  moneymatters
.login                    monkey
.logout                   zebra
.netscape
```

Figure 4.5—Sample Output from an **ls –a** Command

You may combine the different options to Unix commands. For example, the command

%ls -la

lists all material contained in the current working directory in the long form. This produces the same result as entering

%ls -al

The order of the specified options does not matter; they are both applied.

We will describe one final use of the **ls** command. There are times when you want to copy a file from another directory to the current working directory. You may remember the pathname of the directory the file is stored in, but you may not remember the name of the file itself. You can list the contents of this other directory by specifying its name as an argument to the **ls** command.

For example, suppose you are in the directory called

/export/local/home/riddle

and that you would like to copy a file from the directory

/export/local/home/messner/climbs/public

to your directory but cannot remember the name of the file. The command

%ls /export/local/home/messner/climbs/public

executed from your directory will provide you with a list of files in the other directory. Once you locate the name of the file, you can proceed to copy it using the technique described in Section 4.8.

You should execute the command line

%man ls

to learn more about the **ls** command.

Exercises

1. Execute the **ls** command from your home directory. How many files do you have? How many directories? Now execute the command **ls –a**. How many items are listed? How many hidden files are there?

2. How many options to the **ls** command are there on your system? Describe two interesting options different from those covered in this section.

3. What is the full pathname for your home directory?

4.3 Displaying a File—more Command

In Chapter 2 you first encountered the **more** command. The **more** command provides a convenient way to view the contents of a file one screenful at a time. For example, entering the command

```
%more index.html
```

displays one screenful of content of the file **index.html**. Hitting the **Spacebar** brings up the next screenful of text, and typing **q** "quits" the **more** command and brings you back to the Unix prompt. The **more** command only allows you to view the file. To alter the file's contents you need to use a text editor.

Try entering the command

```
%man man
```

on your system. The Unix Reference Manual documentation about the **man** command consists of more than one screenful of information. In the lower left of the screen, the **more** command tells you what percentage of the file has *already* been displayed. Thus, a display such as

```
---More---(13%)
```

indicates you have seen 13% of the file, so there is another 87% of the file that has yet to be displayed. The percentages are very helpful and let you make a mental note of where you are in the file. For example, you may recall that you had seen some important information that was 47% of the way through a file and then be able to easily return to the information. On most Unix systems, you can press **b** while viewing a file with **more** and you will be returned to the preceding screen of information or remain at the first screen if you have not moved forward in the file.

The **more** command also provides you with a mechanism for searching for a user-specified pattern of characters in a file. To execute a search in a file being displayed by **more**, you simply type **/** and then the pattern you are looking for. Suppose you were looking for the pattern **sailboat**. You would type

```
/sailboat
```

The **more** program would then search forward from where you currently are in the file and highlight the first occurrence of the word **sailboat** it found. If the pattern were not present in the file, **more** would indicate that the pattern was not found. To locate subsequent occurrences of a pattern you just entered, you need only type **/** and press **Enter**.

Another convenient feature of **more** is the –s option. This option tells **more** to squeeze consecutive blank lines into a single blank line. In this way additional information can be displayed on the screen. So, for example, to display the file **data.txt** with extra blank lines squeezed out of it, you would enter the command

```
%more -s data.txt
```

The **more** command has a number of other interesting features. You should execute the command line

```
%man more
```

to learn additional information about it.

Two other Unix programs for displaying files are **less** and **pg**. Some users prefer **less** over **more** because **less** allows you to scroll both down and up. The command name **less** was chosen sarcastically; in fact, **less** provides greater functionality than **more**. You can do a **man** on **less** and **pg** to find out how to use them and how they differ from **more**.

Exercises

1. Can the **more** command take several arguments? If so, what is the result?
2. Perform a **man more** command. How many times does the pattern "manual" occur in the **man page** for **more**? How many times does the pattern "Manual" occur? Is the searching done within the **more** command case sensitive?
3. Are the commands **less** and **pg** available on your system? Compare and contrast them with the **more** command.

4.4   Changing Directory—cd Command

The Unix file system is arranged into a hierarchy of directories conveniently represented by a tree. As you organize your work, you will need to be able to navigate through the tree. To move to another directory, you use the **cd** command, short for "change directory." The **cd** command by itself with no arguments will place you in your home directory—regardless of which directory your current working directory is.

To verify a change of directory, you can use the **pwd** command. The output of the **pwd** command is the full pathname of the directory you are in. Suppose Jenny Shelly just logged into her account with userid **shelly**. Figure 4.2 illustrates the location of Jenny's file space graphically. If Jenny executed the command

`%pwd`

for output she would see

`/usr/local/home/shelly`

By specifying a pathname as the argument to the **cd** command, you can change to other directories. For example, consider John Tarvares' file space depicted in Figure 4.6. To transfer into his Web directory (**HTML**), John can enter

`%cd /usr/local/home/tarvares/HTML`

from any other directory in the Unix file system. Notice that John has specified a full pathname. Typing in a full pathname every time you want to change directories is time consuming; it is often more efficient to use a relative pathname. For example, from his home directory, **tavares**, John could have typed

`%cd HTML`

to achieve the same result. That is, relative to his home directory, the directory **HTML** is one level down. The **cd** command followed by an explicit directory name will take you to that directory if it is a child subdirectory of the current working directory. In other words, to move to a child directory called **childsubdirectory** from within its parent directory, you simply enter

`%cd childsubdirectory`

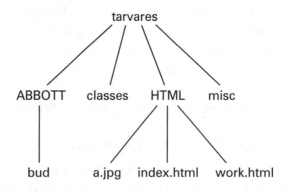

Figure 4.6—John Tarvares' File Space

To move up one level in a directory hierarchy, follow the **cd** command with two dots

```
%cd ..
```

The two dots represent the *parent directory* of where you are currently located. Using relative path names when navigating through the file structure can save a lot of typing time. To move from within his **HTML** directory to his **misc** directory, John can enter

```
%cd ../misc
```

Recall that Unix is case sensitive. Thus, it is important to type directory names exactly as they appear.

The tilde (~) symbol is used to refer to your home directory. For example,

```
~tarvares
```

is expanded automatically to

```
/usr/local/home/tarvares
```

The tilde character can prove very useful for moving around a directory structure. As an example, suppose your current working directory is

```
/usr/local/home/tarvares/brown/bags/computers
```

and you would like your current working directory to be

```
/usr/local/home/tarvares/pool/tables/balls
```

The command

```
%cd ~/pool/tables/balls
```

can be used to accomplish this change of directories. Contrast this with other methods for moving into this directory, which require considerably more typing.

You should execute the command line

```
%man cd
```

to learn more about the **cd** command.

Exercises

1. Consider the directory and file structure shown in Figure 4.7. Suppose you were initially located in the **food** directory. Provide the **cd** commands that require the least number of characters to be typed to perform the following tasks:

   a. move to the **omelette** directory

   b. from the **omelette** directory move to the **cereal** directory

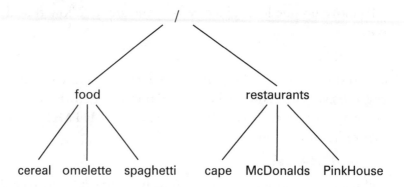

Figure 4.7—Directory and File Structure Used in the Exercises

    c. from the **cereal** directory move to the **cape** directory

    d. from the **cape** directory move to the **omelette** directory

    e. return to the home directory

2. What is the effect of the command **cd .**?

3. What are the child subdirectories of the root directory on your system?

4. Are there any interesting flags to the **cd** command? If so, describe two of them.

4.5   Searching for a Pattern—grep Command

There will be many times when you want to search a file for a pattern. It would be convenient if you could do this without using a text editor. If you could perform such a search from the operating system, you would not have to go through the usual steps of opening the file with a text editor, using the editor's search facility, and then closing the file. Unix provides the **grep** command for searching a file for a pattern. In fact, **grep** allows you to search an entire directory of files or even an entire file system for a pattern. The **grep** command is a powerful search mechanism that provides a convenient notation, allowing you to specify complex patterns to search for.

The word **grep** is an acronym for "global regular expression print." *Regular expressions* are an important concept in computer science. You can think of them as a means to compactly express patterns. We consider a couple of examples involving the use of the **grep** command.

Suppose you are residing in a directory that yields the following display when you execute an **ls** command:

```
annotation.tex     california.tex     game.c          words.favorites
buffalo.txt        denver.txt         golfing.txt
```

To search the file **words.favorites** for the word **zooks**, you enter the command

```
%grep zooks words.favorites
```

The output of this command is a display of all lines in the file **words.favorites** that contain the word **zooks**. In this case, the word appeared twice and the following was displayed as output:

```
yikes—an exclamation, also see zooks.
zooks—an exclamation, also see yikes.
```

If the word were not present in the file, you would have been returned to the Unix prompt without seeing any output.

This example illustrates that the first argument to the **grep** command is the pattern you are looking for, and the second argument specifies the file(s) to search for the pattern in. The pattern can be specified using a regular expression. We will look at various examples of specifying patterns below, and we will also consider several ways of specifying files to search in.

To search for the word **zooks** in the files **games.c** and **words.favorites** simultaneously, you could enter the following command:

```
%grep zooks games.c words.favorites
```

The output in this case is the same as before, since in our case the word **zooks** does not appear in the file **games.c**.

The **grep** command has been optimized and it searches very quickly even when you ask it to look in many large files at once. Suppose you had used the word **elephant** in one of the files in the directory under consideration but could not remember which file. You can use the **grep** command as follows to locate the desired file:

```
%grep elephant *
```

The asterisk (*****) serves as a wildcard. In this context it tells the **grep** command to search all files in the directory for the pattern **elephant**. That is, ***** means match all file names. The **grep** command will search all the files in the directory for the word **elephant**. The output of the command is the name of each file where the pattern was found followed by the lines in the file where the pattern occurred.

The *file extension* is the part of a file name occurring after the last period. For example, the file extension of **main.tex** is **tex**. If a file has an extension of **abc**, we refer to it as an **abc** file. For example, **main.tex** is called a **tex** (pronounced "tech") file.

Suppose you wanted to search only files with an extension of **tex** for the pattern **Peter the Great**. This could be accomplished by the following command:

```
%grep 'Peter the Great' *.tex
```

There are two things to notice about this command. Since the pattern we are looking for contains blank spaces, we put the pattern in single quotes. Otherwise, **grep** would interpret part of the pattern as a file name to search. This would result in an error message since there is no file in our directory called **the**.

The second thing to notice is how we were able to specify all files ending with the **tex** extension using ***.tex**. The star means "match any pattern" and the **.tex** means the file name must end with these four characters: **.**, **t**, **e**, and **x** in order.

If you executed the command **ls *.tex** on this directory, you would see the following output:

```
annotation.txt        california.tex
```

Thus, the **grep** command

```
%grep 'Peter the Great' *.tex
```

searches both **annotation.tex** and **california.tex** for the pattern **Peter the Great**.

The **grep** command provides notation for efficiently specifying patterns. We have already seen that the ***** means "match any pattern." The **.** is used to match any single character. The Unix regular expression

```
a.b.c
```

means match any pattern that consists of five characters, where the first character is an **a**, the third character is a **b**, the fifth character is a **c**, and characters two and four can be any single symbols. For example, the pattern **atbvc** meets these criteria as does the pattern **a\$bZc**.

If you type in a character that has a special meaning to **grep**, for example, ***** or **.**, you should *escape* the character with the \ symbol. This tells **grep** that you want the character to be interpreted literally so that its special meaning is disregarded. For example, suppose you wanted to look for the pattern **a.b.c**. That is, you wanted to find the five characters **a**, **.**, **b**, **.**, and **c** in this order. The following command would search all files with a **txt** extension for this pattern:

```
%grep a\.b\.c *.txt
```

Notice that we have escaped the two dots so that they are matched exactly rather than telling the **grep** command to match any two characters.

The command line

```
%grep '[A-Z]\.' *.tex
```

finds all lines in all files with the extension **tex** that contain a capital letter followed by a period. You can specify a range of characters to **grep** by displaying them in square brackets with a dash in between. A range of lowercase letters may be specified similarly. For example, **[d–g]** is used to match one of the characters **d**, **e**, **f**, and **g**.

There are many other useful ways of specifying patterns to **grep**. You should execute the command line

```
%man grep
```

to learn more about the **grep** command.

Exercises

1. Write **grep** expressions to search the file named **computers** for the following patterns:
   a. the word **personal**
   b. the phrase **personal computer**
   c. the phrase **Personal Computer**
2. On many Unix systems there is a file called **/usr/words/dict**. This file contains a long list of words used by spell-checking programs. Write a **grep** expression to search this file for any words that contain all the vowels in consecutive order. That is, you are looking for words that contain the letters **a**, **e**, **i**, **o**, and **u** in this order. There can be other letters interspersed between the vowels. What words did you find?
3. You will need to read the **man page** for **grep** to complete this exercise. Write **grep** expressions to search all files in a directory for the following patterns:
   a. any line that begins with a capital letter
   b. any line that ends with a capital letter
   c. a pattern consisting of three vowels in a row
   d. the pattern '**a(b)..&***', where the quotes *are* part of the pattern you want to find

4.6 Printing—lpr Command

It is very important to be able to print files from a computer system. Unix provides the command **lpr** for this purpose. The command name **lpr** is an abbreviation for "line printer." On many systems a default printer will be set up for you to use. That is, if you send a file to the printer, the default printer will be the physical printer that actually outputs your file. If a default printer has been set up, you can print the file **banner** from your current working directory using the command line

```
%lpr banner
```

Suppose you want to print the same file to a printer named **laser** rather than to the default printer. You would enter the following command line:

```
%lpr -Plaser banner
```

On some systems you would enter

```
%lp -D laser banner
```

or

```
%lp -dlaser banner
```

The **–d** and **–D** flags stand for "destination." The argument following these flags tells the system the name of the printer on which to print your file. You will need to check to see if your system uses **lpr** or **lp**, or some other print command.

It is important to send the correct file types to the printer. If you send the wrong type of file, the output may be nonsense; you could waste a lot of paper; or you could jam the printer. Today many printers handle *plain text* and *PostScript* files. You should try to learn what formats your local printer can handle.

Many printers do not handle **dvi** files properly. The LaTeX documentation preparation system that we cover in Appendix H generates **dvi** files as output. It is not a good idea to send a **dvi** file directly to a printer. In Appendix H we will explain how to print **dvi** files properly.

There are many options to the **lpr** command that we have not covered. You should execute the command line

```
%man lpr
```

to learn more about it. When you do, you will notice many related commands such as **lprm** and **lpq**. We cover these commands in Chapter 9.

On many systems you have to acquire some local knowledge to be able to print effectively. For example, you will need to obtain the names of the local printers, information about how to process various types of files, information about printing quotas, and which print commands are available. This information is usually posted near the printers or online. Other users or the system administrator will usually be happy to share printing information with you.

Exercises

1. On your Unix system, what is the command line for printing the file **homework** on the default printer? Is more than one printer available to you? What would the command line be for sending the file **homework** to a printer named **laserwriter**?

2. You will need to read the **man page** for **lpr** or **lp** to complete this exercise. How do you print five copies of a document without repeating the print command five times?

3. What does the word *duplex* mean? Can you print in a duplex style? If so, what is the command for doing this?

4. Are there printing quotas on your system? If so, describe them and explain how they are enforced.

4.7   Creating a Directory—mkdir Command

In order to properly organize your work, you will want to be able to create subdirectories. To create a subdirectory, you use the **mkdir** command. The command name is an abbreviation for "make directory." You supply the subdirectory name as an argument to the **mkdir** command, and a subdirectory will be made in the current working directory. For example, to create a subdirectory in the working directory called **datafiles**, you enter the command line

```
%mkdir datafiles
```

You can check that the directory **datafiles** was created by performing an **ls** command. To begin working in the directory, you can execute a **cd datafiles** command.

Directories can be nested so you could create subdirectories of subdirectories of subdirectories, and so on. In practice, personal subdirectories that are more than five or six levels deep become cumbersome.

If you are working in a directory that has a growing number of files, say 20 or more, you may want to think about organizing some of the files into a subdirectory. It is a good idea to have a number of subdirectories set up in your home directory. When you log in, you can then switch to the directory where you want to work.

You should execute the command line

```
%man mkdir
```

to learn more about the **mkdir** command.

Exercises

1. Create a subdirectory called **test** in your home directory. Move into the directory. Can you create another directory called **test** inside of the original directory **test**? Try it and **cd** to the latest **test**. What is the result of executing a **pwd** command?

2. Can you create a subdirectory called **VERYLONGNAMEDIREC-TORY**?

3. A man named Walter has 300 files in his home directory and no subdirectories. What are some of the problems Walter faces when trying to locate one of his files?

4. For this problem do not count hidden directories. How many directories in total would you have if you created directories five levels deep and had five subdirectories (not including hidden directories) in every directory?

4.8   Copying a File—cp Command

There are many times when you will want to copy a file. For example,

❑ when you want to create a local backup version of a file.

❑ when you want to create a duplicate version of a file for test purposes.

❑ when you want a local copy of a file so you can edit it.

❑ when you are beginning work on a new file and have a similar one that serves as a good starting point.

The **cp** command is used to copy a file. The command name **cp** is an abbreviation for "copy." When you copy a file, you simply create a distinct exact duplicate of the file. This is different from renaming a file. We cover renaming files in Section 4.9.

Warning: If you tell Unix to overwrite an existing file using the **cp** command, it will. Be careful not to destroy the contents of a file you want to keep by accidently overwriting it with the **cp** command.

The **cp** command typically takes two arguments. The first argument is the name of the file you want to copy and the second argument is the name of the copy. If you want to make a copy of the file **important.notes** called **NOTES**, you enter the command line

```
%cp important.notes NOTES
```

This command copies the file **important.notes** to the file **NOTES**. If the file **NOTES** previously existed, it is overwritten with the contents of **important.notes**. The original contents of **NOTES** is lost. If the file **NOTES** did not exist, it is created and has the same contents as **important.notes**. To verify that the file was copied, you can execute the **ls –l** command and notice that both files exist and have the same size.

There are times when you want to copy all files from one directory to another. Suppose you want to copy all files from the current working directory to its subdirectory called **BACKUP**. The following command line accomplishes this task:

```
%cp * BACKUP/.
```

Regardless of how many files there are in the current working directory, this simple command copies them all to the directory called **BACKUP** and preserves their names. The * means "match all file names in this directory." The first part of the second argument tells the system the copies of the files are to be put in the (already existing) directory called **BACKUP**; the . tells the system that each file is to be given the same name that it had originally; the / is needed to separate the directory name **BACKUP** from the ..

The usage of the **cp** command can be displayed by typing **cp** without any arguments. You should execute the command line

```
%man cp
```

to learn more about the **cp** command.

Exercises

1. What is the command for making a copy of the file called **equipment**?
2. Describe two interesting options to the **cp** command.
3. Suppose you want to copy all files from a directory called **SYSTEM** to a directory two levels up called **Test**. What command line could you use to achieve this?
4. Create a test file called **junk**. What happens if you try to copy **junk** to itself?
5. Is there a command for copying an entire directory hierarchy that is multiple levels deep? If so, describe it.
6. What is a command to copy all files with a **txt** file extension from the current working directory to a child subdirectory called **Text**?

4.9 Renaming a File—mv Command

There will be many times when you want to rename a file. For example,

❑ when you copy a file from the Web or a friend, and decide you have a better name for it.

❑ when the contents of a file changes significantly.

❑ when you realize a different descriptive name is more appropriate.

❑ when you want to conduct a series of tests using a file and so decide to give it a very short name to save typing time.

The **mv** command is used to rename a file. The command name **mv** is an abbreviation for "move." When you rename a file, you simply change the name of the file. The contents of the file are not altered. This is a different process from copying a file. We covered copying files in Section 4.8.

Warning: If you tell Unix to overwrite an existing file using the **mv** command, it will. Be careful not to destroy the contents of a file you want to keep by accidently overwriting it with the **mv** command.

The **mv** command typically takes two arguments. The first argument is the name of the file you want to rename and the second argument is its new name. To rename the file **black.shoes** to **brown.shoes**, you enter the following command line:

```
%mv black.shoes brown.shoes
```

After entering this command, the file **black.shoes** no longer exists, and the file **brown.shoes** contains the exact same content that the file **black.shoes** used to contain.

There are times when you want to move all files from one directory to another. Suppose you want to relocate all files from the current working directory to its child subdirectory called **VERSION-2**. The following command line accomplishes this task:

```
%mv * VERSION-2/.
```

Regardless of how many files there are in the current working directory, this command moves them all to the directory called **VERSION-2** and preserves their names. The * means "match all file names in this directory." The first part of the second argument tells the system the files are to be moved to the (already existing) directory called **VERSION-2**; the . tells the system that each file is to be given the same name it had originally; the / is needed to separate the directory name **VERSION-2** from the ..

The usage of the **mv** command can be displayed by typing **mv** without any arguments. You should execute the command line

```
%man mv
```

to learn more about the **mv** command.

Exercises

1. What is the command for changing the name of a file called **glasses** to **wine.glasses**?
2. Create a test file called **foo**. What happens if you try to rename a file that does not exist to **foo**?
3. Describe two interesting options to the **mv** command.

4. Suppose you want to move all files from a directory called **SEWING** to a directory three levels up called **CHORES**. What command line could you use to achieve this?

5. Create a test file called **junk**. What happens if you try to rename **junk** to **junk**?

6. How could you use the **mv** command to delete all but one file in a directory?

4.10 Deleting a File—rm Command

There will be many times when you want to delete a file. For example,

❑ the file is no longer needed.

❑ you are running low on disk space.

❑ you copied it to another file and now only want to keep the new version.

The **rm** command is used to delete a file. The command name **rm** is an abbreviation for "remove." When you remove a file, you delete it.

Warning: If you tell Unix to delete a file using the **rm** command, it will. Be careful not to delete a file you want to keep. Once you have deleted a file, you cannot get it back.

To delete the file **velvet** from the current working directory, you enter the following command line:

```
%rm velvet
```

If you execute an **ls** command after deleting a file, the file you deleted will no longer be listed. There is no undelete command, so you cannot undo a mistake. There is also no "recycle bin" from which you can retrieve the file; the file is really gone.

Sometimes you may want to delete all files that end in a certain file extension. The following command line would delete all files in the current working directory whose file extension is **dvi**:

```
%rm *.dvi
```

The following command would delete all **dvi** files, **log** files, and **aux** files:

```
%rm *.dvi *.log *.aux
```

As this example illustrates, the **rm** command can take several arguments. *Note:* The arguments are separated by spaces, not commas.

Warning: If you tell Unix to delete a group of files using the **rm** command, it will. Be careful not to delete files you want to keep. Be very careful when using the **rm** command with an argument involving *****. Once you have deleted a group of files, you cannot get them back.

Once in a while you will want to delete all files that begin with a certain pattern. For example, you may want to delete all files that have the first two letters **he**. However, before you decide to delete these files, it may be worthwhile to execute the command

```
%ls he*
```

in order to determine exactly which files will be deleted. Maybe you forgot that the file **help**, which you wanted to retain, was located in this directory. If you are sure you want to delete all files beginning with **he**, you can execute the command line

```
%rm he*
```

The **–i** option to the **rm** command asks you whether you are sure you want to delete a file before it is actually removed. The **i** stands for inquiry. The **–i** flag is recommended for beginning users, as it can prevent unwanted file deletions. Some users and system administrators redefine the command **rm** to be **rm –i**. This can be accomplished using the **alias** command, which we cover in Chapter 6, by executing the command line

```
%alias rm 'rm -i'
```

This way whenever an **rm** command is executed, the user has the option not to delete the file. Here is a concrete example:

```
%rm -i ponytail
rm: remove ponytail (yes/no)?
```

If you enter an **n**, the file is not deleted. To delete the file, simply enter a **y**.

You should execute the command line

```
%man rm
```

to learn more about the **rm** command.

Exercises

1. Write a command line to delete the files **a**, **a1**, and **a2**.
2. Describe two interesting options to the **rm** command.
3. How could you delete all the files in the current working directory?
4. How could you delete an entire hierarchy of files?
5. How could you delete all files that have a file extension of **bak**?

4.11 Deleting a Directory—rmdir Command

Once you begin creating files and directories, you will find yourself in a situation where you want to do some reorganization. In such a situation you may find that you want to delete a directory. The **rmdir** command, an abbreviation for "remove directory," deletes a directory. When you remove a directory, you delete the directory.

Warning: If you tell Unix to delete a directory using the **rmdir** command, it will, but only if the directory is empty. Be careful not to delete a directory you want to keep.

To delete the directory **cellphone** from its parent directory, you enter the command line

```
%rmdir cellphone
```

If the directory is empty, it will be deleted. Otherwise, you get a message such as

```
rmdir: directory "cellphone": Directory not empty
```

To delete a directory that is not empty, you can use the **–r** or **–R** flag. Before using this flag, make sure you really want to delete everything in the directory. Once you delete the material, it is irretrievable. Sometimes you will want to delete a directory and all of its subdirectories. The **–r** or **–R** flags can be used to recursively delete an entire directory hierarchy.

You should execute the command line

```
%man rmdir
```

to learn more about the **rmdir** command.

Exercises

1. Compare and contrast the two commands **mkdir** and **rmdir**.
2. Describe two interesting options to the **rmdir** command.
3. What command could you use to delete the entire file structure contained beneath and including the directory **GrayBeard**?
4. What happens if you try to delete a nonexistent directory?

4.12 Clearing the Screen—clear Command

Sometimes after performing a **man** command and then quitting **more** with **q**, your screen may have become cluttered. It might be difficult to separate the results of the next command you enter from those of the previous one. Since output on the screen simply scrolls up, you may sometimes find it desirable to start with a fresh screen. Unix provides the command **clear** for this purpose.

The command line

```
%man clear
```

yields a **NAME** section of

```
NAME
        clear - clear the terminal screen
```

We see that typing

```
%clear
```

clears the screen for us and displays the Unix prompt at the top of the screen. Suppose you perform an **ls** command and obtain the following result:

```
GENERALS        conclu.tex      normscite.sty   summary.tex
README          depth.tex       outline.tex     thesis.bib
abstract.tex    examples.tex    prelims.tex     thesis.tex
backgrd.tex     intro.tex       report.sty      uwthesis.sty
bib.tex         model.tex       slides          zoo.tex
breadth.tex     myalpha.bst     subgraph.tex
```

You then decide to delete the file **zoo.tex**, so you enter the command line

```
%rm zoo.tex
```

Now you want to verify that **zoo.tex** has been deleted, so you do another **ls**, resulting in the following display:

```
GENERALS        conclu.tex      normscite.sty   summary.tex
README          depth.tex       outline.tex     thesis.bib
abstract.tex    examples.tex    prelims.tex     thesis.tex
backgrd.tex     intro.tex       report.sty      uwthesis.sty
bib.tex         model.tex       slides
breadth.tex     myalpha.bst     subgraph.tex
```

If you continued to delete individual files in this fashion and then checked to see if they were gone, eventually the screen would become cluttered. At that point you might decide to use **clear**, as it will be easier to read your output on a fresh screen. In such circumstances, you will find the **clear** command very useful.

Exercises

1. Execute the command **man clear** on your system. How many screenfuls of information did you get? Are there any arguments to the **clear** command? Any related commands?
2. If you are using a GUI with your version of Unix, what is the effect of clearing the screen? Once you clear the screen, are you still able to retrieve its former contents?
3. Give two reasons why you might want to clear the screen.

COMMUNICATION

UNIX COMMANDS FOR COMMUNICATING ON A NETWORK

chapter 5

In this chapter we introduce the following commands:

Unix Command	DOS Command	Description
mesg	—	control write access to your terminal
talk	—	exchange messages in real-time with another user online
users	—	find out which users are currently logged onto your system
who	—	display information about which users are logged into the system
write	—	send a message to another user

5.1 Introduction

One great advantage of using computers is that they allow users to communicate very efficiently with one another. In this chapter we explain several Unix commands that are useful for communicating with other users on the same network as you. These commands are useful for short, informal interactive exchanges. More formal correspondence that needs to be archived should be handled via email. We cover the general principles of email in Chapter 6 and one particular email system called **pine** in Chapter 7.

In this chapter you will learn to use commands to

❏ determine who is logged onto your system.
❏ find out information about other users.
❏ carry on real-time conversations with other users via the network.

5.1.1 who Command

There are times when you will be working on your computer system and will want to find out who else is logged in. For example, you may want to ask someone a question or locate a friend to return a lost item to her. The **who** command is useful for doing this. To execute the command simply enter

`%who`

In Figure 5.1 we depict a sample output from the execution of the command. In this case there are three users on the system: **gregg**, **jones**, and **andrew**. Note that **gregg** and **jones** are logged in more than once.

```
gregg     pts/4     May 31 08:56      (mrmazoo)
gregg     pts/6     Jun  2 16:41      (drake)
gregg     pts/7     May 31 08:56
jones     pts/1     Jun  2 18:31      (cervino)
andrew    pts/8     Jun  2 10:51      (reckless)
jones     pts/5     May 31 13:24      (cervino)
```

Figure 5.1—Sample Output from the **who** Command

The output in Figure 5.1 is divided into four columns representing the userids, the terminal id connected to that user's standard input, the date the users logged into the system, and the machine from which they logged into the system, if in fact they logged in from a different machine. In this case all except **gregg**'s third login were from different machines, namely **mrmazoo**, **drake**, **cervino**, and **reckless**. Once you have determined who is logged in, it would be easy to contact them via email.

To learn more about the **who** command enter

`%man who`

Exercises

1. What users are currently logged into your system?
2. Are there any flags to the **who** command? If so, describe three of them. Are any of these options available on your system?
3. Give two uses for the **who** command that were not mentioned in the text.

5.2   Who Is Logged On?—users Command

The **users** command prints a list of those folks logged into the local host on which the command is executed. If you want to have an online conversation, you will want to find out who is logged onto your system. The output of the **users** command is much more compact than that of the **who** command.

For example, entering the command

```
%users
```

on the machine **pluto.uutah.edu** results in a list of the userids of those currently logged into the host **pluto.uutah.edu**. The list is output in the following form:

```
marty jennifer howard jennifer patrick smith jennifer
```

Note that in this case **jennifer** is logged into the system three times. Once you have determined who is on the system, you can communicate with them using the techniques discussed in the remainder of this chapter.

Exercises

1. Are there any flags to the **users** command? If so, describe them.
2. Compare and contrast the **who** and **users** commands.

5.3   Sending a Note—mesg and write Commands

In the last two sections we have seen two commands that can be used to determine who is logged onto your system. In Section 6.5 we will learn about the **finger** command and in Section 9.3.2 about the **w** command. These commands are useful for finding out additional information about a user other than just whether or not they are logged in and what their userid is. In this section we go over the **mesg** command and the **write** command. These commands allow you to communicate with other users on your network who are running Unix and have these commands available.

The **mesg** command is used to control write access to your terminal, so the **mesg** command works in conjunction with the **write** command. In order for someone to be able to send you a message using the **write** command, you must set up your system to allow messages to be written to your terminal. This is where the **mesg** command comes into play. To determine whether or not you are set up to allow another person to write to your terminal, simply enter

```
%mesg
```

You will receive a response of

```
is y
```

if messages are allowed to be written to your account, and a response of

```
is n
```

if messages are not allowed to be written to your account. To turn messages on, you simply enter the command

```
%mesg y
```

and to turn them off, you simply enter the command

```
%mesg n
```

It is a good idea to turn **mesg** off if you do not want to be disturbed.

Suppose that you (say **tammie@amherst.edu**) have turned **mesg** on and have executed the **users** command and determined that **rhonda** is on the system. You can send a message to **rhonda** by entering the command

```
%write rhonda
```

If **rhonda** were not on the local system, you would simply enter her complete address, such as **rhonda@zuma.calstate.edu**. If **rhonda** has messages turned on, she will see a message on her screen such as

```
Message from tammie@amherst.edu on tty1 at 9:33 ...
```

She will need to enter the command

```
%write tammie
```

or (for a nonlocal connection)

```
%write tammie@amherst.edu
```

in order to complete the **write** connection. If after a while you do not receive a message back from **rhonda**, you can assume that she is not logged in any more, has **mesg** set to **n**, or does not want to talk to you now. You may receive a message such as

```
rhonda: write permission turned off
```

If **rhonda** does respond with a **write** command, the connection will be established for you to communicate. Now whenever either of you types something on the screen, your typing will be displayed on both screens. The standard communication protocol is for the originator of the conversation to go first. Once the first person is finished typing, that is, there is a pause, a blank line, or a line such as "(over)"; it is the other person's chance to respond. When the conversation is finished, a message such as

```
you are no longer in my reality
```

is typed by one of the participants to signal this. To close the connection at any time, either party can enter the **Control-D** command. That is, you hold down the **Control** key and then press the **D** key.[1] You can also type **Control-C** to end the conversation.

It is apparent that the **write** command is useful for holding a real-time exchange that is mutually agreeable to two parties. On a windowing system, such as GNOME, it would be straightforward (for a fast typist) to have several windows, each with its own dedicated conversations.

Exercises

1. What is the default on your account: To have **mesg** on or **mesg** off? Why?
2. Are there any flags to the **write** command? If so, describe them.
3. Suppose a user is logged into several different terminals on the same machine. Is there a way to **write** to them at a specific terminal?
4. Can you **write** to yourself by logging into the same machine twice? What about by logging in only once? Explain.

5.4 Holding a Conversation—talk Command

The **talk** command is a more visually oriented communication command that provides essentially the same functionality as the **write** command. Again, the **mesg** command controls whether or not you accept conversations with others on your terminal.

Suppose you (**august@biology.uci.edu**) want to have a conversation with **ronald@gotosleep.org**. Simply make sure you set **mesg** to **y**. Then just enter the command

```
%talk ronald@gotosleep.org
```

If **ronald** is running Unix, has the **talk** command available, and has **mesg** set to **y**; he will see a message on his terminal such as

```
Message from Talk_Daemon@biology.uci.edu at 18:50 ...
talk connection requested by august@biology.uci.edu
talk: respond with: talk august@biology.uci.edu
```

If **ronald** has **mesg** set to **n**, you will see a message such as

```
[Your party is refusing messages.]
```

If **ronald** has **mesg** set to **y**, he simply responds with

---

1. It is not necessary to type a capital D. This is simply the accepted convention for writing "d."

```
talk august@biology.uci.edu
```

in order to have a conversation with you. If **ronald** responds with this message, a **talk** connection will be established. Both his and your terminal screen will be divided in half. Whatever you type in will be displayed on one half of the screen and whatever **ronald** types in will be displayed on the other side. If **ronald** does not respond, you can assume he does not want to talk or is away from his terminal. If **ronald** is not logged in you will get a message such as

```
[Your party is not logged in.]
```

If there is no response, the original output from the **talk** program may be repeated. If you get no response, you can exit the **talk** program by typing **Control-C**.

Once a **talk** connection is established, at any time either party can end the conversation by typing **Control-C**. You will each receive a message such as

```
[Connection closing. Exiting.]
```

Since the **talk** program divides the screen into two halves with each user's typing being displayed in one half, its output is visually more appealing than the **write** program. Both programs are good for short conversations. You will soon become impatient with these programs if your correspondent is a slow typist. For communications that do not need to be done in real-time, email is a less intrusive method of communication. We discuss email in the next chapter.

Exercises

1. Compare and contrast the **talk** and **write** programs.
2. Describe what the necessary and sufficient conditions are for two users to be able to communicate using the **talk** program.
3. Can the **Control-D** command sequence be used to end a **talk** conversation on your system? If not, what happens? If so, what message is printed by the program as it exits?
4. Are there any flags to the **talk** command? If so, describe them.

ELECTRONIC MAIL

chapter 6

In this chapter we discuss the following commands:

Unix Command	Dos Command	Description
alias	—	define another name for a command
finger	—	locate information about a user
unalias	—	remove an alias for a command

6.1 Introduction

Thus far, we have focused our discussion entirely on the Unix operating system. You now have a basic grasp of Unix and should be able to perform many routine functions on your computer. In this chapter we cover *electronic mail*, or *email* for short—the subject of sending and receiving messages over an electronic network.

Email is very important for conversing with other Unix users and in obtaining answers to your questions about Unix. Even if you have already been using email, you may not be familiar with all the relevant terminology nor with a Unix mail program. In this chapter we discuss the most important concepts relating to email, and in Chapter 7 we cover a popular Unix email client named **pine**.

Our goal in this chapter is to acquaint you with the fundamental principles of email. Among other things, you will learn about the following topics in this chapter:

❑ email addresses.
❑ *domain names.*
❑ *aliasing.*
❑ message components.
❑ message composition.
❑ email management.

6.2 Email Clients

Email infiltrates many areas of the Internet and is widely used as a vehicle for communication. If you are not fluent with email, you may find yourself unable to keep up with today's communications. With each passing day, it is becoming more important to become proficient with email. Whether for business or pleasure, everyone needs to learn to use email effectively in order to keep pace with today's rapidly changing world.

Since there are so many different *email clients* (synonyms being *mailers*, *email programs*, and *email applications*), we will stick to a generic description of email. An email client is a program designed for managing, reading, composing, and sending email. The Unix-based **pine** email program is covered in detail in Chapter 7, where we will apply the ideas explained in this chapter. The basic email concepts we discuss carry over directly to most mailers. It is important to grasp the fundamentals of email, since new and improved email programs are frequently being introduced. Additionally, if you switch places of employment at some point in your career, there is a good chance your new employer will use a different email application than the system you are currently using.

Email programs have become very sophisticated in the past few years. This has made using email much easier and more efficient. Some popular email clients are **elm**, **Eudora**, **mail**, **mutt**, **Microsoft Exchange**, **Microsoft Outlook**, **Netscape Messenger**, and **pine**. Most *Web browsers* come with a built-in email application. Many *Internet service providers* (ISPs) provide their own email client. As you can surmise, it is very likely you will need to learn more than one email application over the years.

Exercises

1. Do you use email? If so, for how long have you been using it and which email clients are you familiar with? How many messages do you receive per week? How many messages do you send? Of those you receive, how many do you actually reply to? Are you familiar with any Unix-based email clients?
2. List the names of as many email clients as possible.

6.3 Email Addresses

It is important to have a basic understanding of email addresses. This knowledge will serve you well in remembering and deducing them. The most general form of an email address is `userid@hostname.subdomain.domain`

There are some exceptions, but this format covers most common email addresses. The text before the @ (pronounced "at") sign specifies the **userid** of the individual, while the text after the @ sign indicates where to deliver that individual's mail. We covered userids in Section 2.2, so let us focus on the suffix following the @.

To start off we look at a couple of sample email addresses. For example, consider

`josee@math.ucf.edu`

The first important item to note is that the suffix following the @ sign gets more general from left to right. That is, **math** is a subdomain of **ucf**, **ucf** is a subdomain of **edu**, and **edu** specifies a (generic) *top-level domain name*. In this case, Josee is a math major at the University of Central Florida. The Mathematics Department is one department at the University of Central Florida, which in turn is an educational institution.

If Josee had her own computer called **skiing** that was configured to receive email, the email address

`josee@skiing.math.ucf.edu`

would also work for her.

The number of periods (a period is pronounced "dot") varies from email address to email address. Most addresses have either one or two dots. For example, consider the following email address

`larry@juniper.com`

This address has a top-level domain of **com**. The word **com** is an abbreviation for commercial. The subdomain **juniper** is a commercial entity, and **larry** is a computer user who works at Juniper.

A given field in an email address, that is, a part separated by dots, can be no more than 63 characters long. All fields combined must total fewer than 256 characters. You will rarely encounter email addresses over 30 characters long.

It is important to know how an email address is read out loud so that you can communicate your email address and can record another person's. In our first example the address is read as "josee at math dot u c f dot e d u," and the second one is read as "larry at juniper dot com." When someone specifies an email address to you, it is a good idea to repeat the address back to them in order to make sure that you understood it correctly.

Exercises

1. How many different email addresses do you have? What are they? Explain how your addresses become more specific in going from right to left.
2. Suppose Sara Davis worked at the University of California at San Diego in the Department of Oceanography. Give three plausible email addresses for her.
3. What are the shortest and longest email addresses that you have encountered? What is the theoretically shortest possible email address in terms of the number of symbols?

6.4 Domain Names

Currently only a small number of top-level domain names exist in the United States. The big seven generic top-level domain names in the United States are **com**, **edu**, **gov**, **int**, **mil**, **net**, and **org**. They are listed in Table 6.1 with a brief explanation.

Domain Name	Description
com	commercial business
edu	education
gov	U.S. government agency
int	international entity
mil	U.S. military
net	networking organization
org	nonprofit organization

Table 6.1—The Generic Top-Level Domain Names Used in the United States

In addition to U.S. domain names, every country has its own top-level domain name. In the United States, these are called *country codes*. A few country codes are shown in Table 6.2. It is easy to track down a listing of all country codes online.

Domain Name	Description
au	Australia
ca	Canada
de	Germany
es	Spain (España)
fr	France
hk	Hong Kong
jp	Japan
uk	United Kingdom
us	United States
za	South Africa

Table 6.2—A Small Sampling of Country Top-Level Domain Names

There are proposals to expand the number of top-level domain names. The decision involves economics and politics as much as technology. The number of top-level domain names is an artifact of the early years of the Internet. In total, including all country codes, there are about 150 top-level domain names.

Figure 6.1 provides a convenient way of viewing the organization of the domain names. In the figure we depict a very small portion of the *domain name system* (DNS). This naming scheme provides a unique email address for everyone who is connected to the Internet. The tree structure guarantees the names will be unique. The ... in the figure indicates that many branches of the tree are not shown. Notice how similar the structure in Figure 6.1 is to a Unix directory hierarchy. A full pathname, from a child of the root to a parent of a userid, written down from right to left corresponds to the portion of an email address to the right of the @ sign.

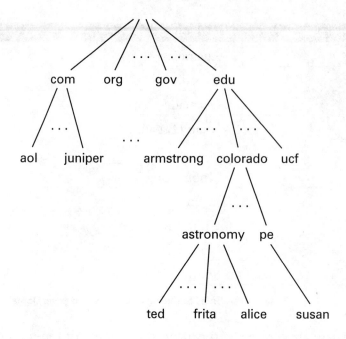

Figure 6.1—A Small Fragment of the Domain Name System

For example, the user **ted** would have an email address of

`ted@astronomy.colorado.edu`

and **susan** would have an email address of

`susan@pe.colorado.edu`

It is important to realize that the domain name space is a *distributed naming scheme* that follows the boundaries of countries and organizations, rather than those of networks. If you know where a user fits in the domain name space, it is relatively easy to determine a corresponding email address.

Exercises

1. List five country codes that are not presented in Table 6.2.
2. Give an example of an existing subdomain for each of the following domains: **com**, **edu**, **gov**, and **org**.

6.5   Figuring Out an Email Address

Once you know the basic principles behind email addresses and you have the picture of Figure 6.1 in mind, it should be fairly easy for you to guess someone's email address. For example, suppose you know that Rossella Vincino has her own company called Suits. An educated guess for her email address would be

```
vincino@suits.com
```

Since you know her company is in business to make money, you guess **com** instead of **org**. Similar principles and some basic deduction can be used to make informed guesses about anyone's email address. For those times when you cannot locate someone, a number of different methods are available for determining an email address:

❑ Ask the person directly.

❑ Go through your browser. For example, Netscape Navigator includes a "search" button that provides access to a group of *white page directories*. White pages are akin to online telephone books.

❑ Use a *search engine*, such as *Yahoo!*, and submit a query on that person's name.

❑ Use a search engine to determine the primary *Web server* for the site or organization where the person is located. Then look for directory information on the site's Web pages by using a search option at that site.

❑ Use a program specially designed for locating people. For example, Unix provides a command called **finger** for doing this.

The **finger** command takes as an argument a name or an email address. If you wanted a detective to investigate someone, you would ask the detective to **finger** the person. This is where the **finger** command derives its name from. The command line

```
%finger johnson
```

returns information about any users on the local system named **johnson** or about anyone with the userid **johnson**. For example, it might return information about Marilyn Johnson, whose userid is **marilyn**, and David Johnson, whose userid is **johnson**.

The **finger** program may return information about when the person last logged in as well as when they "read" email last. Fingering a person is not a reliable way to determine if the person has read the email message *you* sent. This is because the recipient of the email may have opened up the email client but not actually read all the messages since last receiving email.

The command line

```
%finger harris@history.utexas.edu
```

will return information about the person having userid **harris**, who is in the History Department at the University of Texas. If no such userid exists, an error message such as

```
        Login name: harris        In real life: ???
```

is returned.

If **history.utexas.edu** is not a valid computer name an error message such as

```
        unknown host: history.utexas.edu
```

is returned.

There are two special files on Unix systems where you can store information that the **finger** program will display. Their names are **.plan** and **.project**. Notice that both of these file names begin with the . character. Both of these files must reside in your home directory. When someone executes a **finger** command on your userid, the result will be a display of the information about the user. Typically, the first line of the **.project** file is displayed along with the entire contents of the **.plan** file. You can have either one of the files or both. It is common to include contact information and travel information in these files. Thus, other users will know how to reach you.

Here is a prototypical **.plan** file:

```
    Mills Vance            Office: 912.897.8898
    234 Windsor Road       Messages: 912.987.1212
    Savannah, Georgia 31419 Fax: 912.987.1000
    vance@jeep.peachnet.com URL: www.area.scad.edu/vance


    I am currently working on my thesis.


    I will be away from June 1 - June 14 on vacation.
```

The command

```
    %finger vance
```

would display the information in the **.plan** file. Notice this **.plan** provides some very useful information about how to contact Mills and also lets you know when he will be away. If you decide to have your own **.plan** file, remember to keep its information up to date.

Some people like to include funny or sarcastic remarks in their **.plan** or **.project** files. For example, you may see something like

```
    To live forever; or die trying.
```

In summary, the **finger** command can be very helpful for determining someone's
❑ email address (you can **finger** a person via a name).
❑ contact information.

❑ future plans.
❑ time of last login.

Figure 6.2 displays the output of a sample **finger** command.

```
%finger mullins

Login name: mullins        In real life: Deborah Mullins
Directory: /home/mullins   Shell: /bin/csh
On since Feb  1 14:47:50 on console from :0
No unread mail

Plan:

Updated February 26, 2000.
---------------------------
Heading to New England in mid-March and then again in mid-
April. Off to France in May. Off to South Africa in June.
Off to Switzerland in June. Off to California in September.
Off to Seattle in December.


*********************************************************
Deborah Mullins
Department of English
Armstrong Atlantic State University
11935 Abercorn Street
Savannah, Georgia 31419-1997
*********************************************************
```

Figure 6.2—Output from the **finger** Command

To learn more about the **finger** command you should do a **man finger**. Note that on some systems the **finger** command is disabled because it is considered a security risk. You can consult your system adminstrator for further information about the **finger** command and the security risks it poses.

Exercises

1. Is the **finger** command enabled on your system? If so, what is the output of executing the **finger** command on your userid? In either case, can you do a **man finger**? Are there any options to the **finger**

command? What happens if you enter the **finger** command with no arguments?

2. Print out the **.plan** file of someone you know. Critique it. Is it humorous or does it contain any serious information?

3. Try to locate an email address for an old acquaintance following, in order, the various steps outlined in this section. Were you successful? If so, which of the steps worked and which did not? Can you suggest any other means to track down someone's email address?

6.6   Aliasing

Having determined an individual's email address, you may find that the email address is too cumbersome to remember. In that case, an *alias* for the address can be set up within your own email system. An alias is an easy-to-remember name that you create. The email client associates the alias with a particular email address. Each mailer has its own procedure for setting up aliases, but they are similar and are typically called something like "address book" or "nickname feature" by the mailer. For example, if your brother has an email address

> `samueljefferson@intelligentsystems.com`

and you frequently send him email, you may want to set up an alias, such as **sam**. Then, every time you want to send email to him, you would type or select the address **sam** and the mailer would insert your brother's email address (or make it available for you to insert). Typing **sam** is obviously much faster than typing in his entire email address. Conceptually,

> `sam`

gets replaced by

> `samueljefferson@intelligentsystems.com`

You will sometimes see email addresses containing capital letters. You do not need to type them this way, as email addresses are not case sensitive.

An email alias can also be established for a whole group of people to whom you need to send the same message. For example, you may want to send a message to members of a class or a special interest group. To send a message to everyone in your bowling club, you might select an alias of **club** and list all your club members' email addresses. Then simply addressing your email to **club** will result in everyone receiving a copy of the message. Obviously, this is very convenient, because you do not have to look up the email addresses of everyone who is in the club. This type of alias is sometimes referred to as a *distribution list* or *private* *distribution list*. The aliases we have been discussing only affect the email that you send; such aliases are known as *local* or *private aliases*. Someone else's alias of **club** might include the members of a softball team.

In addition to setting up a local email alias, a systemwide or *public alias* can also be established. These are aliases that are usable by everyone on any system that can send email. The primary use of a public alias is to buffer the owner and his correspondents against change. The public alias should be selected to be as stable as possible and to point to the real delivery address, which can be expected to change over time. A secondary use of a public alias is to make it easy or convenient to locate someone. For example, the system administrator might decide that it would be helpful to use an alias, such as **sally**, for herself, so that anyone on the system can easily email her questions and comments. Even though you personally do not have **sally** designated as an alias, the mailer will determine that a message sent to **sally** is a public alias and will direct your message to the correct address.

Sometimes it is useful for the system administrator to set up public aliases for you. This way, if someone is taking an educated guess at your email address, chances are that it will match one of your system aliases. For example, Jacob Thad Henson, whose userid is **jth**, might be assigned email aliases of **jacob**, **henson**, and **jake**.

When a system administrator establishes a global alias for a list of addresses, the result is a private distribution list that allows a user to send a message to a whole group of people. To send messages to each person on the list, the sender addresses the email to the name of the list. The mailing software automatically distributes the message to each name on the list.

Aliasing is used for convenience in many other different areas of computer science. Unix provides a way to rename and redefine commands. The **alias** command allows you to specify a new name for a command. For example, suppose you have trouble remembering to use the **ls** command to list your files because you are used to typing **DIR**. The command line

```
%alias DIR ls
```

lets you type **DIR** to execute the **ls** command. As another example, suppose you nearly always list your files in the long form. It makes sense to define the following alias:

```
%alias ls 'ls -l'
```

This allows you to type **ls** and get the same result as if you typed **ls –l**. Notice the single quotes that are necessary in defining this alias. Later in the text we will see other examples of using single quotes to define things in Unix.

Another intuitive and mnemonic way to define this alias for the **ls** command would be as follows:

```
%alias ll 'ls -l'
```

This defines the command **ll** as a way to list the long form of your files. In this case you can continue to use the original **ls** command as you normally would have.

To remove an alias, you simply use the **unalias** command. For example,

```
%unalias ll
```

deletes the **ll** command. That is, **ll** no longer would stand for any command.

Exercises

1. What is your userid? What are three sensible aliases for it?
2. What groups do you belong to that it would make sense to have a distribution list for? Why?
3. Suppose you defined **ls** to be an alias for **ls –l**. What happens when you enter the command **ls –a**? How about **ls –l**?
4. Devise a naming scheme for aliasing the **ls** command where you use two-character aliases to represent the various options to the **ls** command. For example, you might use **ll** to represent **ls –l**.
5. How would you alias the **rm** command so that it always inquired whether or not you intended to delete a file?

6.7 Email Message Components

Figure 6.3 depicts a sample email message. The first part of a message is referred to as the *email header*. In this case the email header consists of five lines. Each email client will display slightly different header information. Often, header information is part of the email message, but the mail client may not be set up to display that information. Sometimes you can see these extra lines if you save the message in an email client folder and then look at the file with an ordinary text editor or print the message out. The header we have shown is actually an abbreviated email header. The *full header* includes some additional information, such as parts of the route the message took to reach your computer and the unique *message id* associated with this particular message.

```
From: D. Houston <houston@eagle.org> Fri Jan 18 11:03 EDT 2000
Date: Fri, 18 Jan 2000 11:03 -0400 (EDT)
To: gomez@telephonelink.org
Subject: roller coasters
Cc: melissa@psychology.ucla.edu


Dear Diana,

    Ever since that trip to Cedar Point, I have been doing
some research on the largest roller coasters in the world.
My findings about them may interest you. (Melissa, I
think you will be interested in the psychology behind some
of their designs.) I can't type now as someone is knocking
on my door. Be back at you soon.


                      --Davy


*************************************************************
David Houston        |  office: 401.437.8838
55 Eagle Ave.        |  houston@eagle.org
Newport, RI 02900    |  www.eagle.org/houston/main.html
*************************************************************
```

Figure 6.3—A Sample Email Message

While most parts of the message are self-explanatory, we will mention them briefly to familiarize you with the terminology.

The *From* field indicates who sent the message and when. In this case D. Houston, whose email address is **houston@eagle.org**, sent the message on Friday, January 18, 2000, at 11:03 A.M. Eastern Daylight Time (EDT). Note that time is represented using a 24-hour clock.

The *Date* field repeats the date and includes an interesting feature: The -0400. This tells us that EDT is four hours behind Greenwich Mean Time (GMT). Greenwich, England, is the location where standard time is kept. Since email is sent throughout the world, a reference by the mailer to GMT lets us deduce when the user sent the message in relation to our local time. In this example, the message was sent at 3 P.M. GMT. If the message had been sent from Laguna Beach, California, instead of Newport, Rhode Island, we would see a reference to Pacific Daylight Time (PDT) rather than EDT. In general, the date field will include a reference to the time zone the sender is in.

The *To* field specifies to whom the message was sent. In this case, the recipient is

`gomez@telephonelink.org`

The *Subject* field provides a hint as to what the message is about. Here, after only seeing the Subject field, we can assume the message will have something to do with "roller coasters."

The *Cc* field tells us that the message was "carbon copied" to another user. The names of other recipients of the letter who were carbon copied will be listed here. In our example, the message was also delivered to the email address

`melissa@psychology.ucla.edu`

One field that does not appear but is worth mentioning is *Bcc*, which stands for *blind carbon copy*. Additional copies of the message may have been sent out. If the Bcc feature were used, we would not see an indication of it in the heading. *Bcc* is used when you do not want one or more of the recipients to know that someone else was copied on the message.

The opening

`Dear Diana,`

is called the *greeting* of the message.

The main content of the message is called the *text*.

```
Ever since that trip to Cedar Point, I have been doing
some research on the largest roller coasters in the world.
My findings about them may interest you. (Melissa, I
think you will be interested in the psychology behind some
of their designs.) I can't type now as someone is knocking
on my door. Be back at you soon.
```

The final part of the message is known as the *signature*.

`--Davy`

```
**********************************************************
David Houston       |    office: 401.437.8838
55 Eagle Ave.       |    houston@eagle.org
Newport, RI 02900   |    www.eagle.org/houston/main.html
**********************************************************
```

In many business situations involving frequent message exchanges, it is standard to omit the greeting and signature altogether.

The greeting, text, and signature form the *body* of the message. Most email clients recognize the header and body divisions of email messages. A third part of some messages is an *attachment*. An attachment is a file that is sent along with the email message. Attachments often contain specially formatted information.

Exercises

1. Print out a sample email message. Label the parts of the message as described in this section.
2. Why is it important to use a descriptive subject when sending out email?
3. Print out an interesting signature file. Why did you find it interesting? Does your mailer automatically attach your signature file to messages you send? Why is it important to keep signature files short?

6.8 Writing an Email Message

The method by which you compose an email message will vary from email client to email client; however, the basic principles will remain the same. We cover the basic principles of composition in this section.

6.8.1 Message Structure

If you are composing an email message within a mailer, it will prompt you for certain information. Suppose you have selected the compose button or command. Figure 6.4 shows a standard template that a mailer might provide.

```
To       :
Cc       :
Attchmnt :
Subject  :
-----Message Text-----
```

Figure 6.4—Typical Email Template for Message Composition

The mailer's first field is generally the To field. This is where the email address of the person to whom you are sending the message is entered. Many mailers allow you to enter a list of names, separated by commas, on the To line. For example,

```
To: james@firestone.com, regina@subway.nyc.com,
thayes@goliat.upc.es
```

After entering to whom you want to send an email message (either in the form of an alias or an email address), you can specify a file to be attached to this message in the optional Attchmnt field. If you do decide to attach a file, you will be prompted to enter the file name. With many email clients, you will also be prompted to enter a short description of your attachment.

Following the attachment is the Subject line. You should enter a brief descriptive comment for the message subject. If the subject is uninteresting, the recipient may not bother reading your email right away, or even at all. On the other hand, a subject line that is too long may be truncated, or may have its own scroll bar. Including a subject that is concise and descriptive is a good idea, since this data, and your email address, are usually the only information displayed on the recipient's screen. For example, a mailer might display the information shown in Figure 6.5 when you open your mailbox.

```
1 December 25 Pamela Swartz    (3,443)
2 December 27 Ralph Michels    (2,321) Re: donuts
3 January 17 Paul Swanson     (1,111) Missing documents
4 January 21 Jim Lester       (5,332) Great work!
5 January 21 Jim Lester        (876) 1 more thing
```

Figure 6.5—Email Client Display for Multiple Email Messages

In Figure 6.5 the first message contains no subject. If you did not recognize the sender of this message, you might delete it without reading further. The subjects of the remaining messages are

❑ Re: donuts
❑ Missing documents
❑ Great work!
❑ 1 more thing

You can surmise that the message from Paul Swanson is an important one. Usually, it is a good idea to read such a message right away. The message from Ralph Michels is a reply to a message the owner of this account sent.[1] This is indicated by the **Re:**.

A bad habit that you want to avoid developing is the practice of automatically hitting the "reply" button to respond to an email message. After several iterations, the subject deteriorates to the point where it has absolutely nothing to do with the contents of the accompanying message.

Note that some mailers have two reply buttons: One that lets you reply just to the sender of the message, and another that lets you reply to everyone who

---

1. It is possible for a user to enter Re: as part of the subject line but this is considered very bad form. Thus, in all likelihood the recipient of this message originally sent a message with the subject heading **donuts**.

received the first message. Be careful to use the correct button when you reply to a message.

The date and time that the email is sent, as well as your email address, will automatically be filled in by the mailer when you send your message. You have the option of sending copies of the message to others using Cc or Bcc. Simply enter the other email addresses or aliases, as desired. For important correspondence that you want to maintain a record of, it is a good idea either to Cc or Bcc yourself, unless your mailer automatically keeps a copy of sent messages.

Most mailers let you specify your favorite text editor for message composition. That is, if you are composing your message in a separate window, you can usually select the editor you would like to use. If not, you will be provided with a default editor. For example, the **pine** mailer uses the **pico** (standing for "pine composer") text editor by default. The text editor acts as a word processor; it allows you to type in and modify your message.

Most mailers come with a help facility. On nearly all Unix systems documentation is available online to learn about **pine** and **pico**. We discuss both of these pieces of software in Chapter 7.

6.8.2 Network Etiquette

For the most part, when writing your email message, you should follow the rules of informal letter composition. The greeting you select will often set the tone for the message. For example,

> **Dear Dr. Larabie,**

is very different from

> **Hey Doc,**

If the person you are writing to is a close friend, you would naturally be less formal than if you are mailing your resume to a prospective employer.

The overall tone of the message body is also very important. Email messages seem to be inherently direct, so it can be easy to misinterpret, or to phrase a message incorrectly. When we communicate in person (or, to a certain extent, even via the telephone), facial expressions, volume and tone of voice, and gestures all provide clues as to how you and the other person are reacting to the conversation. With written words, all these indicators are absent.

Informal rules of network etiquette, or *netiquette*, suggest practicing restraint when using email to express opinions or ideas, especially when the message will be read by people who do not know you well. When the message is informal, a common practice is to use a *smiley* :-) or a *wink* ;-) to indicate something said in jest. These little symbols and others like them are called *emoticons* and resemble little sideways faces.

Typing a message in capital letters is considered shouting, and doing so signals that the sender is either an email novice, very angry, excited, or ignorant of the rules of netiquette. Not following the rules of netiquette (or sometimes just message content) may result in a *flaming* by someone who took offense to what you said. A flame is a nasty response from the offended party.

6.8.3 Composition

For sending email to friends or to people you know, simply type in a message as you would say it. For people you do not know, or with whom you have had little conversation, be slightly more formal and check your message for typos. When applying for jobs or communicating with people for the first time, you should proofread and spell check your message. Many email applications have a built-in spell checker. A message containing typos may offend your reader and will certainly distract. Most people find that it takes much more concentration to do a thorough job of proofreading on a screen than on a printed page, so it is a good idea to spend an extra minute or two proofreading your messages.

You should always sign your name (that is, identify yourself with your actual name or nickname, not just your email address or userid) or end an email message with your *signature file*. If you opt to use a signature file, many mailers will automatically append it to all messages you send. A signature file should contain standard contact information. For example, it might consist of your nickname, name, phone number, fax number, email address (even though it's already included by the mailer), favorite quote, favorite ASCII graphic,[2] and World Wide Web address. Figure 6.6 depicts a typical signature file.

```
Patrick M. LaMalva
Executive Director
Computing Sciences Accreditation Board (CSAB)
184 North Street
Stamford, CT 06901
ph: (203) 975-1117
fx: (203) 975-1222
em: csab@csab.org
web: http://www.csab.org
```

Figure 6.6—Sample Email Signature

---

2. ASCII stands for American Standard Code for Information Interchange.

After composing your message using a text editor and signing it, you are ready to send. Again, for important correspondence or correspondence you would like to keep a record of, it is a good idea to Cc yourself on the message. Depending on the mailer, you may have to click on a send icon, press the **Control** key and the **d** key simultaneously, or press some other key or combination of keys to indicate that you want the email sent. Before sending the email, you sometimes have the opportunity (again, depending on the mailer) to *attach files* that you would like to append to the message. Some mailers also let you *insert a file* or a graphic at any point in the message body. Up until the time you actually send the email, you can make changes and even decide not to send. Once the message is sent, you cannot get it back. It is like dropping a letter in a mailbox.

6.8.4 Bracketed Text and Include

When replying to a message, keep in mind that a period of time may have elapsed since you received the message. Thus, a reply of **Yes** to a message may have no meaning to the recipient. The recipient may not recall whether you are answering the question "Did you steal $10 from me?" or "What was the name of that '60s rock band that had cool album covers?"

```
Hi Leslie,

I was salmon fishing in Alaska last summer.
I rented a large raft and a motor.

We ended up catching some Kings and a few Pinks.
The local guide told us that this was not a
very good year.

The cost of the trip was worth it though, just to
see the wildlife.

                              --Moe
```

Figure 6.7—Sample Email Message Body

It is a good idea to include the context of the original email message along with your reply. Most mailers allow you to do this very conveniently. The format will look something like the following

original text from sender

if you select the "include option," or

>`original text from sender`

if you select the "bracketed option." The greater than sign (>) is usually inserted at the beginning of each line. In either case the original text is usually indented. When you reply to a message, only include the original text that is pertinent to your response; do not include the whole message, unless it is brief. For example, suppose you received the message body shown in Figure 6.7. You might use the reply with the bracketed include option, as shown in Figure 6.8. If the include option is not available on your email application, be sure to give some background about the message you are responding to when replying.

```
Hi Moe,

> I rented a large raft and a motor.

Did you pump it up by hand?

> The cost of the trip was worth it though, just to
> see the wildlife.

I would pay good money to experience this.

Les
```

Figure 6.8—Sample Email Reply Using a Bracketed Include

Figure 6.8 indicates how important it is to give a context for your response to a message. Without the bracketed indent material included, the response from Les would look as shown in Figure 6.9. Clearly, there is no context for this message. If when Moe received it he had forgotten the context of the fishing trip to Alaska, he would not be able to make sense of the message.

```
Did you pump it up by hand?
I would pay good money to experience this.

Les
```

Figure 6.9—Sample Email Reply without Using a Bracketed Include

The key to becoming competent with your mailer is to explore different options and read the help information. Try to learn a couple of new features about your mailer per week.

6.8.5 Forwarding Email to Friends

Most mailers allow you to pass a message along to another person. This is called *email forwarding*. It is a good idea to exercise restraint in forwarding email to another person since that person typically will not experience the same level of excitement as you did when reading the email. If you forward too much email to someone, the recipient will become annoyed. Future email messages from you may be automatically deleted without consideration.

6.8.6 Forwarding Email to Yourself

At some point, you may have more than one email address. For example, you might have several different computer accounts. Instead of reading email from two different accounts, it is often more convenient to have all email directed to only one account. This is usually possible by forwarding all your email from one account to the other, or, in general, directing a number of email addresses to one. On Unix systems, there is a special file called **.forward**, where you can specify the email address to which you would like the email from that account to be forwarded. The **.forward** file needs to be placed in a user's home directory.

For example, suppose you wanted to forward email from your account on a machine called **june.cs.washington.edu** to the account **tabby** on a machine called **ward.cs.washington.edu**. Then on **june** you would add the line

```
tabby@ward.cs.washington.edu
```

to your **.forward** file. The email you would have received on **june** would now be forwarded to **ward**.

Care must be taken to avoid infinite email loops. For example, do not forward email from account **A** to account **B** and also forward email from account **B** to account **A**. Doing this will cause the email to cycle back and forth.

If you are going to be working at a different location for an extended period of time, it can be very useful to set up email forwarding. This way your correspondents can continue to send you email as before, even if they are not aware you are working at a new location.

Exercises

1. If you Cc yourself on an email message do you get two copies of the message or only one?
2. What is the difference between attaching a file to an email message and inserting a file in an email message?
3. What email client do you use? Can you invoke a spell checker from inside your mailer? If so, how do you invoke it?
4. Compose a signature file for yourself and print it out.
5. Why would you want to send an email message using Bcc?

6.9 Email Hints

You have already seen that email is a complex communication mechanism with many uses. Here we share a few helpful tips. Clearly, you will develop your own email style, but you should not just let it evolve without thought. It is worth spending some time evaluating how you use email and how effective your responses are. Here are some questions to think about.

❑ Does email help you become more efficient at work?
❑ Are you flooded with email from mailing lists?
❑ Are you constantly reading forwarded jokes?
❑ How can email make you more productive instead of less efficient?
❑ Do you receive a lot of useless gossip?
❑ Do you receive lots of junk email?

A new email arrival is usually signaled to you by your mailer. If you are already logged on, there may be a beep when new email arrives, or a mailbox icon with a flag up will be displayed. On most Unix systems, each time you log in the system will notify you if you have new email.

When you decide to view your email, your mailer will provide some sort of index of messages with the subject line displayed (as in Figure 6.5). Usually, the messages are numbered in sequence. They might be displayed in either chronological or reverse chronological order. The mailer typically displays the first or current message.

6.9.1 Processing Options

When a new email message arrives, you have a number of options for dealing with the message. A few of them are listed below.

❑ You might decide, based on the subject line and the address of the sender, that you want to delete the message without reading it. This is one way to deal efficiently with junk email.

❑ You may decide that you do not have time to read the message right away and that you will get back to it later. In this case, you could simply skip over the message or save it to a file.

❑ You may decide to read the current message now. After reading the message, you have the option of deleting the message, replying to it, forwarding the message to someone else, saving the message in a file, or saving the message in your mailbox. Note that it is sometimes worth scanning your entire mailbox before replying to a message, since another later message may supersede the contents of the earlier one.

If you do not receive a lot of email messages (say, fewer than 20 per day), it may be tempting to let them "lie around" in your mailbox. However, if the volume of email you receive picks up, either because you find that you really like communicating via email or because you subscribe to one or more mailing lists, you will need another strategy for dealing with your email.

One recommended strategy, called *triage*,[3] can be summed up as follows:

1. Skim for the most important messages (from your best friend, boss, and so on).
2. Skim for what you can delete unread.
3. Work through the remainder.

Another strategy, called *skim and delete*, works as follows:

1. Skim through your mailbox, reading only those messages that are important to you while deleting the rest.
2. If possible, deal with each message immediately and generate a response as required.
3. If the message requires more than a couple of minutes to address, save it for later if time does not permit handling it now.

If a message is very important, you should save it. Messages can be stored in files and organized in directories by subject, date, and so on, or they can be saved in your mailbox.

Naturally, the mileage you get from such strategies will vary. However, it is critical to develop some sort of protocol for dealing with email, especially if you find it becoming a burden.

6.9.2 Vacation Programs

If you receive a lot of email, you may consider the possibility of configuring a *vacation program* when you go away for an extended period of time. A vacation

---

3. The word "triage" means a system of assigning priorities of medical treatment based on urgency, chance for survival, and so on, and is used on battlefields and in hospital emergency wards.

program is one that automatically replies to your email. Usually, the program sends a brief reply back to each message you receive. For business purposes, it is customary to include the name and telephone number/email address of someone to contact in your absence. Consider the following points before setting up such a program.

❑ Does your vacation message tell recipients whom to contact in your absence?

❑ Do most of your friends know you are going away?

❑ Do most of your business associates realize you are on vacation?

❑ If someone knows you are away for a week, will it make a big difference in terms of correspondence?

❑ Are you subscribed to any mailing lists where 1,000 or so users could be bombarded by your vacation program?

❑ Do you want to generate lots of additional and perhaps unnecessary email?

Not all vacation programs function equally well. With a good program and the right mailing list server software, things can work very well. Nevertheless, at least think about the points mentioned above before installing such a program.

6.9.3 Email and Businesses

When working in a business environment that uses email, you should be aware that it is legal for an employer to read all company email. Very few companies actually do read employees' email, but you should be aware that they can. A company could maintain backups of all email for a long period of time. If necessary, a company could go back and review the email messages of an employee. Such backups can also be subpoenaed.

Businesses sometimes use *email filters*. The filters can work in both directions, to limit either incoming or outgoing email. The filtering mechanism examines each message's email address before deciding whether or not to send the email on. Businesses use email filters to restrict with whom their employees can communicate.

Exercises

1. Outline your strategy for processing email.

2. For a one-week period, chart the number of email messages you receive per day, how many you read, and how many you actually reply to. What fraction of your email would you say is actually necessary? What percentage of your email is just for fun? What percentage of your email may be described as junk?

3. Is your email filtered at work or school?

chapter 7

PINE MAILER

In this chapter we discuss the following commands:

Unix Command	DOS Command	Description
mail	—	run the Unix email program
messages	—	count the messages in a mailbox
pico	EDIT	edit a text file
pine	—	run the pine mail program

7.1 Introduction

This chapter provides an introduction to the *pine mail program*, a popular email client that was developed at the University of Washington in 1989. The name **pine** stands for "Program for Internet News and Email." **Pine** provides an easy-to-use, keyboard-driven interface for composing, sending, reading, and managing email and newsgroup messages.

We explain the basic features of **pine**. Other mailers have similar functionality but their user interfaces may differ. For example, **Eudora** is a popular mouse-driven email program. Nearly all features found in **pine** exist in Eudora and vice versa. In **pine** one or two keystrokes are needed to execute a command, whereas in Eudora several mouse clicks are necessary. Both **pine** and **Eudora** have extensive online documentation.

7.2 Pine's Main Menu

Pine is a text-driven, Unix-based email client; that is, all commands are entered as keystrokes. The mouse is not used, as there is no graphical user interface. Menus, which are located at the bottom of the screen, guide the user by displaying the various commands and options. Online help is easily accessible, making **pine** particularly user-friendly.

Pine software must be installed on your computer (or on the system that your computer is part of) in order for you to use **pine**. Typing **pine** at the Unix prompt or selecting **pine** from a menu of various options are typical ways to start it.

When **pine** starts, a menu similar to that shown in Figure 7.1 is displayed. This is the **pine MAIN MENU** and lists **pine**'s features and options. The top line of the screen indicates the version of **pine** that is running (in this case, 5.01). The title of the screen, **MAIN MENU**, appears next to the version, and to the right of this is a message indicating how many messages there are. In Figure 7.1 we see that there are five messages in the folder named **INBOX**. A folder in **pine** is just a Unix directory containing email messages.

```
PINE 5.01      MAIN MENU      Folder: INBOX 5 Messages


   ?    HELP              - Get help using Pine
   C    COMPOSE MESSAGE   - Compose and send/post a message
   I    FOLDER INDEX      - View messages in current folder
   L    FOLDER LIST       - Select a folder OR news group
   A    ADDRESS BOOK      - Update address book
   S    SETUP             - Configure Pine Options
   Q    QUIT              - Exit the Pine program




  Copyright 1989-2001. PINE is a trademark of the
University of Washington.

  ? Help                        P PrevCmd   R RelNotes
  O OTHER CMDS   L [ListFldrs]   N NextCmd   K KBlock
```

Figure 7.1—**Pine MAIN MENU** Screen

The features available from the **MAIN MENU** are listed on the screen along with their associated commands. They are as follows:

❏ **?** for online help about **pine**.
❏ **C** for composing and sending a message.
❏ **I** for viewing messages in the current folder.
❏ **L** for selecting a folder of messages to view.
❏ **A** for working with the address book.

❑ **S** for customizing **pine**.

❑ **Q** for exiting **pine**.

Notice in Figure 7.1 that in addition to listing the options with their descriptions, the screen offers a summary of **pine** commands along the bottom as well. Since not all of the available options can fit at the bottom of the screen, pressing the **O** key will display other commands that are available. Some of the commands displayed at the bottom of Figure 7.1 include **P** (or **PrevCmd**) for "previous command" and **N** (or **NextCmd**) for "next command." Using the **P** or **N** key highlights the previous or next option in the list of features in the main part of the menu. A highlighted option can be selected by pressing the **Enter** key. Note, we do not show any highlighting in our figures. On a **pine** screen one item is usually highlighted by using reverse video.

Another way to select an option is to press the associated key. It is not necessary to press the **Enter** key. Although the commands are all written as capital letters, you do not need to hold down the **Shift** key while typing them; **pine** is not case sensitive. **Pine** itself displays commands in uppercase letters, and we adopt that convention as well. For example, pressing the **C**[1] key allows you to compose a message and pressing the **Q** key allows you to quit **pine**.

The **R** at the bottom of the **MAIN MENU** screen stands for **Release Notes**. The **Release Notes** describe any changes from the previous version of **pine**, bugs, and so on. The **K** command permits you to lock your keyboard for those times when you want to step away from your computer for a few minutes but do not want to log out.

In addition to the summary of commands at the bottom and the list of options, the **MAIN MENU** screen provides an area for messages and prompts. They are displayed in brackets just below the copyright/trademark declaration. For instance, entering **D** on the **MAIN MENU** screen results in the following message in the command line:

```
[Command "D" not defined for this screen. Use ? for help]
```

Pine's command line is displayed towards the bottom of the screen. Messages are displayed in this part of the screen, and commands are also entered there.

Exercises

1. Start up the **pine** email program. What version of **pine** is running on your system? Read the **Release Notes** and report two interesting facts.

---

1. Pressing the **C** key is shorthand for typing **Shift-c** or **c**.

2. Explore the **pine** help facility. Print out a description of the **P** and **N** commands for the **MAIN MENU**. How do you exit the help facility?

7.3   Text Editing in Pine Using Pico

Before continuing our discussion of **pine**, it is important for you to learn the basics of a text editor that you can use with **pine**. The default text editor for **pine** is **pico**, pronounced "pee co." In this section we give a short tutorial on **pico**. Even if you already know another editor, it is a good idea to learn the basics about **pico** since most Unix systems have the **pico** editor available. You can use **pico** for general editing as well as with the **pine** mailer.

The **pico** editing commands can be conveniently split into the following several groups:

❑   cursor movement.
❑   cutting and pasting.
❑   saving and inserting files.
❑   miscellaneous.

Most editors, including **pico**, let you insert text at the current cursor position simply by typing it in. Pressing the **Enter** key will move the cursor to the next line.

Figure 7.2 shows the **pico** interface. As you will see later, this interface is very similar to that of **pine**. Many **pico** commands are executed by pressing the **Control** (**Ctrl**) key and another key simultaneously. We will use **C** to denote a **Control** key. For example, to get help from inside **pico** you execute **C-G**. Note the **G** does not need to be upper case, as **Pico** is not case sensitive. In Figure 7.2, the **Control** key is shown as a caret (**^**). We describe each of the other commands listed at the bottom of the **pico** interface in a separate subsection below. We follow the **pico** convention and list all letters as capitals.

Note that you can obtain documentation about all of **pico**'s commands online.

```
This is a sample file that is being edited by the pico
editor. This file does not contain any useful
information, but it is useful for illustrating how
to edit a file with pico.




                         [ Read 4 lines ]
```

```
^G Get Help ^O WriteOut ^R Read File ^Y PrvPg    ^K Cut Text
^X Exit     ^J Justify  ^W Where is  ^V Next Pg ^U UnCut Text
```

Figure 7.2—Pico Text Editor

7.3.1 Cursor Movement

The basic cursor movement commands are:

- ❑ **C-F** for forward one space.
- ❑ **C-B** for backward one space.
- ❑ **C-N** for moving to the next line.
- ❑ **C-P** for moving to the previous line.
- ❑ **C-A** for moving to the beginning of the line the cursor is currently on.
- ❑ **C-E** for moving to the end of line the cursor is currently on.

The arrow keys will usually work as well. More specialized movement commands are also available, for example, **C-Y** to return to the previous screen and **C-V** to move forward a page. The command **C-C** reports the current cursor position on the screen. The arrow keys can also be used for repositioning the cursor.

7.3.2 Cutting and Pasting Text in Pico

One of the most important editing operations is the ability to *cut* and then *paste* a piece of text. If done properly, this form of text movement can save lots of time during editing. Cutting deletes text from the screen; pasting allows you to deposit the cut text wherever you would like. In **pico** the cutting is done using the **C-K** command, and the pasting is done using the **C-U** command. By repeatedly typing **C-K**, you can select a number of lines to be cut. For example, five **C-K**'s will cut five lines. Repositioning the cursor and then typing a single **C-U** will paste the cut text.

7.3.3 Saving and Inserting Files Using Pico

Many times when you are editing, you will want to insert a file into the file you are working on. This may be done to save typing time or simply to group together several pieces of information. For example, if five people are each working on a part of a project, it may be necessary to piece together their material into a single file.

To insert a file into the file you are currently editing, you use **C-R**. Simply execute this command, and at the bottom of the editing window you will be prompted for the name of the file to insert. Type in the desired file name and press the **Enter** key. The file you choose will then be inserted at the location of the cursor.

To save a file, you use the **C-O** command. If you have previously saved the file, **pico** will by default display the existing file name to save to. If you press **Enter**, the modified file will be saved under the old name, and the original contents of the file will be lost. If the file is new or you want to save it using a different name, simply type in the name and press **Enter**. The file will be saved under the name you specified.

To exit the editor without saving a file you use the command **C-X**. If you have modified the file but not saved the changes, **pico** will ask if you want to

```
Save modified buffer
```

If you respond with **Y**, the changes will be saved. If you respond with **N**, the changes will be discarded.

To create a new file, you can enter the command **pico** at the Unix prompt, and then edit and save the file using the **C-O** command. After typing **C-O**, you simply enter the name of the file and press **Enter**. Another way of creating a new file is to type

```
%pico new.file
```

where **new.file** is the name of the file you want to create. When you save the file, it will be written to **new.file**, unless you specify otherwise.

7.3.4 Miscellaneous Editing Features of Pico

There are at least three important miscellaneous features that you should learn in conjunction with **pico**. They are for spell checking, searching within a file, and justifying text.

7.3.5 Spell Checking

Pico has a built in spell checker that is invoked by the command **C-T**. If the spell checker finds a word that it thinks is misspelled, it offers you the opportunity to correct the word. On most systems there are many other spell checkers that are available. It is a good idea to run your files through the spell-checking phase. However, just because you do this, do not assume all spelling errors have been corrected. For example, if "there books" should be "their books," the spell checker will not be able to catch this.

7.3.6 Searching

To search for a pattern of text within a file, use the **C-W** command. This command is very useful when you are entering edits from a hard copy. It allows you to search the file to get "close" to where you need to enter a change. Simple cursor movements can then bring you to the exact spot to edit. If you do not need to edit the file, you may want to use the **grep** command to search the file.

7.3.7 Justifying Text

The **C-J** command is used to justify the text of the current paragraph. When composing email, this is very useful for printing a paragraph. That is, **C-J** makes the lines of near equal length. (It does not allow you to set the margins within which justification takes place.) If you are typing in material without paying attention to carriage returns, the **C-J** command can be used to break the text into reasonable length lines. This would make it easier to edit the file in the future.

Appendix D contains a summary of **pico** commands and serves as a handy **pico** reference.

Exercises

1. For efficiency while editing, is there any advantage to keeping narrow text stored (say fewer than 50 characters per line) versus keeping extremely wide text (say over 100 characters per line)? Explain your answer.

2. Explore the **pico** help facility and report two new facts that you learned.

3. Suppose that you were editing the following line:
   ```
   this is no social crisis; this is another trghts
   ```
   and wanted to change it to
   ```
   this is no social crisis; this is just another
   tricky day
   ```
   What is the minimum number of keystrokes required by **pico** to make these edits, assuming the cursor is positioned at the beginning of the line? Assuming the cursor is positioned at the end of the line? In each case list the optimal sequence of keystrokes. Count a control character and key combination as one stroke, and also a shifted key as a single keystroke.

7.4 Composing and Sending Email

Now that you know how to edit an email message using **pico**, we turn our attention to writing email. To compose an email message using **pine**, press the **C** key (or select the **COMPOSE MESSAGE** option by highlighting it and pressing the **Enter** key) from **pine**'s **MAIN MENU**. A new sc reen appears titled **COMPOSE MESSAGE** that contains a template for constructing the message. Figure 7.3 depicts the **pine** email template.

```
PINE 5.01     COMPOSE MESSAGE      Folder: INBOX 5 Messages


To       :
Cc       :
Attchment :
Subject  :
-----Message Text-----







^G Get Help   ^X Send   ^R Rich Hdr   ^Y PrvPg/Top   ^K Cut Line
^C Cancel     ^D Del    ^J Attach     ^V NxtPg/End   ^U UnDel Line
```

Figure 7.3—**Pine**'s Template for Message Composition

Like the **MAIN MENU**, the bottom of the **COMPOSE MESSAGE** screen contains a menu of commands that pertain to it. These commands show a **^** character before a letter, for example, **^G**. These commands are executed by pressing the **Control** key (**Ctrl**) at the same time as the letter key—either uppercase or lowercase. In our discussion we use the letter **C** in referring to these commands; that is, we use **C-G** although what you will see on the screen and in our figures in the **pine** context is **^G**. The conventions are similar to what was used for **pico**.

The **C-G** (**Get Help**) command found on the bottom of the screen provides help about whichever template field is highlighted. The basic template includes a **To:** field, **Cc:** field, **Attchmnt:** field, **Subject:** field, and **Message Text** area. The arrow keys (⬅, ➡, ⬆, and ⬇) or **C-P** (previous line) and **C-N** (next line) may be used to move from field to field.

You will notice that as different fields in the template are highlighted, the commands at the bottom may change. For instance, when the **To**: field is highlighted, selecting the **C-T** option provides access to a list of addresses in the address book. When the **Message Text** field is highlighted, **C-T** invokes the spell checker. **Pine** provides the help menus at the bottom of each screen for easy reference.

As noted earlier, the default text editor associated with **pine** is **pico**. When you highlight the **To**: field and enter the **C-G** command, the help screen provides a short summary of **pico** cursor movement and editing commands.

7.4.1 To Field

When composing an email message, the address of the recipient is entered in the **To**: field. If you position the cursor at the **To**: field, it is highlighted. At this point you can type in an email address. More than one recipient can be specified by separating addresses with commas.

A nickname or alias can be specified in the **To**: field as well. **Pine** will check your address book to determine the full email address(es) and expand the nickname when you proceed to the next field. Remember that an alias can specify a list of email addresses as well as a single address. Nicknames can be specified along with regular email addresses when listing more than one recipient. For example,

```
To: fe@shiloinn.hilltop.com, lucy, striders
```

In this case the nickname **lucy** is an alias for **lucilletemplton@french.wisc.edu** and **striders** is an alias for a list of email addresses belonging to the members of the Savannah Striders Running Club.

7.4.2 Carbon Copy Field

The **Cc**: field allows you to send copies of a message to other people. Email addresses as well as nicknames can be entered in the field. This field is optional and can be left blank by either skipping over it (**C-N**) or by pressing the **Enter** key when positioned at it.

7.4.3 Attachment Field

The **Attchmnt**: field lets you specify the name of files (or attachments) to append to the end of a message. Attachments are appended separately and are not part of the message text. Only files residing on the same machine as the mailer can be appended to the message and only recipients with MIME-capable mail programs (such as **pine**) will be able to immediately view attachments that are other than just plain text. MIME stands for *Multipurpose Internet Mail Extensions*. You can think of a MIME-capable mailer as one that can handle formats other than plain text, for example, *Hypertext Markup Language*. When positioned at the **Attchmnt**: field, the **C-T** command displays a list of files to select from. After entering the name of the file or using **C-T** to select a file, you simply press the **Enter** key to attach the file. You can then insert a comment to go along with the attachment.

7.4.4 Subject Field

The **Subject**: field provides a way to let the recipient know what your message is about. Enter a short, clear description of your message.

7.4.5 Other Header Fields

Entering the **C-R** (**Rich Hdr**) command while on the **COMPOSE MESSAGE** screen causes your template to display other optional fields. To use one of these fields, simply fill it in with the appropriate information. The **Bcc**: field lets you send blind carbon copies so that the addresses of the copied recipients of the message are not displayed. The **Fcc**: field lets you specify a folder in which to keep a copy of the outgoing message. Other fields, including **Newsgrps**: and **Lcc**:, can be explored by using the **C-G** command.

7.4.6 Message Text Field

To type the body of your message, you need to position the cursor so that the **Message Text** field is highlighted. Using **pico** text editing and cursor movement commands, you can then type your message. When you are done, the spell checker can be invoked by using the **C-T** command. The **C-R** command lets you insert a file into the message.

At this point you can either send the message using the **C-X** command, cancel the message with the **C-C** command, or postpone sending the message until a later time using the **C-O** command. Each of these commands causes **pine** to ask you if that is what you really want to do. You respond by either pressing the **Y** key for "yes" or the **N** key for "no." Pressing the **Enter** key will invoke the default selection, which has brackets around it.

Figure 7.4 illustrates a **pine COMPOSE MESSAGE** screen that is filled in and about to be sent. Notice all of the standard fields have been filled in except there is no attachment. To send this message you can type **C-X**. **Pine** will ask if you are sure you want to send the message. This is a good reminder to check that the recipient is correct, to proofread the message, and to double-check that the recipient's address is entered correctly. If the message is okay as it stands, you can enter **Y** and the message will be sent. Otherwise, you can enter **N** and make the appropriate adjustments.

```
PINE 5.01      COMPOSE MESSAGE      Folder: INBOX 5 Messages


To        :diwano@music.maine.edu
Cc        :tls@music.uoregon.edu
Attchment:
Subject   :Saturday's performance
-----Message Text-----
Hi Donna,
    Your playing this Saturday was exquisite.
I think this was one of your best performances.
Do you agree?


    I am really not sure how you were able to hold
up under all of the pressure. I can't remember
anyone rising to the occasion like you did.
Great job. Your performance was inspiring
to all :-)


        Yours, Mandy


PS: Hope to see you perform again soon.
```

Figure 7.4—Sample **Pine COMPOSE MESSAGE** Screen

Exercises

1. Compose a message to yourself that in two paragraphs explains the concept of email to a novice. Mail the message to yourself and print it out when you receive it. What command did you print it out with?

2. Give two examples of when you would *not* want to carbon copy yourself on a message.

7.5 Reading Email

When you receive email messages, **pine** places them in a folder called **INBOX**. To view the messages in your **INBOX** folder, press **I** (**FOLDER INDEX**) from the **MAIN MENU** to bring up a screen called **FOLDER INDEX**. This screen displays information about each message in the **INBOX** folder. Figure 7.5 shows a sample **INBOX** folder screen.

```
PINE 5.01    FOLDER INDEX    Folder: INBOX Message 4 of 4 ANS


+   D  1 December 25 Pamela Swartz    (3,443)
+      2 December 27 Ralph Michels    (2,321) Re: donuts
       3 January 17 Paul Swanson      (1,111) papers
    A  4 January 21 Jim Lester        (5,332) Great work!




               ʼ

? Help  M Main Menu P PrevMsg - PrevPage    D Delete R Reply
O OTHER V [ViewMsg] N NextMsg Spc NextPage U Undel  F Forwd
```

Figure 7.5—**Pine FOLDER INDEX** Screen

The **FOLDER INDEX** screen does not display email messages that you have received, just a little information about each message so that you can decide which (if any) messages you want to read. In Figure 7.5, four messages are shown on the sample screen. This is also indicated on the top line of the screen, where it identifies the folder as **INBOX** and the highlighted message as **4 of 4**.

For each message displayed on the **FOLDER INDEX** screen, seven pieces of information are provided:

❑ Column 1: Either a blank or a **+** symbol, where a **+** indicates that this message was sent directly to you (as opposed to being carbon copied, for instance).

❑ Column 2: Message status—either **A**, **D**, or **N**. An **A** means that the message was answered using the **Reply** command, a **D** signifies that you have read the message and have marked it for deletion, and an **N** indicates that the message is new.

❑ Column 3: Message number.

❑ Column 4: Date the message was sent.

❑ Column 5: Sender of the message.

❑ Column 6: Size of the message in bytes. (You can think of each byte as representing a single character.)

❑ Column 7: Subject of the message as specified by the sender.

To read a particular message, select it by using the arrow keys or by pressing the **P** (**PrevMsg** for **Previous Message**) key or the **N** (**NextMsg** for **Next Message**) key. The selected message is highlighted in reverse video and indicated on the top line: **Message 4 of 4**, for instance. Pressing the **V** key displays the entire message on another screen (or perhaps replaces the original screen) called the **Message Text** screen. Simply pressing the **Enter** key does the same thing since **V** is the default. The commands to continue reading messages are listed on the bottom of the screen: **N** (**NextMsg**) to view the next message or **P** (**PrevMsg**) to view the previous message in this folder. To return to the **INDEX**, press **I**.

After reading a particular message, you might decide to respond to it. One way to do this is to go to the **COMPOSE MESSAGE** screen, fill in the header information, write the message, and send off your response. Another possibility is to use the **Reply** command, **R**, right from the **Message Text** screen. From the command line, **pine** will ask if you would like to include the original message in the reply. Responding "no" (the default) causes the **COMPOSE MESSAGE Reply** screen to appear with the header information already filled in. The **Subject**: field will contain **Re**: followed by the subject line of the original message.

Responding "yes" to the command line causes the text of the message sent to you to be copied into the message text area with header information filled in as well. The copied message text is preceded by a line identifying who wrote the original text and when. For example, if Betsy were using the **R** command to respond to a message sent by Steve (**hudson@georgiapacific.com**), **pine** would fill in the following in the **Message Text** area of the template:

```
On Sat, 23 Jul 2001, hudson wrote:
```

Steve's original message would appear after that with each line from his original message marked by a less than (>) symbol along the left margin. Lines can be added, deleted, and modified using the **pico** text editing commands.

After completing your reply, use the same commands that appear on the **COMPOSE MESSAGE** screen to finish the process:

❑ **C-X** to send the message.

❑ **C-C** to cancel the message.

❑ **C-O** to postpone sending the message.

The **Forward** command (**F**) is similar to the **Reply** command. It allows you to forward the message you are currently reading to another email address. A screen containing a copy of the message appears and you must fill in the **To:** field. Like the **Reply** command, the original message can be modified and added to.

Exercises

1. Send yourself a simple email message. Read the message and then forward it to yourself. Describe the differences in the **FOLDER INDEX** between the two messages.
2. Send yourself a simple email message. Read the message and mark it for deletion. Now exit the **pine** mailer. Describe what happens.
3. Describe two commands that are available to you from the **FOLDER INDEX** screen but which are not listed at the bottom of the initial screen.
4. Send yourself an empty message. How many bytes long does the **pine** mail program think the message is? Explain.

7.6 Managing Email with Pine

Managing email involves deleting unwanted messages and organizing those messages that you want to save. The saved messages can include copies of email that you have sent, as well as email you have received. Messages are organized and kept in directories. In **pine** the word *folder* is a synonym for *directory*. **Pine** provides the following three default folders for each account:

❏ **INBOX**—The folder where new incoming messages are stored.
❏ **saved-messages**—The default folder for saving copies of messages.
❏ **sent-mail**—The folder where copies of messages that you have sent are saved.

In addition to these three folders, **pine** allows you to create your own folders as needed. If you receive a lot of correspondence from a user named Jed, then you may decide to store all of this email in a folder called **jed**.

To move around between folders, press **L** (**FOLDER LIST**) from the **MAIN MENU**. A **FOLDER LIST** screen appears with *collections* of folders listed. To select a collection, highlight the phrase

```
[ Select Here to See Expanded List ]
```

below the desired collection and press the **Enter** key. The folders within that collection are displayed on a new **FOLDER LIST** screen (possibly replacing the original screen), and you can highlight a folder to view. A menu of commands is listed at the bottom of the screen. These let you view what is in the selected folder (**V** for **ViewFldr**), as well as delete (**D** for **Delete**), add (**A** for **Add**), and rename (**R** for **Rename**) folders. Another way to access the index of another folder is to use the goto folder (**G** for **GotoFldr**) command that prompts you to enter the name of the folder you want to view.

7.6.1 Deleting Email Messages

It is important to delete unwanted messages since they clutter up folders, making it difficult to keep track of more important correspondence. Also, accounts have a limited amount of memory allocated to them, so cleaning out folders is necessary to conserve disk space.

Deleting an email message is done in two parts. First, the message is *marked* for deletion by selecting the message from the **FOLDER INDEX** screen. Using the **D** command marks an email message for deletion. A message can also be marked for deletion when viewing the message from the **Message Text** screen. If you decide later that you do not want to delete the email message, it can be unmarked by using the undelete command, **U**, from either the **FOLDER INDEX** screen or **Message Text** screen.

The second part of deleting a message involves *expunging* the messages that have been marked for deletion. You can explicitly expunge a message from the **FOLDER INDEX** screen by using the **X** command. Otherwise, **pine** asks if you want to expunge messages marked for deletion when you terminate **pine** or when you leave a folder (other than the **INBOX** folder). Note that a message marked for deletion can be undeleted. However, once a message is expunged, it is gone for good and **pine** cannot restore it.

7.6.2 Saving Email Messages

Incoming messages are automatically put in your **INBOX** folder. After reading a message (and possibly responding to it), you may decide to save a copy of it. If you are reading the message from the **Message Text** screen, pressing **S** saves a copy of the message and marks the **INBOX** copy of the message for deletion. The **saved-messages** folder is the default folder where messages are saved, but you can specify another folder. After pressing **S**, **pine** prompts you with

```
SAVE to folder in <mail/[]> [saved-messages]:
```

Pressing the **Enter** key selects the default folder (**saved-messages**), or you can enter another folder name. If the folder name that you specify does not exist, **pine** will ask if you want it created. Otherwise, **pine** saves the message to the file specified.

Messages can also be saved from the **FOLDER INDEX** screen by highlighting a message to select it and then using the **S** command in the same way as from the **Message Text** screen.

7.6.3 Email Address Book

Another aspect of managing email involves organizing email addresses. **Pine**'s address book provides a way to create *nicknames* (also called "aliases") for groups as well as individuals, and to save the aliases. Storing addresses in the address book simplifies the task of filling in the **To**: and **Cc**: fields when composing a message. Rather than manually typing in an email address, you have two convenient choices. One, you can type a nickname, which **pine** will automatically expand to the full address as specified in the address book. Two, you can go to the address book by using the **C-T** command and select the address(es) as desired. **Pine** will then fill in the **To**: or **Cc**: field automatically with the appropriate address(es).

Entering addresses into the address book is done by selecting the **A** option from the **MAIN MENU** screen. The **ADDRESS BOOK** screen will appear with a list of the entries in the address book including the nickname, name, and email address. The menu of commands at the bottom of the screen permit updating (**V** for **View/Edit**) and deleting (**D** for **Delete**) selected addresses, composing a message (**C** for **ComposeTo**) to send to the selected address, and adding new addresses (**A** for **AddNew**) to the address book. Using the **A** command will let you manually enter a new address or a new list of addresses to create a distribution list.

Another way to add addresses to the address book is to "take" them from a message that you are viewing from the **Message Text** screen or from the message information listed on the **FOLDER INDEX** screen. Use the **T** (**TakeAddr**) command. Note that **T** is visible at the bottom of the screen only if you display the other commands available. The command line will direct you to select the address to be taken (if there is more than one to pick from) and then to enter a new or existing nickname.

In order to take addresses to build a distribution list, press **L** (**ListMode**) from the **Take Address** screen before selecting the addresses. To indicate which addresses are to be added to the list, select the address by highlighting it, and press **X** (**Set/Unset**) to mark it in the box to its left. When done marking all the addresses, press **T** (**Take**), and **pine** will ask you to enter the nickname.

7.6.4 Additional Features

We have covered the most important features of the **pine** mailer, however, **pine** includes many other features as well. To explore these features we encourage you to experiment with **pine**, especially the **S** (**SETUP**) command from the **MAIN MENU**, which will, among other things, allow you to create a signature file. Exploring the various commands and trying them out—sending email to yourself, if necessary—is the best way to become proficient at using **pine**.

Exercises

1. Enter three of your most commonly used email addresses into your address book. What are the addresses? How many keystrokes do you save by using **pine**'s automatic address insertion as opposed to typing in the actual addresses?
2. In the help facility, read the documentation about the **setup** command. Describe three customizations you can perform.
3. Compare and contrast **pine** with another email program that you are familiar with.
4. Why do you think deleting a message in **pine** is a two-step process?
5. Is there a way an experienced user can suppress **pine**'s help information? Why might someone want to do this?

7.7 Unix Mail Program

We have focused this chapter on the **pine** mail program. There are several other mailers that are available with most Unix systems. In this section we explain how to send a message using the Unix **mail** program. There may be times when this is the only mailer that you are familiar with on a given system. In such cases, when you really need to send a message, the material we cover in this section will prove very useful.

Suppose you have created a file, perhaps using **pico**, called **message**, and that you want to send **message** to **holly@notebook.com**. Further, suppose that the file **message** is located in your current working directory. You can send **holly** this email as follows:

```
%mail holly@notebook.com < message
```

The file **message** will be emailed to **holly@notebook.com**. No confirmation will be given; you will be returned to the Unix prompt. The less than sign (<) is used to redirect the file **message** to the **mail** program. We will cover redirection in detail in Chapter 18.

Suppose the email message you wanted to type in was not already saved in a file. For example, suppose you wanted to send **billytownsend@cold.uminn.edu** a short note. This could be accomplished using the **mail** program as follows:

1. Type **mail** at the Unix prompt and press **Enter**.
2. Type in your message.
3. Type **C-D**.

Although you will not receive any confirmation that the message was sent, the **mail** program will deliver your message if you follow these steps.

Of course, Unix also provides programs to read your email. However, since **pine** is more user-friendly than other Unix mailers, we will not discuss them.

You should execute the command line

```
%man mail
```

to learn more about the **mail** command.

Exercises

1. Create a file called **foo** with a few lines of text. Send yourself the file using the Unix **mail** program. What information does the email header contain?
2. Send yourself the message "test message using the Unix mail program" by invoking the **mail** program from the command line. What information does the email header contain?
3. How can you include a subject line using the **mail** program? Suppose you wanted to send a long email message to a friend. Which of the methods for sending email that were discussed in this section would you use? Why?

7.8   messages Command

It is convenient to know how many new email messages you have waiting for you each time you log in. The **messages** command displays the number of messages in your mailbox. If run automatically when you log in, you will always know how many messages you have awaiting your attention.

To run the **messages** command, simply enter

```
%messages
```

You will receive a number in response indicating how many times the word "From" occurs at the beginning of a line in your mailbox. This number is usually the same as the number of messages you have received.

Exercises

1. Is the **messages** command run automatically each time you log in?
2. Run the **messages** command. What was the result? Did this agree with how many messages you had in your mailbox? Explain.

UNIX SYNTAX
AND ADDITIONAL
COMMANDS

chapter 8

UNIX COMMAND SYNTAX

In this chapter we discuss the following commands:

Unix Command	DOS Command	Description
cat	TYPE	concatenate and display files
rlogin	—	log in to a remote computer

8.1 Introduction

We have already seen many of the most important Unix commands. In this chapter we focus on the *syntax* of Unix commands. The syntax of a command specifies the precise details about how a command needs to be entered into the computer. The syntax tells you the arguments that the command may take. For example, among other possibilities, the **man** command may take **–T**, **–s**, **section**, **–k**, or **keyword** as arguments. Here **section** and **keyword** stand for a section number of the Unix Reference Manual and any word, respectively. The **ls** command may take arguments such as **–a**, **–l**, **filenames**, or **directorynames** as arguments. Here **filenames** and **directorynames** stand for a list of any file names and a list of any directory names, respectively. The syntax of a command is described under the **SYNOPSIS** heading of the **man page** for the command. Thus, it is easy to look up the syntax of any Unix command online. As we describe syntax in this chapter, it is worthwhile thinking about how this idea relates to the commands you are already familiar with.

Many computer users confuse the concept of *semantics* with that of syntax. The semantics of a command is the meaning of the command. Think of the syntax of the command as the form of the command. That is, the rules for describing how to enter the command properly. Contrast this with the semantics, which describes how the command actually behaves. That is, the semantics tells you what the command actually does when you execute it, whereas the syntax describes the way in which you can enter a command to the computer. Since computers are programmed to interpret their input literally, you need to get the syntax right in order for a command to execute properly.

Abstractly, the syntax of a Unix command has the following form:[1]

```
commandname -flag1 arg1 -flag2 arg2 ... -flagk argk
```

Notice a blank space is left between flags and arguments. The word **commandname** is a placeholder for any Unix command. For example, **commandname** could stand for **login**, **ls**, or **man**. In this general abstract command form, we have depicted k flags to the command interleaved with k arguments. The ith flag is denoted by **flag$i$**, whereas the ith argument is denoted as **arg$i$**. The ... represents the third through k-1 flags and arguments. It is rare that you will use more than two or three flags with any given command. As an example, flags you are already familiar with to the **ls** command include **–a** and **–l**. In our command abstraction, any or all of the placeholders for flags and arguments may be omitted (appear as "missing") in an actual command. For example, a command might take two flags and a single argument. This is represented in our abstraction as

```
commandname -flag1 -flag2 arg2
```

Note that **arg1** has been omitted and appears to be missing. We will examine additional examples in this chapter to further clarify Unix command syntax. In practice, you will typically use one or two arguments with a command. For example, in using the **rm** command, you might want to specify the names of two files to be deleted. These would be the arguments to **rm**.

As a complete specific example, let us see how the familiar **ls** command fits this syntactic template. To list hidden files in a directory, you can use the **–a** flag to the **ls** command. To list all of the files in the long form, you can use the **–l** flag to the **ls** command. Finally, to sort the files by time stamp instead of alphabetically by name, you can use the **–t** flag to the **ls** command. Suppose you want to list all files in two subdirectories called **aasu** and **letters**, and list all of the above-mentioned properties of the files. The command

```
%ls -a -l -t aasu letters
```

would achieve the desired result. In Figures 8.1 and 8.2, we show some sample output from the execution of this command.

```
%ls -a -l -t aasu letters
aasu:
total 18
drwxr-xr-x 30 smith faculty 2048 Mar 31 17:21 ..
```

---

1. We have oversimplified the description of syntax to avoid getting bogged down in too many technical details. For example, some flags require an argument.

```
drwx------  2 smith faculty  512 Mar 27 19:10 curriculum
drwx------  4 smith faculty  512 Mar 27 10:29 student
drwx------  4 smith faculty 1024 Mar 20 10:05 yamacraw
drwx------  2 smith faculty 1024 Feb 25 16:04 misc
drwx------  2 smith faculty  512 Feb 16 18:29 equipment
drwx------  2 smith faculty  512 Feb 8 18:44 literature
drwx------  2 smith faculty  512 Feb 8 09:21 tenure
drwx------  2 smith faculty  512 Jan 25 15:54 annual
drwx------  2 smith faculty  512 Jan 20 11:42 office
drwx------ 17 smith faculty  512 Dec 17 00:25 .
drwx------  4 smith faculty 1024 Dec 17 00:24 hiring
drwx------  7 smith faculty  512 Dec 17 00:18 fmeet
drwx------  2 smith faculty  512 Dec 9 19:24 faculty
drwx------  5 smith faculty  512 Dec 8 20:10 activities
drwx------  6 smith faculty  512 Sep 24 1999 CSAB99
drwx------  4 smith faculty  512 Jan 5 1999 CSAB93
```

Figure 8.1—Output from a Complex Usage of the **ls** Command

```
letters:
total 48
drwxr-xr-x 30 smith faculty 2048 Mar 31 17:21 ..
drwx------  2 smith faculty  512 May 4 1999 .
-rw-------  1 smith faculty 1037 Mar 26 1999 upe.tex
-rw-------  1 smith faculty 6447 Dec 18 1998 rosen.tex
-rw-------  1 smith faculty 2045 Dec 9 1996 johnson.tex
-rw-------  1 smith faculty 1104 Apr 26 1996 mayr.tex
-rw-------  1 smith faculty 1227 Apr 26 1996 lange.tex
-rw-------  1 smith faculty 1128 Apr 26 1996 jenner.tex
-rw-------  1 smith faculty  794 Apr 26 1996 jacobo.tex
-rw-------  1 smith faculty 1856 Jan 21 1996 savage.tex
-rw-------  1 smith faculty 6497 Dec 9 1995 papa.tex
-rw-------  1 smith faculty 3864 Apr 20 1995 beigel.tex
-rw-------  1 smith faculty 1381 Apr 18 1995 mcnamara.tex
-rw-------  1 smith faculty 6106 Apr 12 1995 dewdney.tex
-rw-------  1 smith faculty 5773 Jan 23 1995 wood.tex
```

Figure 8.2—Second Half of Output from a Complex Usage of the **ls** Command

The output depicted in Figures 8.1 and 8.2 lists all the files in the **aasu** and **letters** directories. Notice all the files in the directories are listed, in the long form, and in decreasing chronological order. (If no year is shown, the date is for the current year.) Dissecting the command line,

```
%ls -a -l -t aasu letters
```

we see three flags, namely –**a**, –**l**, and –**t**, followed by two arguments: **aasu** and **letters**. It is easy to see how this command line fits our general model:

```
commandname -flag1 arg1 -flag2 arg2 ... -flagk argk
```

In this case the form of the command is

```
commandname -flag1 -flag2 -flag3 arg3 arg4
```

Note that the same command could have been written

```
%ls -alt aasu letters
```

That is, the options to the command do not need to be specified separately. In contrast, the arguments always need to be separated by a space. Otherwise, the operating system has no way of telling where one argument begins and the next argument ends.

Some Unix commands do not require any arguments. For example, the **cd** command without any arguments specified will take you to your home directory. The **clear** command without any arguments will clear the screen. There are other Unix commands that must take an argument. We say that such commands *require* an argument. The copy command, **cp**, requires two arguments, one specifying the file(s) to be copied and the other specifying the name of the resulting file(s). When a command may or may not require an argument, we say the command takes an *optional* argument. For example, the **man** command has an optional argument for specifying the section of the Unix Reference Manual to search for information about the command. The command line

```
%man 3 login
```

tells the operating system to look for information about the **login** command in Section 3 of the Unix Reference Manual. In **man page** descriptions, optional arguments are often written between square brackets, [and]. So, in the description of the **man** command on your system, you might see a part of it that looks something like

```
man [section] commandname
```

The [**section**] simply means that you have the option to enter a section in order to restrict the search in the Unix Reference Manual to a specific section. Since

commandname is not in square brackets, this argument is required and always needs to be specified; it is a required argument of the **man** command.

In order to make our discussion of command syntax more concrete and to cover several additional important points, we will focus on the syntax of two additional commands: **cat** and **rlogin**. First, we briefly mention the semantics of each command. The **cat** command is used to display a file on the screen, whereas the **rlogin** command is used to log in to another computer from the computer you are currently using.

8.2   Displaying a File—cat Command

Before delving into the syntax of the **cat** command, we consider an example of how it is used. One of **cat**'s primary uses is to display a file on the screen. Suppose you are in a directory that has a file called **signature** in it. To display the contents of the file **signature**, you can enter the command

```
%cat signature
```

The result is that the contents of the file **signature** are shown on the screen. If the file is more than one screenful long, the display simply scrolls (and rather quickly) until the bottom of the file is reached. The **cat** command works well to view files that are less than one screenful in length. However, to view longer files, the **more** command is probably a better bet.

The general syntax of the **cat** command is

```
cat -flag1 -flag2 ... -flagm filename1 filename2 ... filenamen
```

That is, **cat** takes several optional flags followed by the name of a file or several files. In our general syntax abstraction, arguments 1 through $m-1$ are missing, whereas arguments m through n are present. As we saw already,

```
%cat signature
```

can be used to display the contents of the file **signature**. One useful flag to the **cat** command is $-n$. By specifying this option, the **cat** command will consecutively number all of the lines in its output. In Figure 8.3, we show the contents of a file called **README**. The contents are easily displayed by invoking the **cat** command on the file **README**. Contrast this output display with the output of the

```
%cat -n README
```

command shown in Figure 8.4. In Figure 8.4 notice that all of the lines in the file have been numbered consecutively.

```
Directory for a book about Unix.

To make the index do the following:

makeindex -s index.isty main

The A group in the index is not getting done properly.
Edit main.ind on final pass and change the first
A to indexgroup A.
```

Figure 8.3—Contents of a File Called **README**

```
1 Directory for a book about Unix.
2
3 To make the index do the following:
4
5 makeindex -s index.isty main
6
7 The A group in the index is not getting done properly.
8 Edit main.ind on final pass and change the first
9 A to indexgroup A.
10
```

Figure 8.4—Contents of a File Called **README** with Lines Numbered by **cat**

Notice that the file **README** ends with a blank line and in total the file contains ten lines. The **cat** command is very useful for generating numbered output. The **–b** flag to the **cat** command allows you to number only nonblank lines. The result of the

```
%cat -b README
```

command is shown in Figure 8.5. There are only six nonblank lines in the **README** file.

```
1 Directory for a book about Unix.

2 To make the index do the following:

3 makeindex -s index.isty main

4 The A group in the index is not getting done properly.
5 Edit main.ind on final pass and change the first
6 A to indexgroup A.
```

Figure 8.5—Contents of a File Called **README** with Nonblank Lines Numbered by **cat**

When we specified the syntax for the **cat** command, we indicated that it could take several files as arguments. For example, the command

```
%cat README signature
```

means to join two items together, one followed immediately by the other. The **cat** command lists items from left to right. That is, the files are joined together with the leftmost item displayed first, followed by the next leftmost, and so on until finally the rightmost item is displayed. Thus, in our example, first the contents of the file **README** are displayed followed immediately by the contents of the file **signature**. The **cat** command does not insert any extra space between the files. The **–n** flag can be used to number the lines of a group of files that are concatenated together. Figure 8.6 displays the results of the command

```
%cat -n README README
```

```
1 Directory for a book about Unix.
2
3 To make the index do the following:
4
5 makeindex -s index.isty main
6
7 The A group in the index is not getting done properly.
8 Edit main.ind on final pass and change the first
9 A to indexgroup A.
10
11 Directory for a book about Unix.
12
13 To make the index do the following:
```

```
14
15 makeindex -s index.isty main
16
17 The A group in the index is not getting done properly.
18 Edit main.ind on final pass and change the first
19 A to indexgroup A.
20
```

Figure 8.6—Numbering the Lines in Two Copies of the File **README**

It is helpful to think of the **cat** command as taking a number of files and gluing them together. Notice that when we glued **README** together with itself, we doubled its length.

Adding the –s flag to the **cat** command "squeezes out" consecutive blank lines. That is, by specifying the –s flag **cat** will replace any series of t blank lines with just a single blank line. In this way more information can be displayed on the screen. The command

     `%cat -s -n README martha test.one`

displays the contents of the three files—**README**, **martha**, and **test.one**—in the specified order with consecutive blank lines removed and with lines numbered consecutively. Comparing this command line with the general syntactic description of the **cat** command

     `cat -flag1 -flag2 ... -flagm filename1 filename2 ... filenamen`

helps us to understand the abstract syntactic description for **cat**. In general, the **cat** command takes a series of flags followed by one or more file names. There are other interesting flags to the **cat** command and many other interesting uses of the **cat** command. To learn more about the **cat** command, you should execute the command

     `%man cat`

Later in the book we will cover some additional uses of the **cat** command.

It is worth mentioning that sometimes the word **cat** is used as a verb. If you are sitting down at a keyboard typing, someone looking over your shoulder might ask you to **cat** a file for them. This means the person wants you to display the file using the **cat** command.

Exercises

1. Why might you want to **cat** multiple files?
2. Is there a flag to the **cat** command that allows you to number the lines in a file in decreasing order?
3. Suppose you have a file called **blankending** that ends in four blank lines. If you **cat** this file with itself using the –s flag, are the blank lines between the files "squeezed out"?

8.3 Remote Login—rlogin Command

Suppose that you have two computer accounts on two separate Unix machines and that both computers are connected to the same network. The machines may be in the same room or in different parts of the world. There will be times when you are working on one of the machines and want to gain access to the other machine.[2] That is, maybe you want to look up a piece of information on the other machine. The **rlogin** command allows you to do this. The abbreviation **rlogin** stands for "remote login." In this section we discuss the syntax and semantics of the **rlogin** command.

To make this scenario more concrete, suppose Marvin has accounts on machines A and B. He is currently logged into machine A but wants to do some work on machine B without logging out from machine A. Figure 8.7 depicts the two computers. It is important to keep in mind the geographical locations of the two computers. The computers need not be housed in close proximity. The only requirement is that they are connected to the same network and that they can communicate over this network.

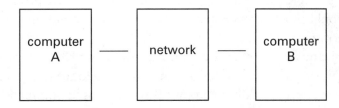

Figure 8.7—Computers A and B on the Same Network

Suppose the domain name of computer A is **white.bc.edu** and the domain name of computer B is **yellow.nyu.edu**. Computer A is located in Boston, Mas-

---

2. The **rlogin** command often only works between computers that are under the domain of the same systems administrator. However, about 90% of the time the **telnet** command can be used to connect to and log in to any remote system where you have an account.

sachusetts and computer B is located in New York City, New York. Suppose also that Marvin's account name on computer B is **barnes**. If Marvin is logged into computer A, he can remotely log in to computer B by executing the following command

```
%rlogin yellow.nyu.edu
```

After entering this command, Marvin will be presented with a login prompt on computer B. He simply enters his account name **barnes** and then types in his password for the account **barnes** on machine B. Once successfully logged into computer B, Marvin can enter commands. All commands he executes will be performed on computer B. Upon completion of his work on computer B, he can log out, and then he will be working on computer A again. The **rlogin** command is thus very useful for users with multiple computer accounts on the same network.

Now we focus on the syntax of the **rlogin** command. A simplified view of the general syntax of the **rlogin** command is

```
%rlogin [-l username] host
```

The first thing to notice about this description is that **–l username** is an optional argument, whereas **host** is a required argument. The **host** is used to specify the name of the remote computer you want to log into. In our example, Marvin logged into the **host** named **yellow.nyu.edu**. The optional **–l username** arguments can be used to specify a particular account name to log into. For example, Marvin could have logged into his account at New York University by entering the command

```
%rlogin -l barnes yellow.nyu.edu
```

Having entered this command, Marvin would then be prompted for his password. He would not have to enter his user name as he did previously when the **–l** flag was not specified.

Like many other Unix commands, the word **rlogin** is also used as a verb. For example, it is common to hear someone say "**rlogin** into your machine at home." There are several additional options to the **rlogin** command that you may investigate by entering the command

```
%man rlogin
```

Exercises

1. Why would you want to have multiple computer accounts?
2. Is it possible to be logged into a computer and then **rlogin** into the *same* computer again?

3. Give two examples of when it would be convenient to **rlogin** into another computer.
4. Research the **.rhosts** hidden file. What is its purpose and how is it used?

8.4   Summary

In this chapter we have covered command syntax both at abstract and concrete levels. We presented the notions of required and optional command arguments looking at specific examples involving the **cat** and **rlogin** commands. Beginning users often have trouble making heads or tails of the Unix Reference Manual's **man page** descriptions. When you begin reading a new **man page** and have difficulty figuring something out relating to command syntax, keep in mind the examples we went over in this chapter. Also, keep in mind that you may need to experiment with a command a few times before becoming comfortable with its syntax (and semantics). For trying out commands, it is a good idea to set up a test directory so that you do not end up deleting or overwriting any important files. Also, keep in mind that even experienced users sometimes have trouble figuring out command syntax. This may be because programmers who were intimately familiar with Unix wrote the documentation for the commands.

chapter 9

BASIC UNIX COMMANDS

In this chapter we introduce the following commands:

Unix Command	DOS Command	Description
cal	—	display a calendar
date	DATE	display the current date and time
find	TREE	locate a file
fortune	—	print a random epigram
ispell	—	run the interactive spelling checker
lpq	—	check the print queue
lprm	—	remove a job from the print queue
ping	PING	check the status of another computer
spell	—	spell check a file
touch	—	change the time stamp on a file
uptime	—	display runtime statistics about the computer system
w	—	display runtime statistics about the computer system and determine who is logged onto the system and what commands they are executing
whereis	FIND	search for source, binary, and man page files for a Unix command

which	FIND	determine where a command is located
whoami	—	print effective userid

9.1 Introduction

You have already learned the most fundamental Unix commands. The commands described so far are the commands that you will use every day and that will probably represent about 80% of your command usage. In this chapter we cover a number of utility commands. You will likely find yourself using these commands from time to time. We divide the presentation of the commands as follows:

❏ Commands relating to time. You will learn how to
– display the current date and time.
– make use of a calendar program.

❏ Commands relating to the system. You will learn how to
– find out what the load average is on your system.
– determine which users are logged into the system.

❏ Commands relating to printing. You will learn how to
– determine which print jobs are in the print queue.
– delete one of your jobs from the print queue.

❏ Commands for locating information. You will learn how to
– search a directory structure for a file.
– determine the version of a particular command you are using.
– locate the executable and source code for a given command.

❏ Miscellaneous commands. You will learn how to
– spell check a file.
– determine the effective userid of a terminal session.
– change the time stamp on a file.
– print a random saying on your screen.
– check to see if another computer is running.

9.2 Commands Relating to Time

In this section we describe a number of Unix commands relating to time.

9.2.1 date Command

The **date** command can be used to display the current system time and date. For example, entering the command

```
%date
```

on our system results in the Unix response

```
Fri Jul 14 16:05:57 EDT 2000
```

This tells us that today is Friday, July 14, the year is 2000, and it is 4:05:57 P.M. Eastern Daylight Time. Programmers often forget what day of the week it is or what day of the month it is. The **date** command comes in very handy in these situations. The **date** command has a wide variety of optional arguments. Many of the arguments are used to format the information returned by the **date** command. For example, on our system the command

```
%date +%x
```

returns

```
07/14/00
```

Other arguments to the **date** command may be used to determine other facts involving the current date. For example, the command

```
%date +%e
```

displays

```
28
```

This is the week number of the year that today's date occurs in. That is, July 14 is in the 28th week of the year 2000. Your typical use of the **date** command will likely be just to determine the day of the month, day of the week, and time.

To explore other options of the **date** command on your system, enter the command

```
%man date
```

9.2.2 cal Command

The Unix **cal** (short for "calendar") command displays a calendar. For example, suppose you needed to determine which day of the week a specific day fell on or what numbered day of the year a certain day was. This type of information is easy to obtain once you know how to use the **cal** command.

The general command syntax for the **cal** command is

```
cal [-mjy] [month [year]]
```

This means the optional flags to the **cal** command are –m, –j, and –y. There are two other optional arguments. They are **month** and **year**.

The result of entering the command

```
%cal
```

is a display of this month's calendar as illustrated below:

```
      July 2000
Su Mo Tu We Th Fr Sa
                   1
 2  3  4  5  6  7  8
 9 10 11 12 13 14 15
16 17 18 19 20 21 22
23 24 25 26 27 28 29
30 31
```

By specifying the **–m** flag to the **cal** command we can display the calendar (as in many countries, Monday occurs as the first day of the week). For example,

```
%cal -m
```

results in

```
      July 2000
Mo Tu We Th Fr Sa Su
                1  2
 3  4  5  6  7  8  9
10 11 12 13 14 15 16
17 18 19 20 21 22 23
24 25 26 27 28 29 30
31
```

The **–j** flag can be used to display Julian dates. That is, the number of each day from the beginning of the year. The author's sister's birthday is July 27. We can figure out what day of the year that is by using the command

```
%cal -j
```

This results in the following display:

```
           July 2000
Sun Mon Tue Wed Thu Fri Sat
                        183
184 185 186 187 188 189 190
191 192 193 194 195 196 197
198 199 200 201 202 203 204
205 206 207 208 209 210 211
212 213
```

By comparing this calendar with the original one, it is easy to see the author's sister's birthday is the 209th day of the year. Notice also that the **cal** command expanded the abbreviations of the names of the days of the week to match the width of the three-digit Julian days.

The **–y** option to the **cal** command lets you display the calendar for an entire year. For example,

```
%cal 2000
```

displays the full calendar for the year 2000 as follows:

```
                                  2000

         January                 February                  March
Su Mo Tu We Th Fr Sa     Su Mo Tu We Th Fr Sa     Su Mo Tu We Th Fr Sa
                   1            1  2  3  4  5               1  2  3  4
 2  3  4  5  6  7  8      6  7  8  9 10 11 12      5  6  7  8  9 10 11
 9 10 11 12 13 14 15     13 14 15 16 17 18 19     12 13 14 15 16 17 18
16 17 18 19 20 21 22     20 21 22 23 24 25 26     19 20 21 22 23 24 25
23 24 25 26 27 28 29     27 28 29                 26 27 28 29 30 31
30 31

          April                    May                      June
Su Mo Tu We Th Fr Sa     Su Mo Tu We Th Fr Sa     Su Mo Tu We Th Fr Sa
                   1         1  2  3  4  5  6                     1  2  3
 2  3  4  5  6  7  8      7  8  9 10 11 12 13      4  5  6  7  8  9 10
 9 10 11 12 13 14 15     14 15 16 17 18 19 20     11 12 13 14 15 16 17
16 17 18 19 20 21 22     21 22 23 24 25 26 27     18 19 20 21 22 23 24
23 24 25 26 27 28 29     28 29 30 31              25 26 27 28 29 30
30

          July                   August                 September
Su Mo Tu We Th Fr Sa     Su Mo Tu We Th Fr Sa     Su Mo Tu We Th Fr Sa
                   1         1  2  3  4  5                        1  2
 2  3  4  5  6  7  8      6  7  8  9 10 11 12      3  4  5  6  7  8  9
 9 10 11 12 13 14 15     13 14 15 16 17 18 19     10 11 12 13 14 15 16
16 17 18 19 20 21 22     20 21 22 23 24 25 26     17 18 19 20 21 22 23
23 24 25 26 27 28 29     27 28 29 30 31           24 25 26 27 28 29 30
30 31

         October                 November                 December
Su Mo Tu We Th Fr Sa     Su Mo Tu We Th Fr Sa     Su Mo Tu We Th Fr Sa
 1  2  3  4  5  6  7            1  2  3  4                        1  2
 8  9 10 11 12 13 14      5  6  7  8  9 10 11      3  4  5  6  7  8  9
15 16 17 18 19 20 21     12 13 14 15 16 17 18     10 11 12 13 14 15 16
22 23 24 25 26 27 28     19 20 21 22 23 24 25     17 18 19 20 21 22 23
29 30 31                 26 27 28 29 30           24 25 26 27 28 29 30
                                                  31
```

To obtain the calendar for the year 1187, you can enter the command

```
%cal 1187
```

The command

```
%cal 4 1187
```

results in a display of the calendar for the month of April in the year 1187. The result of this command is shown below.

```
        April 1187
 Su Mo Tu We Th Fr Sa
              1  2  3  4
  5  6  7  8  9 10 11
 12 13 14 15 16 17 18
 19 20 21 22 23 24 25
 26 27 28 29 30
```

From the examples we have presented, you can see that the **cal** command is an effective way of locating various calendar dates. From time to time you will want to use the **cal** command to look up information about dates. For further information about the **cal** command, you can enter the command

```
%man cal
```

Exercises

1. Is there a flag to the **date** command so that you can determine which numbered day of the year today is? If so, what is it?
2. Is there a way to display the date without using a 24-hour clock?
3. What numbered day of the year is your birthday? Your best friend's?
4. In the year 1266 what day of the week did April 12th fall on?
5. Print the Julian calendar for March of the year you were born.
6. What day of the week did December 25th fall on in the year 1000?

9.3   Commands Relating to the System

There are several Unix system commands that are worth describing even in an introductory book on Unix. These commands will help you become more knowledgeable about your system.

9.3.1   uptime Command

From time to time you will want to check some basic information about the computer you are using. For example, if the machine is running very slowly, you may want to check the load average on the system. Think of the load average as the amount of computing resources the system is using. A light load means the system is not being taxed, whereas a heavy load indicates there are large computing demands on the system. In the latter case the system performance will be less. You may want to figure out how long the system has been up and running without a crash or reboot. The uptime command can be used to determine these and other basic statistics about a system.

A typical output of the command

```
%uptime
```

is as follows

```
5:05pm  up  3:48,  1 user,  load average: 0.00, 0.02, 0.00
```

This one-line description of the system tells us that

❏ it is currently 5:05 P.M.
❏ the system has been up for 3 hours and 48 minutes.
❏ there is only one user on the system.
❏ the system load averages for the past 1, 5, and 15 minutes were 0.00, 0.02, and 0.00 respectively.

The load on the system where we ran the **uptime** command was negligible. That is, the system was very lightly loaded. For our purposes it suffices to say that as the load numbers increase, you will see your performance decrease. For example, a load of 10 or more would indicate the system was very heavily loaded. At this load you would notice a huge degradation in performance and would begin to wonder what was wrong with the system.

9.3.2 w Command

Unix provides a command that essentially performs the functions of the **uptime** command and the **who** command (described in Section 5.1.1) simultaneously, and then some. This command is called **w**. To execute the command simply enter

```
%w
```

In Figure 9.1 we display some sample output from the command. You will already recognize most of the information here from our explanations of the **uptime** command and the **who** command; therefore, we only describe what is new.

```
   6:58pm  up 2 day(s), 13:21,  5 users,  load avg: 0.00, 0.00, 0.01
User      tty            login@  idle   JCPU    PCPU   what
andrew    pts/0          Wed 5am 8:37  17:00      3    csh
andrew    pts/1          Thu 8am 8:38                  -csh
gregg     pts/2          Thu11am 2:15    12           -bash
andrew2   pts/3          Thu 2pm 9:59                  -csh
greenlaw  pts/4          6:58pm                         w
```

Figure 9.1—Sample Output from the **w** Command

In the first line of the output, we are told that the system has been up for two days. This means the system has not crashed or rebooted within the past two days and has been running continuously since then. The third column of the **who** portion of the output tells us when the users logged into the system. The fourth column indicates when they last executed a command. For example, **andrew**'s first login last executed a command eight hours and 37 minutes ago. The fifth and sixth columns indicate the amount of CPU time the user has consumed by all of his processes and by his currently active processes, respectively. The last column indicates the command the user is currently executing. For example, **andrew2** is executing **csh**.

To learn more about the **w** command, you can enter

```
%man w
```

Exercises

1. How long has your computer system been up and running?
2. What were the loads on your computer system for the past 1, 5, 10, 15, and 20 minute periods? Explain how you were able to determine this information.
3. Monitor your system twice a day for a week. What was the greatest load on the system? Did the system shut down at all during the week? What was the maximum number of users you noticed on the system at any given time? How about the minimum number of users?
4. What users are currently logged into your system? Are any of them logged in from other machines?
5. Compare and contrast the first line of output of the **w** command with the output of the **uptime** command.
6. Can all of the information provided by the **w** command pertaining to runtime statistics be obtained via the **uptime** command?
7. Is there any reason to prefer the **who** command (described in Section 5.1.1) to the **w** command?
8. Print out an execution of the **w** command on your system. Describe the meaning of the output in a couple of paragraphs.

9.4   Commands Relating to Printing

In this section we cover a number of important printing-related commands.

9.4.1 Introduction

In Chapter 4 we covered the most important command pertaining to printing, namely, **lpr** for sending a *print job* (or *job* for short) to the printer. On most Unix systems, printers are shared by several users. Each printer available on a system has a unique name. On a multi-user system you will be competing with other users for the use of the printer. In order to keep track of different user's print requests, the operating system maintains a list of jobs known as the *print queue*, or *queue* for short. Each printer has its own associated print queue.

It is best to think of a queue as a line where items wait to receive service. For example, when you wait in line to buy tickets for a concert, you are in the ticket queue. When a new person arrives to buy tickets, (in theory) the person joins the queue at the end. The print queue operates analogously. If there are no jobs in the print queue for the printer named **HP** and Joseph sends a job to **HP** using the **lpr** command, then Joseph's job becomes the first job in **HP**'s print queue. If moments later Lucille sends her job to the printer **HP**, it will be queued behind Joseph's. Once Joseph's job finishes printing, Lucille's job will print.

Table 9.1 shows two sample print queues for two printers: **laser** and **duplex**. The first column in the table indicates the position of the job in the queue. The job in position 1 is at the *head* of the queue. It will be the next job to print. Jobs with higher numbers will be printed only after all lower-numbered jobs are printed, so job 2 can print only after job 1 has been printed, job 3 can print only after jobs 1 and 2 have been printed, and so on. The last job in the queue is said to be at the *tail* of the queue. In the print queue for **laser**, Betty is at the tail and she is printing the file called **book.txt**. Moses' job is at the tail of printer **duplex**'s queue and he is printing the file **lineup**.

Queue Position	User/Job Name	User/Job Name
	LASER	**DUPLEX**
1	Walt/**rangers.ps**	Sandra/**baby.txt**
2	Walt/**rangers2.ps**	Michael/**knitting.dvi**
3	Fatuma/**boston.txt**	Ricky/**chair**
4	Moses/**lineup**	Moses/**lineup**
5	Becky/**friends**	
6	Walt/**rangers.ps**	
7	Betty/**book.txt**	

Table 9.1—The Print Queues of Two Printers

Unix assigns a unique job number to each print job it queues. In Section 9.4.3 we will see how to make use of these job numbers to remove an item from the queue.

The second column of Table 9.1 provides the user name associated with a given print job plus the name of the file being printed for the printer named **laser**. The third column of the table provides the same information for the printer named **duplex**. In Table 9.1 we see that Walt has three jobs in the print queue for **laser**: two copies of **rangers.ps** are to be printed and one copy of the file **rangers2.ps**. Notice Moses has sent his job **lineup** to both printers.

It is generally accepted practice to send a print job to the printer located closest to your office or to the nearest one that is lightly loaded. You probably should not use more than one printer at a time as this delays others from printing.

Unix provides a command for checking which jobs are in the print queue. This is useful so that you can make sure your job was properly sent to the printer and so that you can see where in line your job is. Checking the queue will give you a sense of when you can expect your job to print out. Unix also provides a command that allows you to delete a job from the print queue. We will cover these two useful print commands in the next two sections.

9.4.2 lpq Command

The **lpq** command is used to check the print queue of a specific printer. The abbreviation **lpq** stands for "line printer queue." If you type in

```
%lpq
```

without any arguments, the print queue for the *default printer* will be displayed, as will the name of the default printer. The default printer is the printer where your account automatically prints unless you specify otherwise. Your system administrator has probably configured your account to print to a specific printer. You should find out where that printer is located; its location is where you will find output that you send to the printer. It is generally a good idea to pick up your output shortly after printing. This avoids the output getting lost and can help avoid a mess at the printer. At some installations where printers are heavily used, there will be a person who places the output in bins. The output is typically sorted alphabetically either by user name or last name. A good practice is to retrieve your output from such bins in a timely manner.

There probably will be times when you need to send sensitive information to the printer; that is, information that you do not want other users to read.

For example, you might be sending your résumé, a poem you composed, or the answers to a take-home exam to the printer. In such cases you will probably want to check the print queue before sending the job to the printer. If the print queue on a given printer is *empty*, meaning there are no jobs in line to print, then you might decide to send your job to that printer. If the print queue on a printer has several jobs in, you can assume someone else may be hanging around the printer already waiting for output, in which case this person might accidentally see your output as well.

Suppose you have access to two printers: **laser** and **duplex**. Furthermore, suppose that **laser** is your default printer. By entering the command

```
%lpq
```

you can check **laser**'s print queue. To check the print queue on **duplex**, you can enter the command

```
%lpq -P duplex
```

Notice that there is a space between the **–P** flag and the name of the printer whose print queue you are checking. On some systems this space is not required, while on others it is. Figure 9.2 shows what the resulting display might look like. The first line indicates the name of the printer, **duplex**, and that the printer is currently working. That is, the printer is "ready and printing." If the printer is not working, you will see a different message here, such as "not responding." The remainder of the output is divided into several columns. We explain each of these in turn.

```
duplex is ready and printing
Rank      Owner       Job     File(s)          Total Size
active    harris      2204    book.ps          938366 bytes
1st       elizabeth   2205    blueprints       7712 bytes
2nd       elizabeth   2206    blueprints.rev   7796 bytes
3rd       jean        2207    roses            555 bytes
```

Figure 9.2—Sample Output from an **lpq** Command

The first column indicates the "rank" of each job in the queue. The head of the queue is where the active job is. In this case the file **book.ps** is at the top of the queue and is currently printing out. Jobs with higher ranks are printed later. The job numbers are assigned by the operating system. Most printers typically schedule jobs in *first-in, first-out* (*FIFO*) order. That is, the position of your job in the queue is determined by when you submitted the job to the queue and not by some other priority. Therefore, the sooner you submit your print job, the sooner it will be printed. Note that there are other scheduling algorithms in computer science for which this statement would not be true.

The second column specifies the userid or "owner" of the job. This column indicates that the job was submitted from the account of the owner. For example, the active job was submitted from the account **harris**. It is usually a good idea to submit your own print jobs and not to submit print jobs for others. At some installations some number of pages may be printed free, and beyond that quota there is a charge.

The third column specifies the "job." This column depicts the job number assigned by the system. These numbers are assigned in increasing order, each number being one larger than the previous value. For example, userid **elizabeth** has two jobs in the queue numbered 2205 and 2206. This means she submitted **blueprints** before she submitted the revised version of the file **blueprints** called **blueprints.rev**. Since the numbers are consecutive, we can deduce no job was submitted after **blueprints** and before **blueprints.rev**.

The fourth column provides the name of the file of the corresponding job. Elizabeth has two jobs in the print queue, **blueprints** and **blueprints.rev**.

The last column indicates the size of each job in bytes. The active job is 938,366, or almost 1 *megabyte*. A megabyte is equated with 1,000,000 bytes. This is a large job, as its name suggests, and will likely take a long time to print out, perhaps 20–30 minutes. The other jobs in the queue have sizes 7,712; 7,796; and 555, respectively. These small jobs are likely just a page or two long. They will print out very quickly once their turns arrive. Since these jobs are queued behind a large job, it will be a long time before they are actually printed.

The –l option to the **lpq** command is used to display more detailed information about the jobs in the queue. In particular, it displays the name of the host from where the job was submitted. This option is also useful so you can gauge how long it will take for your job to print. In Figure 9.3 we depict some sample output from the execution of the command

```
%lpq -l -P laser
```

```
laser is ready and printing

nagoya:    active      [job 1128 sailboat]
           1128-1      8675 bytes
melinda:   1st         [job 1129 matterhorn]
           1129-1      309 bytes
```

Figure 9.3—Sample Output from an **lpq -l** Command

Notice that the output includes the owner of the job, the job number, the name of the host from which the job was submitted, and the size of the job. In this case there are two jobs in the queue. The active job was sent from userid **nagoya** from the machine **sailboat**. The next job in the queue was sent from the userid **melinda** from the computer **matterhorn**.

In summary, the **lpq** command is used to view the contents of a print queue. This is useful for the following reasons:

❑ to verify that a job you sent to the printer properly arrived at the printer.

❑ to check how many jobs are already in a queue so you can decide whether or not to send your job, and to get a sense of how long it will take for your job to print out.

❑ to obtain the status of a job in the print queue.

❑ to determine the job number of an item you sent to the printer (as we will see in the next section, this is useful in case you decide to delete the job from the print queue).

To learn more about the **lpq** command, you can execute the command

```
%man lpq
```

9.4.3 lprm Command

Occasionally, you will need to delete a job from the print queue. This process of removing a job from the queue is known as *dequeuing*. For example, maybe by accident you sent a file to the printer in a format that the printer cannot print properly. When we describe the L A T_EX document preparation system in Appendix H, you will see that the output L A T_EX produces is a file in **dvi** format. This format needs to be converted to the **postscript** format before it is sent to the printer. If you send a **dvi** file to the printer, the output will not be printed correctly. In fact, a document that is only two pages long may result in 40–50 pages of bogus output. Always be careful to send the correct file formats to the printer.

Sometimes the job you send to the printer may get caught behind a large number of other jobs, and you may not have the time to wait for the file to print out. If the material is sensitive, you may decide to remove the job from the print queue rather than letting it print out while you are not around to retrieve the output. In situations like these you need to be able to delete a job from the print queue.

Unix provides the **lprm** command for deleting jobs from the print queue. The command name **lprm** is an abbreviation for "line printer remove." Recall that the command **rm** is used to delete a file and the command **rmdir** is used to remove a directory. Thus, it is appropriate that **lprm** is the command name used for the command to remove a job from the print queue.

In order to remove a job from the print queue, you need to know the job's number. You can look up a job's number by invoking the **lpq** command on the desired printer. Suppose you wanted to delete job number 887, which you had earlier sent to the default printer. To remove the job from the print queue, you simply enter the command

```
%lprm 887
```

After executing the command, you will see a message such as

```
887 dequeued from laser
```

The word "dequeued" means that the job was taken out of the print queue. In this case the name of the default printer is **laser**. To verify that the job was removed, you can execute another **lpq** command on the default printer.

Of course, you are allowed to remove only your own print jobs from the print queue; that is, only print jobs sent from your account. In addition, if a job has already started printing, you will not be able to stop all of it from printing. For a large job, you might be able to stop a portion of it from printing. So, for a large job, it is still worth trying to remove it from the queue even if it has begun printing.

On some systems when you dequeue a job, you are sent email notification from the "Line Printer Administrator" that the job was dequeued. The Line Printer Administrator is a program that helps manage the printers on a system. Suppose you sent a print request to the printer called **hp** and then decided to remove the job using the **lprm** command. In response to this dequeue request, the Line Printer Administrator might send you a message such as that shown in Figure 9.4. This indicates that job number 4279 was deleted from the queue. Note that if your job was the active job, then part of it may have already printed. It is a good idea to check at the location of the printer and obtain the pages of the job that were "accidentally" printed.

```
Your request hp-4279 destined for hp
The job title was:      4279-1
submitted from:         sailboat
at:                     Thu Jun  1 08:38:36 2000
was canceled by the lpsched daemon.
```

Figure 9.4—Message from the Line Printer Administrator

We consider one additional example of removing a job from a printer that is not the default printer. Suppose you sent a job to a printer name **csmath** and decided that you really did not want to print the file after all. The first thing to do is to look up the job number using the **lpq** command as follows:

```
%lpq -P csmath
```

Suppose the job number for the file you sent to the printer was 1231. Once you know the job number, you can remove the file from **csmath**'s print queue as follows:

```
%lpq -P csmath 1231
```

After executing the command, you will see a message such as

```
1231 dequeued from csmath
```

You can verify that the job was removed by typing

```
%lpq -P csmath
```

You can learn more about the **lprm** command by executing the command

```
%man lprm
```

Exercises

1. What is the name of your default printer?
2. How many printers are available for your use? What are their names? Check their print queues. What job numbers were scheduled at each printer?
3. Is there a way to print multiple copies of a job using the **lpr** command only once? If you do this, does the job appear in the print queue multiple times or only once?
4. Send a job to the default printer. Check its job number using the **lpq** command. What was its job number? Now delete the job using the **lprm** command. What was the system response?
5. What happens if you try to dequeue a job from a printer that someone else sent to the printer?
6. Are there other flags to the **lprm** command? If so, report on two of them.
7. Can you dequeue multiple jobs at once?

9.5   Commands Relating to Locating Information

Unix provides a number of utility features to help you determine the location of various commands and files. In this section we cover the most useful of these commands.

9.5.1   which Command

On some Unix systems there are different versions of the same command available. That is, there may be two separate versions of a command available where the commands do not always behave exactly the same way. For example, the two commands may use slightly different flags or may perform slightly different functions. The **which** command is useful for determining the particular version of a command you are using. It displays the pathname indicating where a given command is located or provides the user-defined alias for the command. The **which** command will provide information only for commands that are located in your *path*. We will cover the concept of path in detail in Chapter 17, but for now think of your path as specifying a series of directories to search in for any command that you execute.

As an example, consider the execution of the following command:

        %which lp

This will typically return a result such as

        /bin/lp

indicating that the **lp** command you are using is the one located in the **/bin** directory.

On some systems, executing the command

        %which lpr

might return the following:

        /usr/ucb/lpr

indicating that the **lpr** command you are using is the one located in the **/usr/ucb** directory. There may be another **lpr** command located in the **/bin** directory. To use this version of the **lpr** command instead of the one located in the directory **/usr/ucb** you could enter the command

        %/bin/lpr

That is, you could specify the full pathname for the command.

In the examples we have shown a pathname indicating where the command was located. Suppose the command had been aliased. For example, when some people use the *emacs* text editor, they prefer to open a new window to edit in. By supplying the **–nw** flags to the **emacs** command, a new editing window will be opened. Let us suppose you had executed the command

```
%alias emacs emacs -nw
```

so that entering the **emacs** command results in the command **emacs –nw** being executed. Now performing the command

```
%which emacs
```

would result in the following display

```
emacs: aliased to emacs -nw
```

Thus, when an alias exists, the **which** command indicates the command that its argument is aliased to.

If you use a command that is not behaving as you expected, it may be because you are not actually executing the command that you thought you were. The **which** command is most helpful for checking this.

9.5.2 find Command

The Unix **find** command is useful for locating files and also for checking the properties of certain files. For example, you may want to check which of your files were recently modified. There are many different options to the **find** command. However, the most common use of the command is simply to locate a given file among your directories. Suppose you wanted to locate all of your files called **email.tex**. The **find** command could be used as follows to do this:

```
%find -name email.tex
```

The **–name** flag to the **find** command tells **find** to search the directory structure for the file named **email.tex**. One set of results from the execution of this command is shown in Figure 9.5. In this case there were eight files found with the name **email.tex**. As shown in the figure, **find** reports the directories where it located the file. For example, the file was found in the user's directory as follows:

```
books/Web/SOLUTIONS/STUDENTSIO/email.tex
```

```
./books/EMAIL/email.tex
./books/Web/BOOK/email.tex
./books/Web/SOLUTIONS/ENGINEER/email.tex
./books/Web/SOLUTIONS/IO/email.tex
./books/Web/SOLUTIONS/STUDENTSIO/email.tex
./books/Unix/BOOK/email.tex
./books/Unix/BOOK1/email.tex
./misc/email/email.tex
```

Figure 9.5—Results from Executing the **find** Command for the File **email.tex**

Once you have found the file that you were searching for, you can change to the appropriate directory and perform the desired action on the file. If the file you are searching for is not found, you will see a message such as

find: mouse.txt: No such file or directory

In this case the user was searching for **mouse.txt** and no such file or directory with this name existed in the domain of the search.

In nearly all cases when using the **find** command, you will be searching for a file whose location you have forgotten. As you become a more advanced user, you will want to learn more about the powerful **find** command. Let us investigate one additional specialized use of the command.

Suppose you were working on a project and had recently edited a series of files spread over a number of different directories. Furthermore, suppose all of the directories were subdirectories of a directory called **project**. Perhaps you went in and entered some changes to make the file formats consistent. You may have been interrupted (sound familiar?) and were not yet able to complete all of the changes that you had intended. Now on returning to the work, you realize that you have forgotten which files you edited over the past three days when the modifications where being done. The **find** command can be used to print a listing of the files that were modified. The following command will do the trick:

%find project -ctime 3 -print

The argument **project** tells the **find** command to search in the **project** directory hierarchy, the **–ctime** flag with its argument **3** tells the **find** command to locate all files that have been modified within the last three days, and the **–print** flag tells the command to print the names of these files on the screen.

The **find** command has many other interesting uses and we encourage you to enter the command

```
%man find
```

to learn more about this powerful but sometimes difficult-to-use command.

9.5.3 whereis Command

The **whereis** command is used to determine the location of *source*, *binary*, and **man page** files relating to a Unix command. The source files contain programmer's code for implementing the Unix commands. The binary files are the actual executable commands. The **man page** files contain the information that is displayed when you use the **man** command. By location, we mean the directory where the associated files reside. There may be times when you need to determine all the **man pages** that are available to you pertaining to a certain command or when you need to locate the source or binary files for a particular command. We consider a couple of examples.

Suppose you want to determine the location of the source files for the **man** command. By entering the command

```
%whereis -s man
```

you can do this. The –s flag to the **whereis** command specifies that you are interested in the location of only the source files. In this case, the system responds with

```
man:
```

indicating that the source files are not available. If they had been available, you would have been given a complete specification of where they were located. Note that the **whereis** command responds with the command name you are looking up followed by a colon, and then with the locations of the information you were looking for.

Now suppose you want to look for the binary files corresponding to the **man** command. This can be accomplished by using the command

```
%whereis -b man
```

The –b flag to the **whereis** command specifies that you are interested in the binary files only. The result of this command will be something like the following:

```
man: /usr/bin/man /etc/man.config /usr/local/man
```

This tells you that binary files relating to the **man** command are located in the files or directories **/usr/bin/man**, **/etc/man.config**, and **/usr/local/man**. You can then **cd** to these locations to track down the information you are looking for. In this case the executable file for the **man** command is contained in the file **/usr/bin/man**. Rather than typing in **man** at the command line prompt, you could type in **/usr/bin/man**, which would also execute the **man** command. (Later in the book we will explain why typing **man** is in fact sufficient to execute the **man** command rather than typing in its real location, **/usr/bin/man**.)

Now suppose you want to look for the **man pages** corresponding to the **man** command. This can be accomplished using the command

```
%whereis -m man
```

The **–m** flag to the **whereis** command specifies that you are only interested in the associated **man page** files. The result of this command will be something like the following:

```
man: /usr/man/man1/man.1 /usr/man/man7/man.7
```

This tells us where the information in the Unix Reference Manual relating to the **man** command is stored.

We have now seen how to determine the location of the source, binary, and **man pages** separately. Now suppose you want to determine the location of the source, binary, and **man pages** for the **man** command all at once. By entering the command

```
%whereis man
```

you can determine this. You will see a response such as

```
man: /usr/bin/man /etc/man.config /usr/local/man
/usr/man/man1/man.1 /usr/man/man7/man.7
```

You can then explore these directories and files to learn more about where different files relating to the **man** command are located.

In summary, the **whereis** command is used to determine the location of files associated with a Unix command. To learn more about the **whereis** command, you can enter

```
%man whereis
```

Exercises

1. Where are the versions of the **login**, **logout**, and **alias** commands that you are using located?
2. As an experiment, alias a command name. Execute the **which** command on the alias. What is the result on your system?
3. Suppose you had aliased the **ls** command. How can you determine where the command is located?

4. Write a **find** command to locate all the files named **test** residing in a directory called **experiments**. Now write a **find** command to locate all the files named **test** in a directory called **experiments** or within any of the subdirectories below **experiments**.

5. Is there a way to locate all files that were modified within the last ten days on a given user's account?

6. How many flags are there to the **find** command on your system?

7. Report on two interesting flags from Exercise 6 and provide a sample use of each flag. Is there more than one **login** command on your system? How about for the **lp** command? Explain how you derived your answer.

8. Contrast and compare the **find** and **whereis** commands.

9. What are the locations of the source, binary, and **man page** files for the **cat** command on your system? How about the **cal** command?

10. Are the source files for any Unix commands available on your system? If so, where are they located?

9.6 Miscellaneous Commands

In this section we cover a variety of other interesting and useful commands.

9.6.1 ispell and spell Commands

The **spell** and **ispell** programs are spell-checking programs. The command name **ispell** is an abbreviation for "interactive spell checker." We describe only the more general and useful **ispell** command; however, information about **spell** can be obtained by entering the command

```
%man spell
```

It is a good idea to spell check any important documents or correspondence. Of course, spell checkers will not catch errors such as "their beers" if this phrase were intended to be "there bears." Thus, in addition to spell checking, it is necessary to proofread your work.

To invoke the interactive spell checker on the document **paper.tex** (which is not currently opened with any other program), simply enter the command

```
%ispell paper.tex
```

The result is that the spell checker opens the file **paper.tex** and then positions the cursor on the first "spelling error" it has found. A sample output from the **ispell** command is shown in Figure 9.6. The top line of the output lists the first potential spelling error: "cal" followed by the file name **paper.tex** being checked.

The second line displays the line in the file **paper.tex** where the potential spelling error occurred. This gives you a context from which to decide if the word was really misspelled. Following these two lines is a list of potential corrections to choose from. In this case there are 20 suggested corrections to the spelling of "cal." The possible corrections are displayed in alphabetical order. To select one of them, you simply enter the corresponding number. For example, if "cal" should have been "Sal," you would type in **19**. If "cal" was spelled correctly to begin with, you simply type **a** for accept as is. In either case, you will then be positioned at the next potential spelling error. Again, you will be faced with a list of possible replacements. When the spelling checker no longer finds any possible spelling errors, it returns you to the Unix prompt. The file is saved along with all of the spelling corrections that were made.

```
cal File: paper.tex
This line may have an error cal.
00: Al
01: cab
...
18: pal
19: Sal

[SP] <number> R)epl A)ccept I)nsert L)ookup U)ncap
Q)uit e(X)it or ? for help
```

Figure 9.6—Results from **ispell**

Notice that at the bottom of the display of **ispell** is a list of commands available. These are largely self-explanatory; however, if you cannot figure something out, you can enter **?** to obtain the corresponding **ispell** documentation. One command worth describing is the **r** command for "replace." Note that typing a lowercase **r** is fine. If **ispell** finds a misspelled word, it may be the case that it does not display the actual correction you want to make. This is sometimes the situation if you horribly misspelled a word. In this case, you simply press **r** and then type in the correct word. Once you have typed in the word, **ispell** will spell check the new word and then continue processing the file in its normal fashion.

It is worth noting that when you process a special type of file such as a LaTeX file, **ispell** will report more spelling errors than there really are. This is because certain command names are not English words. Nevertheless, if you get familiar with **ispell**'s output, you will quickly adjust to hitting the **a** key for such words.

You will need to slow down only on English words. If you accidentally pass by a real error, just make a mental note of it. Then go in and edit the file by hand to correct the error after your **ispell** session is finished. This technique is particularly time saving on a very large file that does not contain just English words.

9.6.2 whoami Command

There will be times when you are working on multiple computers using several different userids. In such situations it is actually possible to forget which account is logged in where. Unix provides the **whoami** command to display the userid that is logged into a given terminal. For example, entering

```
%whoami
```

would result in

```
larryfender
```

if the current effective userid were **larryfender**. Hopefully, if you use the **whoami** command on a terminal you logged into, you will recognize the reported userid. If you find a terminal left unattended, entering the **whoami** command can determine who is logged into the terminal.

9.6.3 touch Command

As we initially learned in Chapter 4, the **ls –l foo** command can be used to print out extensive information about the file **foo**. Among other things, the output will display the date that **foo** was last saved. Occasionally, you may find it necessary to alter this time stamp. For example, maybe you just read a file using the **more** command and want to update its time stamp to denote to yourself that you read it. The Unix **touch** command is useful for doing this. By entering

```
%touch foo
```

you can change **foo**'s time stamp to the current time.

Sometimes, it is useful to **touch** a group of files that you brought over from a different system as a way of marking them. The **touch** command also comes in handy during program development. It can be used to make one file look "newer" than another, thereby causing a file to be recompiled. In Chapter 23 on program development, this use of the **touch** command will become more apparent to you.

You can learn more about the **touch** command by typing

```
%man touch
```

9.6.4 fortune Command

The **fortune** command is a simple command that prints a random saying. Many people execute this command when they log in, and some execute it when they log out. The command is not available on all systems.

To have a random saying printed on your screen, simply enter the command

```
%fortune
```

Here is a sample execution of the command:

```
What's another word for "thesaurus"?
                    -- Steven Wright
```

Usually, the originator of the adage is provided as well, in this case Steven Wright.

There are a number of flags to the **fortune** command that specify what type of sayings will be displayed. For more information on **fortune**, enter the command

```
%man fortune
```

9.6.5 ping Command

Occasionally, you will want to check to see if another computer is working. For example, you may be sending a message to a person on the system, **vegas.unlv.edu**, and are not sure if this host is up and running. You would like to try to confirm that the recipient's machine is up as an indication that your message will arrive. By entering the command

```
%ping vegas.unlv.edu
```

you can check this. The response from **ping** that you will receive in this case is one of the following:

❑ **ping: unknown host vegas.unlv.edu**
    In this case **ping** does not know about this machine. You may want to check the spelling of the host's name.

❑ **vegas.unlv.edu is alive**
    This means the host is up and running.

❑ **no answer from vegas.unlv.edu**
    This means **ping** sent a message out to **vegas.unlv.edu** but never got an answer back. This usually indicates there is a problem with the host.

The **ping** command is useful for computer scientists working on networking projects. They can use the command to find out information about various hosts on the network.

We have provided only a glimpse of the **ping** command. To learn more about **ping** and some other uses of this command, enter

```
%man ping
```

Exercises

1. Run **ispell** on a sample file. Print out the last line of **ispell**'s output. Explain what each option means and how to use it.

2. Why does **ispell** not number possible replacement choices for misspelled words consecutively starting from zero? That is, why are the choices in our example not numbered 0, 1, 2, and so on?

3. Enter the **whoami** command on your terminal. What was the result? Are there any flags to the **whoami** command? If so, describe them.

4. Create a test file called **timestamp**. Perform an **ls –l timestamp** command and jot down the time. Now alter **timestamp**'s last-saved date to the current time. Perform an **ls –l timestamp**. Jot down the time. How much time elapsed between the first and second time stamps? Can you do this more quickly?

5. Without using the **touch** command, how could you alter the time stamp on a file?

6. Is the **fortune** command available on your system? If so, run it a number of times until you find two sayings that you feel are interesting.

7. Describe five flags to the **fortune** command. (*Note:* Even if the **fortune** command is not available on your system, its **man page** probably is.)

8. Can you run the **ping** command on your system? If so, **ping** another host. Print out a copy of **ping**'s response.

9. Can **ping** be used to determine "how far away" another computer is from your location? Explain.

FILE STRUCTURE
AND DIRECTORIES

OVERVIEW OF THE UNIX FILE SYSTEM

chapter **10**

In this chapter we introduce the following commands:

Unix Command	DOS Command	Description
du	—	estimate file space usage
quota	—	display disk space and limits

10.1 Introduction

Most users spend a great deal of time working with files while online. For example, they are editing files, writing programs and saving them into files, or reading files. Early on in this book you learned a wide range of commands for working with files. You learned the **ls** command for listing your files, the **grep** command for searching for a pattern in a file, the **rm** command for deleting a file, the **cp** command for copying a file, the **mv** command for renaming a file, and so on. You now have a good sense of what a file is.

What we have been calling a file is technically called an *ordinary file* in Unix jargon. For the purposes of this introductory book though, it is not necessary to distinguish between a file and an ordinary file, so we use the word file to denote an ordinary file.[1] For our purposes, we will classify files into two basic categories:

❑ *text file*—a file containing just text characters. This type of file is also called an *ASCII file* or *plain text file*. ASCII stands for *American Standard Code for Information Interchange* and is pronounced "ask key." You can think of ASCII characters as those on a standard keyboard, so a text file is the type of file we have most often talked about in this book. You will usually be working with text files.

❑ *binary file* or *data file*—a file containing any type of information. *Note:* A binary file may contain characters other than just ASCII characters. For example, a binary file might contain special characters coding an image. For our purposes a binary file is any file that is not a text file. Note that we consider the

---

1. The concept of file is much more general in Unix, encompassing several other elements as well.

text files to be a subclass of the binary files. Another example of a binary file is an executable file. An executable file is a program that you run. For example, the file containing the executable code for the **man** command is an executable file. You should not run **cat** or **more** on a binary file containing special characters. If you do, it will result in garbage being displayed on the screen and probably lock your terminal as well.

We should note that we have been distinguishing between Unix directories and Unix files, although both have the same properties. Again, for our purposes no harm is done in thinking of directories as a separate class of objects. (Technically speaking, directories are a type of file.)

In the remainder of this chapter we examine the tree-like structure of the Unix file system, several special types of files, and commands for determining how much file space you have available. In Chapters 11 and 12 we look at a handful of additional commands to manipulate files.

10.2 Structure of the File System

In Chapter 1 you were introduced to the structure of the Unix file system. Here we examine some key elements of that structure in further detail. In Figure 10.1 we show a small portion of a Unix file system. The figure illustrates the tree-like structure of any Unix file system.

Recall that the / at the top of the figure denotes the root directory. In Figure 10.1, four child subdirectories are depicted beneath the root directory; namely, **bin**, **dev**, **etc**, and **usr**. The ellipsis in the figure denotes that in fact there are many other subdirectories typically present as well. Some of the subdirectories of the root directory not shown here are **boot**, **home**, **lib**, **lost+found**, **mnt**, and **tmp**. A few remarks about several of these directories are in order.

The **bin** directory is the "binary" directory where executable command files are stored. By performing a directory listing in this directory, you can obtain a (partial) listing of the Unix commands that are available on your system. Figure 10.2 depicts one such listing. You will be familiar with many of the commands shown in the figure; others we will cover later in this book, and still others can be researched using the **man** command.

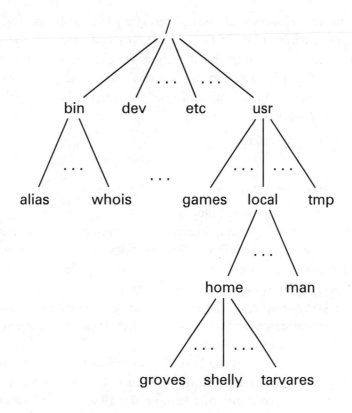

Figure 10.1—Structure of a Unix File System

arch	df	igawk	nice	su
ash	dmesg	ipcalc	nisdomainname	sync
ash.static	dnsdomainname	kill	ping	tar
aumix-minimal	doexec	linuxconf	ps	tcsh
awk	domainname	ln	pwd	touch
basename	echo	loadkeys	red	true
bash	ed	login	remadmin	umount
bash2	egrep	lpdconf	rm	uname
bsh	ex	ls	rmdir	userconf
cat	false	mail	rpm	usleep
chgrp	fgrep	mkdir	rvi	vi
chmod	fsconf	mknod	rview	view
chown	gawk	mktemp	sed	vimtutor
consolechars	gawk-3.0.4	more	setserial	xconf
cp	grep	mount	sfxload	ypdomainname
cpio	gtar	mt	sh	zcat
csh	gunzip	mv	sleep	zsh
date	gzip	netconf	sort	
dd	hostname	netstat	stty	

Figure 10.2—Sample Directory Listing of a **bin** Directory

The **etc**, pronounced "ed c," directory is an abbreviation for "et cetera" and contains a wide range of files relating to system administration. The two best known files contained in this directory are the **passwd** file, which we will discuss further in Section 10.4, and the **terminfo** file, which contains a database of information about terminal capabilities. The **terminfo** file replaces its predecessor **termcap** file. You can enter

```
%man terminfo
```

or

```
%man termcap
```

to learn more about these files.

The **lib** directory, an abbreviation for "library," contains assorted utility files. The **dev** directory, an abbreviation for "devices," contains files with information about physical devices. A user rarely needs to access these directories. The **tmp** directory, an abbreviation for "temporary," is a place where temporary files are stored. For example, a **tmp** directory might be where a document preparation system writes temporary font files. The files located in the **tmp** directory are usually deleted on a regular schedule.

The **usr** directory is the "user" directory where a wide variety of information relating to users can be found. In Figure 10.3 we show a portion of a listing of the directory contents of a sample **usr** directory. All of the items shown are themselves directories. Notice the **usr** directory contains subdirectories having the same name of some of the directories we have already explored. For example, there are **bin**, **etc**, **lib**, and **tmp** directories. There is also a **man** subdirectory, where information about **man pages** is located, and a **games** directory, where user games are found. Finally, the subdirectory **local** typically contains another subdirectory called **home**, as shown in Figure 10.1, beneath which user accounts are located. In Figure 10.1 we show the accounts of three users: **groves**, **shelly**, and **tarvares**.

```
X11R6    doc      include   libexec      man      src
bin      etc      info      local        sbin     tmp
dict     games    lib       lost+found   share
```

Figure 10.3—Sample Directory Listing of a **usr** Directory

As the brief overview presented in this section illustrates, the Unix file system is set up as a hierarchy. This hierarchical structure is very useful for organizing information. It is convenient for grouping related files together. By knowing the broad topic that a particular item falls under, one can look through the directory structure in search of the item. For example, if you were looking for a game to play, you might search for one as follows:

1. **cd** to the root directory and obtain a directory listing there.
2. **cd** to the **usr** directory, where software relating to users is kept, and perform an **ls** command.
3. **cd** to the **games** directory and perform an **ls** command to see if there is anything of interest.

This example illustrates that by learning about the structure of the Unix file system and the location of a few key directories, you can become very efficient in your search for specific information.

For any of the directories that we have discussed in this section, remember that you can get a full listing of their contents using the **ls** command. We encourage you to explore the Unix file system structure so that you can learn more about where different types of files are located.

Exercises

1. How many subdirectories are there of the root directory on your system?
2. How many different Unix commands are there in your system's **bin** directory?
3. How many different games are in the **games** directory on your system? What are their names? Are they available to you? Does your system have restrictions on game playing?
4. What is the longest directory path you can locate on your system?

10.3 Hidden Files

Earlier in Section 4.2, when learning about the flags to the **ls** command, we mentioned the concept of *hidden files*. In this section we revisit these files in further detail.

The Unix file system has some special files (and directories) that are called hidden files or *dot files* (*hidden directories*). The names of these files begin with a period (.) symbol. As we noted in Section 4.2, every directory contains the hidden files **.** and **..** Recall that these refer to the current working directory (the directory itself) and the directory's parent directory. Some other examples of hidden files are **.cshrc**, **.login**, **.newsrc**, and **.pinesrc**. The **rc** stands for "run command" and is a historical artifact of some old operating systems. These hidden files usually contain configuration or initialization information. That is, each time you log in, these files are executed. One item some users place in their initialization file is the

fortune command. In Chapter 17 we will examine in detail the type of information that goes into these files in order to make your Unix environment more user-friendly.

It is a good idea not to edit hidden files unless you are absolutely sure of what you are doing. Even when you are confident in the changes you are making, it is wise to make a "backup" copy of any of these files you intend to edit. Some of these files are not intended to be edited by hand, but only by programs. To list hidden files and directories, you can use the **–a** flag, standing for "all," to the **ls** command. Since it is very rare that you will want to see or edit these files, the default is for the **ls** command not to list them.

Exercises

1. How many hidden files are there in your **home** directory?
2. Suppose you prefer that all your hidden files are always listed when you perform an **ls** command. Is there a way to set up **ls** so that it does this? Explain.
3. Do directories other than your **home** directory contain hidden files? If so, what are they and what is their purpose?

10.4 Unix Password File

There are many important files on a Unix system. You have learned how to move around the Unix file system and examine files on your own. One very important file worth mentioning a few things about is the *password file*. The full pathname for this file is

```
/etc/passwd
```

In Figure 10.4 we show a small portion of a sample password file. The file contains a number of important pieces of information relating to user accounts. Not all of the information contained in the password file is important to us; however, there are a couple of items worth expanding on.

```
...
scott:x:5109:50:Swartzentruber:/home/scott:/bin/csh
paul:x:5111:50:Paul Kass:/home/paul:/bin/csh
janice:x:5112:50:Janice Zeigler:/home/janice:/bin/csh
pam:x:5114:50:Pam Culberson:/home/pam:/bin/csh
ms:x:5115:50:Michelle Shinholster:/home/ms:/bin/csh
oracle:x:150:150::/home/oracle:/sbin/sh
ted:x:202:10:Schmidt:/home/ted:/bin/ksh
caugh:x:5204:50:ed caughran:/home/caugh:/bin/csh
studwww:x:1203:10:Student Web Server:/var/spool/http/htdocs:/bin/ksh
zehrmich:x:4016:50:Michael Zehr:/home/zehrmich:/usr/local/bin/bash
kolodny:x:4022:50::/home/kolodny:/bin/csh
...
```

Figure 10.4—Portion of a Password File

The password file contains an entry for each user with an account on the system. The entry corresponding to a given user is listed on a single line. The information stored includes the following:

❑ userid.

❑ user's actual name.

❑ in some cases an encryption of the user's passwords (not shown in Figure 10.4).

❑ location of the user's home directory.

❑ an indication of the user's shell (shells are discussed in Chapter 17).

By examining Figure 10.4, it is easy to see the different fields corresponding to this information. The various fields are separated by using the colon as a delimiter. Notice that in Figure 10.4 the user's password is not displayed. When passwords are displayed in the **/etc/passwd** file, they are encrypted so that allowing access to the password file does not compromise security. The only time you might want to look at the password file is if you wanted some of this information about a specific user. Of course, the **finger** command can usually be used to track down more detailed information about a given user.

Exercises

1. Can you display the password file on your system? If so, how many different fields appear to be associated with each user? Describe them.
2. Print the line corresponding to your account in the password file. Describe how you located the line.
3. Do all encrypted passwords appear to be of the same length in the password file? If so, does this imply that all passwords must be of the same length? Explain.

10.5 Amount of File Space

If you are working on a time-sharing system, there is a limit to the amount of *disk space* you can use. The phrase *disk space* refers to the amount of room you have to store your files. The system administrator will generally specify that each new user gets a prescribed amount of disk space, called your *quota*. Unix provides the **quota** command for you to check your disk quota. Suppose **annabelle** wants to check her disk quota. She simply enters the command

```
%quota
```

The system will respond with a message such as

```
Disk quotas for user annabelle (uid 712): 512
```

This means **annabelle** can use up to 512 Kbytes or roughly 512,000 bytes. This is a small quota when you consider that some image files may take as much as 100,000 bytes or more to store. A more generous quota would be 5,000 Kbytes or 5 *megabytes*. A megabyte is 1,000,000 bytes[1] or 1,000 Kbytes. If you are a student working at a university, it is a good idea to delete unwanted files so you do not bump up against your disk quota. On the other hand, if you are doing legitimate school work, your system administrator will usually increase your disk quota (if you ask politely and supply a good reason).

How can you check to determine how much disk space you are actually using? After all, it would be a good idea to know when you were about to bump up against your disk quota. Unix provides the **du** command for this purpose. The name **du** is an abbreviation for "disk usage." To check your disk usage, enter the command

```
%du
```

---

1. Technically, 2^{20} or 1,028,576 bytes.

This command will report back the total number of Kbytes used in your current working directory and all of its subdirectories. In Figure 10.5 we show some sample output for the command. The last line of the figure shows that there are 7,524 Kbytes in use, or roughly 7.5 megabytes. The directory **papers/science** takes up the vast majority of disk space. The first dot (**.**) shown in each line is used to represent the current working directory.

```
188        ./.gnome/apps-redhat/Utilities
356        ./.gnome/apps-redhat
4          ./.gnome/apps
...
296        ./.netscape
4          ./nsmail
6492       ./papers/science
6496       ./papers
20         ./house
7524       .
```

Figure 10.5—Sample Output from the **du** Command

A user who needed to reduce the amount of disk space usage on an account could run the **du** command to find out where the majority of space was being used, and then try to selectively delete files from these space-intensive areas. Certain software applications that you run such as LaTeX and the C programming language compiler may generate auxiliary files. For example, LaTeX generates **log** files, **dvi** files, and **aux** files; and the C compiler produces object files with an **o** extension. These files often take up a lot of space, but are needed only temporarily. It is a good idea to delete such files when they are no longer in use.

If you have cleaned up your file space but still are bumping up against your quota, you have the option of trying to *compress* certain files. Unix provides compression commands that allow you to shrink the space a given file requires. In Section 12.6 we will go over the various commands for compressing and uncompressing files. Such commands will come in very handy as you begin to approach your disk quota. It is also useful to compress files before transferring them since the transfer of smaller files requires less time.

To learn more about either the **quota** command or the **du** command, take a look at their **man pages**.

Exercises

1. Do you have a disk quota? If so, what is it and how close are you to bumping into it?
2. Which of your directories is consuming the most disk space?
3. How can you determine how much disk space an individual file is taking up?
4. What types of files do you usually delete when trying to reduce the amount of disk space you are using? Why?

FILE AND DIRECTORY PERMISSIONS

chapter 11

In this chapter we introduce the following commands:

Unix Command	DOS Command	Description
chmod	ATTRIB	change the protection of a file or a directory

11.1 Introduction

In the last chapter we described the Unix file system and explained where various items reside on a typical system. Using the **cd** command, you can move around the file system. The question arises of how to maintain privacy if any user can locate your home directory. The answer lies in the concept of file and directory *permissions*. Permissions provide a measure of security by establishing *who* is able to access what files and directories, and *how* they can access them. The phrase "file permissions" is an abbreviation for file and directory permissions. Recall that a directory is really just a special type of file. Statements we make in this chapter about files also pertain to directories.

In this chapter we explain

❏ the various access methods for files.
❏ how to interpret Unix file permissions.
❏ how to set file permissions.
❏ how to safeguard against others accessing your private files.

11.2 File Access—Who and How?

In this section we answer the questions "Who can access a file?" and "With what capabilities can a user access a file?" Unix provides three identifiers for specifying *who* can access a particular item. They are

❏ the *user* who owns a file, designated **u**.
❏ users who are members of the same *group* as the owner of a file, designated **g**. (The system administrator, when setting up your account, places you in a

group. For example, if you are a student, you will probably be placed in a group named **student**. Your account will have the privileges afforded to students.)

❑ all *other* users, designated **o**. (This means everyone.)

In summary, the three "who identifiers" are **u**—user, **g**—group, and **o**—other.

Coincidentally, Unix provides three different levels of file permissions as well. That is, there are three different ways *how* a file can be accessed. The permissions are

❑ *read*, designated **r**.
❑ *write*, designated **w**.
❑ *execute*, designated **x**.

Read access to a file means you have permission to view the file's contents but do not have permission to alter the file. *Write access* to a file means you have permission to write to the file. For example, if you have write access to a file called **test**, you can copy (**cp**) or move (**mv**) another file to **test**. Note that you cannot edit the file. *Execute access* to a file means you have permission to run or execute the file. For example, if you have execute access to an object file that computes prime numbers, then you have permission to run the file. A program cannot be run by a user unless the user has execute access to it. A file that has only execute access cannot be read from nor written to. To be able to **cd** to a subdirectory, you need to have execute access to it. Without execute access, you cannot enter a subdirectory.

Write permission also means the ability to delete. That is, if someone has write permission to a file (directory), they also can delete the file (or directory). This is a very important point. *Write access* means the ability to delete.

In summary, read access means you can only look at the file, write access means you can write to the file or delete the file, and execute access means you can run the file.

Exercises

1. Who can access the files in your home directory and how? (*Hint:* Use the **ls** command.)
2. Suppose the permissions on a file are set so that others have read, write, and execute permissions, but all permissions for the user and group are turned off. Can a member of the group edit such a file? How about the user? Explain your answer.

11.3 File Permissions

File permissions can be conveniently displayed by using the **ls –l** command. The result of executing this command is a listing of all files and subdirectories in the current working directory along with their permissions as specified by a string of ten characters. Suppose the current working directory has just one file in it called **bicycle**. The command

```
%ls -l
```

will return a response such as

```
-r--r--r-- 1 peter student 1591 May 9 06:43 bicycle
```

We now delve into the details of what this line actually means.

The first character in the line identifies the *type* of item. In this case a dash (–) is displayed, meaning an ordinary file. The other important type for us is directory, represented by a **d**. The next nine characters in this string require some explanation.

It is helpful to think of the remaining nine characters broken up based on their semantics as

$$\underbrace{\texttt{rwx}}_{u} \quad \underbrace{\texttt{rwx}}_{g} \quad \underbrace{\texttt{rwx}}_{o}$$

This picture partitions them into three blocks of three characters each. The first three characters are associated with the user (**u**), the second three with the group (**g**), and the final three with other (**o**). The order **ugo** is very important in the permissions listing. If you read the order out loud as "you go," it may help to remember it.

For each block of three characters, an **r** in the first position indicates that the item can be read by members of the corresponding category. By category, we mean either **u**, **g**, or **o**. Sometimes the word "who" is used as a synonym for "category." Similarly, a **w** in the second position indicates write permission and an **x** in the third slot indicates execute permission. If any of the permissions is denied, the corresponding symbol is replaced by a dash. In this way, it is possible to have any combination of read, write, and execute permissions for each category. There are 8 ($2 \times 2 \times 2$) such combinations of – (none), **r**, **w**, and **x** possible for each category. Thus, there are 512 ($8 \times 8 \times 8$) different possible ways to set the permissions on a single file. Fortunately, only a few of these combinations occur in practice.

In order to make this discussion more concrete, we consider several examples. First, we revisit our initial example.

```
-r--r--r-- 1 peter student 1591 May 9 06:43 bicycle
```

The file name is shown at the far right. This listing means the user, group members, and others can read the file named **bicycle**. That is, everyone can read this file since there is an **r** in each category. No one has permission to write or execute the file, as each of these fields has a dash in it. The permissions

```
-r-------- 1 peter student 1591 May 9 06:43 bicycle
```

indicate that only the user can read the file. The **r** has been removed from the group and other categories. Again, no one can write or execute the file. The permissions

```
-rw-r----- 1 peter student 1591 May 9 06:43 bicycle
```

mean that the user can read and write the file, and that group members can read the file. No other permissions are set. The permissions

```
-rwxr-xr-x 1 peter student 1591 May 9 06:43 bicycle
```

mean that everyone can read and execute the file, but only the user can write the file.

We now take a look at the remainder of the permissions line. The **1** in the second column indicates the number of *hard links* to the file. Initially, for all your files this will have a value of one. In each of the examples presented above, the user of the file is identified in the third column as **peter**. The group is identified as **student** in the fourth column. Finally, the **1591** in the fifth column tells us that the size of the file **bicycle** is 1,591 bytes. That is, the file contains 1,591 characters.

As explained in Chapter 21, certain file and directory permissions are required so that others can view your Web pages over the Internet. In the next section we describe how to set file permissions.

Exercises

1. List the eight possible combinations of file permissions for a given category.
2. Perform an **ls −l** command on a single file. Diagram the meaning of each entry in the listing.
3. Write a one-page paper using your own words to explain Unix file permissions to a beginning user.
4. Research the concept of *hard link* and write a couple of paragraphs explaining it.

11.4 Setting File Permissions—chmod Command

Unix provides the **chmod** command for setting file permissions. The name **chmod** is an abbreviation for "change mode." There are two ways to use the command—symbolically and numerically. We will describe only the symbolic method in this book. If you are more numerically inclined, you may prefer the numerical method for setting file permissions. After having read this section and the **man page** for the **chmod** command, you can easily begin using the numerical method.

The **chmod** command takes the categories to be altered and a permissions setting as arguments. We look at a couple of examples to make the use of this command clear. Suppose you execute an **ls –l** command and receive the following listing:

```
-rw-r----- 1 peter student 1591 May 9 06:43 bicycle
```

To add read permission for others to the file **bicycle**, we can enter the command

```
%chmod o+r bicycle
```

That is, to add read permission for others we have specified others using **o** and used the plus (**+**) sign followed by an **r** flag. The intuitive nature of the syntax, using **+** to add permissions, makes the command easy to use. Similarly, to remove permission we use the minus[1] (**–**) sign. For example, to remove the write permission on **bicycle**, we perform the following command:

```
%chmod u-w bicycle
```

An **ls –l** command would now result in the following listing:

```
-r--r--r-- 1 peter student 1591 May 9 06:43 bicycle
```

Suppose that we need to add write permission for the user and the group, and execute permission for the user, the group, and other. One way to accomplish this in two steps is to execute the command

```
%chmod ugo+wx bicycle
```

followed immediately by

```
%chmod o-w bicycle
```

Notice that the first command temporarily gives write permission to everyone. Be careful to not accidentally forget to carry out the remaining steps of such

---

1. This is the same symbol as dash but we call it minus to indicate the removal of permission.

169

a "shortcut"; otherwise, the final permissions may not end up as you desired. We should point out that this result could have been achieved in one step by executing the command

```
chmod ugo+wx,o-w bicycle
```

We explain this syntax in more detail at the end of this section.

When permissions in all three categories (**ugo**) are turned on (display as **r**, **w**, or **x** across the board), we say that permission is *world*. For example,

```
-r--r--r--
```

denotes a *world readable* item,

```
--w--w--w-
```

denotes a *world writable* item, and

```
---x--x--x
```

denotes a *world executable* item. We should point out that some users say a permission is *world* whenever an **o** permission is turned on. For example, the permissions

```
------r--
```

would be considered world readable under this definition.

To change permissions in a directory on all items to be world readable, you can enter the following command:

```
%chmod ugo+r *
```

The star (*****) is a "wild card" that matches the name of every item in the directory. By replacing **r** with **w** or **x**, you can make all files in a directory world writable or world executable, respectively.

We should note that the order of the symbols **u**, **g**, and **o** and, separately, the order of the symbols **r**, **w**, and **x** as presented to the **chmod** command is not significant. That is,

```
%chmod og+rx
```

is equivalent to

```
%chmod go+rx
```

is equivalent to

```
%chmod go+xr
```

and so on. It is required that the categories come before the permissions. That is,

```
%chmod x+g
```

is not legal syntax for **chmod**. It is also worth pointing out that **chmod** may be used in a more general way than we have described. In a given line, the permissions for "who" can be set independently. For example, the command

```
chmod u+r,g+r,o-r test
```

adds read permission for the user and group, while taking away read permission from others for the file **test**. Note that no spaces are allowed between the permissions settings. To explore the **chmod** command in more detail, you can enter

```
%man chmod
```

It is always a good practice to check file protections after using the **chmod** command just to make sure permissions were really set the way you had intended.

Exercises

1. Create a file called **junk** and save the word **test** in it. What are the permissions on the file? Explain them.
2. Suppose you have a world readable file. Give a command to remove read permissions for others. Now give a command to remove read permissions for group members. Now specify a command to make the file world readable again.
3. Suppose you have a file that is completely accessible in every way to everybody. Write a minimum number of **chmod** commands to achieve the following permissions:

    ```
    ---xrw-r--
    ```

4. Suppose a file has the permissions

    ```
    -------r--
    ```

    Can someone who is the user or in the group for the file read the file? Explain. Suppose a file has the permissions

    ```
    -----wx-wx
    ```

    Can the owner of the file write or execute the file? Explain.
5. (Requires mathematical reasoning.) We say a permissions setting
    $-a_1b_1c_1a_2b_2c_2a_3b_3c_3$
    is t-steps hard for **chmod** if given the starting permissions

    ```
    -rwxrwxrwx
    ```

it takes at least t uses of the **chmod** command (without using the numerical method and only one of the operators – or + per command) to convert the permissions

```
-rwxrwxrwx
```

into the permissions

$$-a_1b_1c_1a_2b_2c_2a_3b_3c_3$$

where $a_i \in \{-, \mathbf{r}\}$, $b_i \in \{-, \mathbf{w}\}$, and $c_i \in \{-, \mathbf{x}\}$ for $i = 1, 2, 3$. Give a permissions setting that is 2-steps hard for **chmod**. If one exists, give a permissions setting that is 3-steps hard for **chmod**. Determine the minimum value y, such that no string is y-steps hard for **chmod**. Explain your answer in each case.

11.5 Safeguarding Your Files

In general, unless you are specifically sharing your files, it is a good idea to set just the minimum necessary permissions. For example, if you are going to be the only one editing a text file, the permissions on it should be set to

```
-rw-------
```

This way no one else can access the file. You should never provide write permission on a file to a nontrusted user. Remember that write permission allows for file deletion.

If you have some files that you would like to share with others, it is a good idea to create a subdirectory in your home directory called **public**. You will need to set the permissions on this directory to **r–x** for the folks you want to be able to access it. You will also need to set the permissions on your home directory to **r–x** in order for people to access a subdirectory of it. To make your home directory world readable and executable, you can enter the command

```
%chmod og+rx ~
```

In doing this, people can get a listing of the files that are in your home directory. However, if the permissions on the files in your home directory are set to

```
-rw-------
```

then only you can actually read the files. You will need to set the permissions on the files in the directory **public** to grant the access to others that you desire. For example, to make all files in the **public** world readable, you could enter the command

```
%chmod uog+r *
```

Always be careful to verify that you have set permissions correctly by using the **ls** command. If you are not sure your file permissions are set properly, check with the local Unix guru. If you suspect someone has been tampering with your files, contact your system administrator.

Exercises

1. What types of files would go in a **public** directory?
2. List all the permissions on a specific file that would give others the right to delete it.
3. If you give someone write access to a directory, can he delete it? Explain.

FILE MANIPULATION

chapter 12

In this chapter we introduce the following commands:

Unix Command	DOS Command	Description
compress	COMPACT	compact the storage space used for a file
diff	COMP	find the difference between two files
file	FTYPE	determine the type of a file
gunzip	EXPAND	decode a file that has been compressed via the gzip command
gzip	COMPRESS	compact the storage space used for a file
head	—	display the first part of a file
sort	SORT	sort the lines of text files
tail	—	display the last part of a file
uncompress	EXPAND	decode a file that has been compressed via the compress command
uudecode	—	decode a uuencoded file
uuencode	—	encode a binary file
wc	—	count the lines, words, and characters in a file

12.1 Introduction

In Chapters 4, 10, and 11 you learned some commands to manipulate files, the structure of the Unix file system, and how to set file permissions, respectively. You now have a great deal of knowledge about day-to-day file manipulation. However, the Unix operating system is extremely versatile and provides another series of commands for performing more specialized file manipulation. In this chapter we cover a number of the most important such commands.

Our goals in this chapter are to acquaint you with Unix commands for performing the following tasks:

❑ determine the type of a file.
❑ display the beginning and ending portion of a file.
❑ compress and uncompress a file.
❑ sort the lines of a file.
❑ count the number of lines, words, and characters in a file.
❑ compare two files.

12.2 File Type—file Command

Unix provides the **file** command for determining the type of a file. You might ask why is such a command necessary since you can easily determine a file's type by viewing it with the **cat** or **more** commands. If you try to view an executable file using one of these commands, you are likely to lock your terminal. Thus, it is important to have a command such as **file**.

The **file** command works by performing a number of different tests on its argument to determine what type of file it has been given. The command usually responds with answers fitting into one of the following broad categories:

❑ **text** means the file consists of just ASCII characters and is likely safe to display on your terminal screen.
❑ **executable** means the file is the result of a compilation and is probably not safe to display on your terminal screen.
❑ **data** means the file is neither text nor executable code. Such a file is probably not safe to display on your terminal screen.

The **file** command will provide more precise answers about the type of file you have given it when possible.

We now consider several examples to illustrate the **file** command. Suppose you have a LaTeX file called **chapter.tex** that contains just ASCII characters. The command

```
%file chapter.tex
```

will result in a response such as

> `chapter.tex: LaTeX document text`

If you have a C program called **fastsearch.c**, the command

> `%file fastsearch.c`

will result in a response such as

> `fastsearch.c: C program text`

As our final example, if you compile **fastsearch.c** to obtain the file **a.out**, the command

> `file a.out`

will result in a response such as

> `a.out: ELF 32-bit LSB executable, Intel 80386, version 1,`
> `dynamically linked (uses shared libs), not stripped`

indicating the file is an executable one.

To learn more about **file**, enter the command

> `%man file`

Exercises

1. Experiment with the **file** command. What are the responses you are able to get from your system's **file** command? If you try to rename a file using a different extension, are you able to fool the **file** command?
2. Report on three interesting flags to the **file** command.

12.3 File Display—head and tail Commands

We have already described the **more** and **cat** commands for displaying files, and we have briefly discussed the **less** and **pg** commands. The **more** command is particularly useful if you want to page through a large file. The **cat** command is very useful for viewing a small file. In this section we cover the **head** and **tail** commands, which display the beginning and ending parts of a file, respectively.

There are times when you will want to take a quick look at just the initial part of a file. Unix provides the **head** command for this purpose. The command

> `%head miscellaneous.stuff`

will display the first 10 lines of the file **miscellaneous.stuff** or the entire file if it contains fewer than 10 lines. A useful flag to the **head** command is **–n**. It provides you with a method to specify that you want the first **n** lines of a file displayed. For example, entering the command

```
%head -n 15 miscellaneous.stuff
```

will result in a display of the first 15 lines of the file **miscellaneous.stuff**, or the entire file if it contains fewer than 15 lines. There are several other flags to the **head** command. To learn about these, enter the command

```
%man head
```

There are times when you will want to take a quick look at just the latter part of a file. Unix provides the **tail** command for this purpose. The command

```
%tail miscellaneous.stuff
```

will display the final 10 lines of the file **miscellaneous.stuff** or the entire file if it contains fewer than 10 lines. A useful flag to the **tail** command is –**n**. It gives you a way to specify that you want the last **n** lines of a file displayed. For example, entering the command

```
%tail -n 15 miscellaneous.stuff
```

will result in a display of the last 15 lines of the file **miscellaneous.stuff** or the entire file if it contains fewer than 15 lines. There are several other flags to the **tail** command. To learn about these, enter the command

```
%man tail
```

Exercises

1. Give an example of when you would want to print out just the initial part of a file. Give an example of when you would want to print out just the last part of a file.

2. Suppose you have a file called **alphabet**, which contains 26 lines, where each line contains a single character of the alphabet and the lines are in sorted order from **a** to **z**. Furthermore, suppose your computer screen will display at least 30 lines. What are the results of entering the following commands?
   a) `%head alphabet`
   b) `%tail alphabet`
   c) `%head -n 3 alphabet`
   d) `%tail -n 14 alphabet`
   e) `%head -n 30 alphabet`

3. Describe the –**f** flag to the **tail** command. Give an example of when this option would be useful. (*Hint:* System administrators frequently use this flag.)

12.4 Sorting Lines in a File—sort Command

From time to time you will want to sort a text file. For example, you may have a file of words that you want to put in alphabetical order, or perhaps you have a bibliography that you want sorted by author's last name. Unix provides the **sort** command for sorting the lines in a text file. In this section we will look at a simple use of the **sort** command. When used in conjunction with other Unix commands as described in Chapter 18, **sort** becomes an even more powerful tool.

Suppose you have a file called **fruit** whose contents consist of the following lines of text:

```
orange
pear
grape
banana
apple
strawberry
peach
```

To sort the lines in this file, and hence the words in the file, you simply enter the command

```
%sort fruit
```

This results in the following output:

```
apple
banana
grape
orange
peach
pear
strawberry
```

Similarly, **sort** can be used to sort any lines of text.

One important flag to the **sort** command allows for sorting in reverse order. To sort the file **fruit** in reverse order, you simply enter the command

```
%sort -r fruit
```

This results in the following output:

179

```
strawberry
pear
peach
orange
grape
banana
apple
```

You will encounter a wide variety of applications of the **sort** command if you continue to use Unix. To learn more about **sort**, enter the command

```
%man sort
```

Exercises

1. How can you determine the order **sort** uses to order various characters? What order do the following characters come in, according to the **sort** command: **4**, **9**, **=**, **.**, **a**, **A**, **p**, **P**, **z**, **Z**, and **g**? Can you draw any general conclusions about the ordering of characters based on the ordering of this group of characters?

2. Give an example of a situation in which you would want your data sorted in reverse order.

3. Does **sort** put decimal numbers in increasing order according to their numerical size? Explain.

12.5 Counting Parts of a File—wc Command

Somewhere along the line you may have had a teacher who said, "Turn in a paper of at least 500 words on the subject of swimming pool maintenance." Well, how did you make sure you wrote enough words about this interesting topic? Researchers are often told to include a 200-word or shorter abstract in their papers. Do they actually count the words by hand? In fact, some of them do count the words by hand, but others are familiar with the Unix **wc** command. The name **wc** is an abbreviation for "word count." This command is extremely useful for counting the number of characters, words, and lines in a file.

As far as **wc** is concerned, a character is just a single byte, a word is any string of characters that does not contain a blank space, and a line is just a usual line of text consisting of words followed by a carriage return. For example, **a** is a character, **7yh53–,,;]kk** is a word, **sail boat** is two words, and

```
a sample line of text 12345
```

is a line. When you run the **wc** command on a file, it returns three numbers: the total number of lines, the total number of words, and the total number of characters in the file. We now consider an example of the **wc** command to make these concepts concrete.

The previous chapter of this book resides in a file called **protections.tex**. We ran the **wc** command on it by entering the command

```
%wc protections.tex
```

The results of this command were

```
533    2858  17846      protections.tex
```

This means the file had 533 lines, 2,858 words, and 17,846 characters. From this information, we can see that the average word length in **protections.tex** is 17,846/2,858 = 6.3, and that the average number of words per line is 2,858/533 = 5.4. These numbers may seem a bit unusua l for a book chapter. However, the file **protections.tex** is not just a textual description of the chapter, it also contains LaTeX formatting commands. This example illustrates the point that **wc** counts all characters in a given file (not just the ones you want it to). The author leaves many blank lines in his files when writing book chapters. In fact, the file **protections.tex** is not full of five-word lines, but rather consists mainly of 15-word lines with lots of blank lines in between. Again, this shows that one must exercise care in interpreting **wc**'s output.

To count all the lines, words, and characters in an entire directory, you can enter the command

```
%wc *
```

This results in a single line display of **wc**'s statistics for each file, plus a grand total for the entire directory. We ran this command on a preliminary version of the directory containing this book and obtained the grand total results of

```
59171     156992     4443867
```

This means there were 59,171 lines, 156,992 words, and 4,443,867 characters in the files contained in the directory.

An interesting feature of the **wc** command is that it can be used to determine the maximum length line in a file. For example, executing the command

```
%wc -L protections.tex
```

yields the output

```
83 protections.tex
```

indicating that the longest line in the file **protections.tex** consists of 83 characters.

Thus, in general, you would not need to scroll horizontally to view an entire line in the file **protections.tex**, since a screen typically displays 80 columns.

You can learn more about **wc** by entering the command

```
%man wc
```

Exercises

1. How could the **wc** command be used to help determine a typist's typing speed?
2. How can the **wc** command be used to determine the length of the second-longest line in a file?
3. Can the **wc** command be used to display only the number of characters in a file? Only the number of words? Only the number of lines?
4. Can a file ever have the same number of characters and words? The same number of characters and lines? The same number of words and lines? The same number of characters, words, and lines? Explain.

12.6 File Compression

File compression is the idea of reducing the amount of space needed to store a file. For example, suppose you have a file called **large.txt** that is 1 megabyte in size. Recall that a megabyte is approximately 1,000,000 bytes. If the same information in the file can be stored in less than 1 megabyte, we say the file can be *compressed*.

You may be wondering how a file can be compressed; after all, a file "contains what it contains." Computer scientists have developed a number of clever compression algorithms that allow you to shrink the amount of space required to store a file. The compressed version of the file is not actually the same as the original (for one thing, its size is much smaller); however, the original file can be reconstructed precisely from the compressed version.

We should point out that general algorithms for file compression are very interesting but somewhat complicated. You can find information about them by looking in any introductory computer algorithms textbook, or by searching on the Web. For example, enter the query of "file compression algorithm" to your favorite search engine.

It is worth describing an intuitive example of how file compression works before explaining the overall compression process. Suppose the file **large.txt**, mentioned earlier, actually contained 1,000,000 **x** characters. A description of **large.txt** could be coded as

```
1,000,000 x characters.
```

This description is only 23 characters long, including the two blanks and the ending period. Thus, with this description of the file, we have achieved a *compression ratio* (old size/new size) of 1,000,000/23 or 43,478. This is a huge storage savings. With the compressed version of the file, we may not be able to accomplish what we could have with the original one. For example, maybe the purpose of the original file was to illustrate how large the number one million is to a group of children. Perhaps someone had intended to print out **large.txt** to illustrate this. Obviously, printing out the compressed version does not get this point across as well. Also, notice that to go from the compressed version

```
1,000,000 x characters.
```

to the original file will take some time. That is, to generate 1,000,000 x's will require some processing. The processing time required to convert from the compressed version to the original version of the file is referred to as the *decompression time*. Similarly, to determine that there were originally exactly 1,000,000 x's in the file required some processing time. The processing time required to convert from the original file to the compressed version of the file is referred to as the *compression time*. Good compression algorithms both compress a file quickly and *decompress* a file quickly, and they achieve a high compression ratio. The process of restoring a file back to its original form is called *uncompression* or *decompression*.

The entire compression process can be outlined as follows:

1. Possess an initial file to compress.
2. Run a compression program on the file.
3. Perform the desired action on the compressed file.
4. Uncompress the file, restoring it to the original form.
5. Make use of the file as desired.

We make these steps more concrete by discussing a specific example. Suppose you would like to send your latest book via email to your publisher, who lives on the other side of the country. Assume that the book is stored in a file called **greatmountains.ps** and that the size of this file is 20 megabytes. This is a very large file to send in an email message. In fact, many email programs cannot handle a file this large. Good compression algorithms exist that may be able to reduce the storage space for such a file to $\frac{1}{20}$th of its original size.

Suppose **greatmountains.ps** is compressed to the one-megabyte file **greatmountains.ps.Z**. The file **greatmountains.ps.Z** likely contains many special characters (inserted by the compression algorithm as part of its compression process) and so cannot yet be sent via email. Unix provides the **uuencode** command that can be used to encode any file into an appropriate format so that it may be sent as email. The name **uuencode** is an abbreviation for "Unix-to-Unix encode." By entering the command

```
%uuencode greatmountains.ps.Z > greatmountains.ps.Z.U
```

you can recode the file **greatmountains.ps.Z** so that it can be emailed. (We elaborate on the use of the symbol > in Chapter 18. For now, think of it as saying "place the output of the **uuencode** command in the file **greatmountains.ps.Z.U**.") This recoding causes the file to expand by about 37%. In our case, the file to be sent grows to about 1.37 megabytes. The file can now be sent using email in the standard way.

When the publisher receives the file, she can save it to the file **greatmountains.ps.Z.U**. She then needs to run the **uudecode** command, standing for "Unix-to-Unix decode," on the file as follows:

```
%uudecode greatmountains.ps.Z.U
```

This will result in the compressed file **greatmountains.ps.Z** being restored to its original form. This file now needs to be uncompressed using the decompression algorithm corresponding to the original compression algorithm. Once the file has been decompressed, the publisher has the original file and can begin working on it.

Compression and decompression algorithms come in matched pairs. There is only one decompression algorithm that works for a given compression algorithm. Thus, to decode a compressed file you need to make sure you use the decompression command corresponding to the original compression command.

To learn more about **uuencode** or **uudecode**, refer to their corresponding **man pages**.

As our example just illustrated, it is useful to *compress* files that are to be transferred between two computers. In our case, compressing **greatmountains.ps** made it small enough that the recipient's email program could handle the file.

In general, compression makes a file smaller, and therefore, the compressed version of the file can be transferred over a network faster. Thus, it makes sense to compress and uuencode large files you are transferring over a network, assuming the recipient on the other end can uudecode and uncompress the file appropriately.

If you are bumping up against a disk quota, you may want to compress some of your files. Note that if you do compress some files to save space, you should not leave the original file around as well as the compressed file. The compressed file should replace the original file to achieve a space savings.

A wide variety of compression tools exist. Unix provides two commands for compression: **compress**, with its corresponding decompression algorithm **uncompress**, and **gzip**, with its corresponding decompression algorithm **gunzip**. The **g** in these latter two commands stands for GNU—the free version of Unix that we discussed in Chapter 1. We will only explain how to use the **compress** and **uncompress** commands since **gzip** and **gunzip** work analogously.

Suppose you want to compress the file **iceland.map**. This can be accomplished by entering the command

```
%compress -f iceland.map
```

The command has the effect of replacing the file **iceland.map** with the compressed version of the file **iceland.map.Z**. Note that the original file is no longer present. In order to make use of the file **iceland.map**, you would need to restore it to its original form using the **uncompress** command.

As another example, the previous chapter of this book is 17,846 bytes long and resides in a file called **protections.tex**. We executed the following command

```
%compress -f protections.tex
```

followed by the command

```
%ls -l protections.tex.Z
```

which resulted in an output showing the compressed file is 8,221 bytes. Thus, a compression ratio of a little over two was achieved. In general, you can expect a similar compression ratio for text files when using **compress**. Note that compression ratios will vary widely for different types of files. To restore the file **protections.tex.Z** to its original form, you simply enter the command

```
%uncompress protections.tex.Z
```

For files in this size range, **compress** processes them almost instantaneously, as does **uncompress**.

File extensions will usually alert you as to how a file was compressed. You need to know this in order to decompress the file. The file extension **Z** means the file was compressed by **compress** and the extension **gz** means the file was compressed by **gzip**. You will need to decompress any compressed file in order to use it.

To learn more about any of the compression commands discussed in this chapter, you can read their corresponding **man pages**.

Exercises

1. What is the largest file in your home directory? Compress it using **compress**. Compress it using **gzip**. Which compression program worked better? Was there a significant difference in the compressed file sizes?

2. In general, which process do you think takes longer, if either: file compression or file decompression? Explain your answer.

3. Can you create a file that when compressed by either **compress** or **gzip** has the same size as the original? Actually increases the file in size? Explain.

4. Suppose you want to transfer a 20-megabyte file over a line that transfers data at the rate of 16,000 bytes/second. How much time will it take to transfer the file? Now suppose that you are able to compress the file to one megabyte. How long will it take the compressed file to transfer using the same transmission rate? Is the savings significant?

12.7 Comparing Two Files—diff Command

When you are working on a computer editing files, it is a good idea to keep backup copies of the files. Some text editors save a separate copy of a file for you. For example, when you begin to edit the file **hwone.tex**, your editor might automatically create a second version of the file. The emacs text editor does this by calling the original version of the file something like **hwone.tex.bak**. When you go to save the new version, it will be saved under the name **hwone.tex**; that is, the original name of the file. In this way, if you accidentally destroy the copy of the file you are editing, you still have the backup from which to recover.

Suppose Mariah is working on her first C program, called **hello.c**. After a series of edits and compiles, suppose she has created a new version of her program called **hello2.c**. If she wants to compare the two programs to see how they differ, she can use the **diff** command. The command name **diff** is an abbreviation for "difference." The **diff** command performs a line-by-line comparison of two files. The basic syntax of the command is

```
diff file1 file2
```

where **file1** and **file2** are the two files to be compared.

The output of the **diff** command consists of a series of lines of the following forms:

❑ `lines1start, lines1end a lines2start, lines2end`
❑ `lines1start, lines1end d lines2start, lines2end`
❑ `lines1start, lines1end c lines2start, lines2end`

Here **lines1start** (**lines2start**) denotes a starting line number in **file1** (respectively, **file2**), and **lines1end** (**lines2end**) denotes an ending line number in **file1** (respectively, **file2**). These line numbers denote the lines that need to be altered in order to make the two files identical. In traditional Unix fashion, if **linesistart** equals **linesiend**, where **i** has a value of **1** or **2**, then only one number is listed. We will see an example of this shortly. It is best to think of the **a** as representing "add," **d** as representing "delete," and **c** as representing "change." The idea behind **diff** is to describe what modifications to **file1** would be necessary in order to convert it into **file2**.

To make the discussion more concrete, we display Mariah's C code for program **hello.c** in Figure 12.1 and her code for program **hello2.c** in Figure 12.2. To check for differences between the two programs, Mariah can enter the command

```
%diff hello.c hello2.c
```

```
/* Mariah's first C program. */

#include <stdio.h>
main()


{
printf("Hello to my family.\n");
}
```

Figure 12.1—The C Program **hello.c**

The **diff** command compares the two programs, remarkably quickly, and then outputs the differences between the two. The output in this case is

```
7a8
> printf("This is a cool programming language.\n");
```

There are several things to notice about the output of **diff**. First, we see the line affected in **hello.c** is line 7. In our abstraction above, this would be represented as **line1start** equals 7 and **line1end** equals 7. Since the starting and ending lines are equal, only one number is specified. Similarly, the line affected in **hello2.c** is line 8. To convert **hello.c** to **hello2.c**, we need to add the line following the > sign to **hello.c** after line 7. This is easy to see by inspecting Figures 12.1 and 12.2.

Secondly, notice that lines to be added to the first file from the second one are prefaced by a > sign. Although not illustrated by this example, lines to be deleted from the first file are prefaced by a < sign. Also, lines that need to be changed in the first file are shown first prefaced by a < sign followed by the lines they need to be changed to in the second file prefaced by a > sign.

```
/* Mariah's first C program. */

#include <stdio.h>
main()


{
printf("Hello to my family.\n");
printf("This is a cool programming language.\n");
}
```

Figure 12.2—The Revised C Program **hello2.c**

Since **diff** is a very useful command, it is worth considering a more complex example. In Figures 12.3 and 12.4, we depict two separate modifications of the program **hello2.c**; the first one is called **hello3.c**, and the second one is called **hello4.c**. These examples are for illustration purposes only, as neither file is a valid C program.

```
/* Invalid C program. */

#include <stdio.h>
main()


{
printf("Hello to my family.\n");
printf("is a cool programming language.\n");
a
b
a
b
a
b
c
This is a test.
```

```
This is a test.
This is a test.
This is a test.
testing
}
more to follow
more to follow
more to follow
more to follow
more to follow
```

Figure 12.3—The **hello3.c** File

The results of executing the command

```
%diff hello3.c hello4.c
```

are shown in Figure 12.5. There are essentially three key differences between the files. The first is described by the part of **diff**'s output that begins with 0a1,4. In this case, to transform this part of file **hello3.c** to that of file **hello4.c**, the following four lines (lines represented by 1,4) of **hello4.c**:

```
> more to follow
> more to follow
> more to follow
>
```

need to be added after line 0 of file **hello3.c**. Notice the last one of these lines is a blank line. The second key difference is described beginning with 16,20c20,29. In this case, lines 16–20 of file **hello3.c** need to be changed to lines 20–29 of file **hello4.c**. The third change is reported by **diff**, beginning with 25,27d33. In this case lines 25–27 of file **hello3.c** need to be deleted in order to transform the file into **hello4.c**. Notice the last line of **hello3.c** is a blank one.

```
more to follow
more to follow
more to follow

/* Invalid C program. */

#include <stdio.h>
main()
```

```
{
printf("Hello to my family.\n");
printf("is a cool programming language.\n");
a
b
a
b
a
b
c
printf("Hello to my family.\n");
printf("is a cool programming language.\n");
a
b
a
printf("Hello to my family.\n");
printf("is a cool programming language.\n");
a
b
a
}
more to follow
more to follow
more to follow
```

Figure 12.4—The **hello4.c** File

This example illustrates an addition (**a**), a deletion (**d**), and a change (**c**). Unix users who have become familiar with the **diff** command can quickly determine all the changes that exist between two files. It does take some practice before one adapts to **diff**'s output.

```
0a1,4
> more to follow
> more to follow
> more to follow
>
16,20c20,29
< This is a test.
< This is a test.
```

```
< This is a test.
< This is a test.
< testing
---
> printf("Hello to my family.\n");
> printf("is a cool programming language.\n");
> a
> b
> a
> printf("Hello to my family.\n");
> printf("is a cool programming language.\n");
> a
> b
> a
25,27d33
< more to follow
< more to follow
<
```

Figure 12.5—Results of **diff hello3.c hello4.c** File

Programmers who are working together on a piece of code will make use of the **diff** command regularly in order to see the changes their partners have made. This is true for researchers writing papers together or for students working together on a joint project. The **diff** command has a number of interesting flags as well. To explore these you can execute the command

> %man diff

Exercises

1. Suppose you have a file called **test**. What is the output of the command

   > %diff test test

2. Create a file with three blank lines and another with five blank lines. What is the output of the **diff** command on these two files? Does the order you compare them in matter? Explain.

3. Create the smallest two files you can in terms of number of lines so that you end up with an **a**, **d**, and **c** in **diff**'s output. That is, an addition, deletion, and change are needed to convert the first file into the second one.

4. Will **diff** ever output two consecutive **a**'s, **d**'s, or **c**'s? Explain your answer.

chapter 13

MANAGING DIRECTORIES

In this chapter we introduce the following commands:

Unix Command	DOS Command	Description
shar	BACKUP	create a shell archive
tar	BACKUP	create a tape archive
unshar	BACKUP	unpack a shell archive

13.1 Introduction

You now have an excellent understanding of the tree-like structure of the Unix file system. An obvious question to ask is "How do I take advantage of this system to organize my work?" In this chapter we address this question.

To work effectively and efficiently online, you must be able to organize your material well. Directories are the key element to setting things up appropriately. Towards the end of helping you develop the skills to devise a good organization for your files, we first revisit the concept of directory paths, then suggest ways to organize your files into directories, and lastly describe how you can package an entire directory into a single file. By combining the information you learn in this chapter with the skills you have already developed with respect to file manipulation, you will have essentially mastered the Unix file system.

13.2 Directory Paths and Structure

In this section we review how to move up and down the Unix file structure, and point out several considerations you will want to take into account while organizing your files. In Figure 13.1 we show a portion of Dana's file space; Dana's userid is **dana**. We will use her file space to make the ideas discussed in this section concrete.

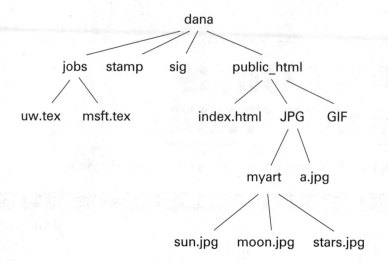

Figure 13.1—Dana's File Space

At the top level Dana has organized her file space into two directories, namely **jobs** and **public_html**. She also has two files sitting in her home directory, **stamp** and **sig**. Dana frequently needs to use the files **stamp** and **sig**, which are two separate signature files containing her contact information, so she has positioned them right in her home directory. It is usually a good idea to place frequently used items in your home directory; however, a balance needs to be achieved because you do not want your home directory to become too cluttered. Note that not every item can be a frequently used item unless there are very few total items.

Dana's **jobs** directory contains two files, namely **uw.tex** and **msft.tex**. Her **public_html** directory contains the file **index.html**, the **JPG** directory, and the empty **GIF** directory. The **JPG** directory contains the file **a.jpg** and the subdirectory **myart**—which is home to three **jpg** files.

Suppose Dana's current working directory is her home directory. To move into the **myart** directory, she could enter the command

```
%cd public_html/JPG/myart
```

From there, to move into the **GIF** directory, she could enter the command

```
%cd ../../GIF
```

or

```
%cd ~/public_html/GIF
```

To move from there to the **jobs** directory, she could enter the command

```
cd ../../jobs
```

These commands illustrate that with a directory structure that is only three *levels* deep, it is very easy to move from any given location in the hierarchy to any other place in the hierarchy. Note that a level consists of items that are the same path length from Dana's home directory. In Figure 13.1 the first level consists of **jobs**, **stamp**, **sig**, and **public_html**. The second level consists of **uw.tex**, **msft.tex**, **index.html**, **JPG**, and **GIF**. The third level consists of **myart** and **a.jpg**. The fourth level consists of **sun.jpg**, **moon.jpg**, and **stars.jpg**.

If you will be moving up and down your directory hierarchy frequently using the **cd** command, it is important to think about the following issues:

❑ choose short but descriptive names for directories.

❑ place related material in the same "branch" of the directory structure.

❑ balance the *width* of the directory structure with its *depth*. (The width of a directory structure refers to the maximum number of items included in any individual directory, and the depth refers to the maximum number of levels in the directory structure. The width of Dana's directory structure is four and its depth is coincidentally also four.)

The type and amount of information you have dictates how it is most effectively arranged. Two rules to remember when trying to weigh various possible trade-offs in organizing material are

❑ five minutes spent up front organizing is worth one hour of time later trying to reorganize.

❑ very few people ever take the time to recast a poor organization,[1] so they typically operate inefficiently every day.

From these two rules we can conclude that it is very important to spend some time organizing your material initially and that it is very important to reorganize your materially periodically. This way you can operate efficiently on a daily basis. In the next section we provide some additional hints as to how to organize your information.

Exercises

1. Frank has eight different topics he is studying. Each topic consists of four subtopics and each subtopic seven additional topics. Sketch a file structure that would be appropriate for organizing his work. How many levels deep is the structure and what is its width?

2. Suppose you were moving around a file structure in which all directory names were exactly five characters long. Further, suppose the

---

1. They simply do not have the time since they are operating so inefficiently.

structure were three levels deep and had a width of two. What is the maximum number of characters you would ever need to type in changing from any directory to any other directory? Explain your answer.

3. Eagle has 1,000 files that are all very closely related. She insists on putting them all in a single directory or giving each its own separate directory. Explain some of the possible problems with either of these arrangements.

13.3 Organizing Files and Directories

You have total control to create and maintain both files and directories in your home directory. The main reason for using subdirectories is to organize files. For example, in Figure 13.1 we saw that Dana has subdirectories in her home directory for jobs and her Web material. Also in her home directory, she has a file called **sig** and a file called **stamp**. You will certainly want to create subdirectories to better organize your online material. To create a subdirectory in your home directory, you can use the **mkdir** command.

The most difficult issue to face when organizing material is that when you begin to get organized, you have only a very small fraction of the material that you will ultimately have to organize. That is, new material will pop up unexpectedly. For example, you may get a lot of interesting email correspondence that you want to save outside of your mailer; you may find lots of cool images on the Web that you want to store; or you may find yourself doing a project for a class that you had not anticipated (sound familiar?). Thus, whatever organizational scheme you adopt, it needs to be one that can grow to accommodate additional information.

Over the years, we have developed a few rules of thumb that may help you in deciding how to organize your material. Such guidelines will not apply to all situations, so apply them judiciously. These hints are intended to apply to individual users. The suggestions are

1. Create subdirectories in your home directory only for the most general topics.

    You do not want to clutter your home directory. From your home directory, you should be able to take a listing, at a glance determine where to go next, and then quickly jump to the next directory to move closer to the information you are trying to find.

2. Limit the number of subdirectories of a directory to 20.

    If you begin to get more than 20 directories in any directory, it may be time to add a level to your organization. The new branching point will give you room to grow and maintain an efficient organization as new material arrives.

3. Limit the number of files you place in your home directory to just a few; the ones you do place there should be extremely important.
   Placing a lot of files in your home directory will make it more difficult to pick out the item of interest from the "crowd."

4. Limit the number of files in the lowest level directories to 50.
   It is hard to pick out individual files efficiently from a listing that is much larger than 50. If you have directories containing hundreds of files, you may want to subdivide them.

5. Do not mix files and directories in most directories. (Recall that in this book we distinguish between a file and a directory.)
   If you maintain just files or just directories in a given directory, then you will only have to look for files in directories that contain files and only have to look for directories in directories that contain them. This can speed up your search time.

6. Choose descriptive directory names.
   As your work space grows, it will be hard to remember where everything is located. A good naming scheme can prove very valuable several years down the road.

As you organize your material into an efficient structure, you will primarily be making use of the **cd**, **ls**, **mkdir**, **mv**, **pwd**, **rm**, and **rmdir** commands.

Exercises

1. Suppose a directory structure consists of five levels, that each directory not containing a file has five subdirectories, that each directory containing a file contains exactly ten of them, and that directories at level four are the only directories containing files. How many files could such a directory structure hold?

2. A student goes to college for five years. Each semester the student takes three classes. For each class the student completes an online project and five online assignments. Suggest two different possible directory structures to organize the student's work. One arrangement should have the top-level organization based on semesters, and the other should have the top-level organization based on classes.

3. At a maximum, how many files or directories can a file structure that is four levels deep and three items wide contain?

13.4 Bundling Up a Directory

There will be times when you want to group together the contents of an entire directory and all of its subdirectories into a single file. For example, if you are working on a joint project and need to transfer the files to your collaborator, if you are a graduating student and want to bring all of your school files with you when you graduate, if you are relocating your Web material, or if you are changing jobs and want to move your files over to a new system. In this section we cover two commands that are very useful for packaging up a group of files into a single file.

The first command we look at is called **tar**. The name **tar** is an abbreviation for "tape archive." There are many different options available to the **tar** command. We illustrate how to use the **tar** command to pack the contents of a directory and all of the contents occurring in its subdirectories. Suppose you want to create a file called **Project.tar** that contains all of the information in the directory **Project**. Simply change to the location where the directory **Project** is housed. Then enter the command

```
%tar -cvf Project.tar Project
```

The effect of this command is to create the file **Project.tar**, which will contain all of the material in the **Project** directory and below. The flags we have used are **c** standing for "create," **v** standing for "verbose," and **f** standing for "file." The **Project.tar** file can then be compressed and uuencoded for emailing, or moved to a new location and unpacked. To restore the material once it has arrived at the desired location, simply execute the command

```
%tar -xvfBp Project.tar
```

This restores everything in the current working directory. The flags we have used are **x** standing for "extract," **v** standing for "verbose," **f** standing for "file," **B** standing for "block," and **p** standing for restore the files to their original "protections."

In both creating a **tar** file and extracting the contents of a **tar** file, we have specified the verbose option. When the verbose flag is on, **tar** prints out the actions that are being carried out. It is helpful to have this information printed on the screen so that you can see exactly what the **tar** command is doing.

It is clear that the **tar** command is very useful for creating a backup copy of a file space. There are other interesting uses of the **tar** command as well. To learn more about the other options to the **tar** command, you should enter

```
%man tar
```

The second command we look at for bundling up a directory and its subdirectories is called **shar**. The name **shar** is an abbreviation for "shell archive." This command, like **tar**, is useful for packing up a group of files into a single file. The **shar** command is very versatile but our primary interest is simply to illustrate how to bundle up files located in a single directory. To package all files in a directory and its subdirectories into a file called **ALL.shar**, you enter the command

```
%shar * > ALL.shar
```

This creates the file **ALL.shar** containing everything in the current working directory and below. To unpack everything so that it is returned to its original state and structure, you enter the command

```
%unshar ALL.shar
```

As a second example, suppose you have a directory called **Cproject** that contains, among other things, a lot of C programs having a **c** file extension. By entering the command

```
%shar *.c > Cproject.shar
```

you can collect all of the files in the directory **Cproject** having a **c** extension into the single file **Cproject.shar**. The **c** files remain unchanged. The **shar** file can be manipulated as desired, and when it arrives at its final destination, the file can be unpacked as follows:

```
%unshar Cproject.shar
```

This results in copies of all of the original **c** files being deposited in the current working directory.

Like the **tar** command, you can see that **shar** is very useful for creating a backup copy of a group of files. To learn more about the many different flags to **shar**, you should enter the command

```
%man shar
```

Exercises

1. Create a directory in your work space where you can experiment. Put 10 files of varying sizes into the directory. Build a **tar** file consisting of the contents of the directory. Is the size of the **tar** file the same as the sum of the sizes of the individual files? Explain.

2. Create a directory in your work space where you can experiment. Put 10 files of varying sizes into the directory. Construct a **shar** file consisting of the contents of a directory. Is the size of the **shar** file the same as the sum of the sizes of the individual files? Explain.

3. Compare and contrast the **tar** and **shar** commands.

4. Describe all of the steps you would need to take to send another user (via email) a **tar** file containing your entire work space.

UNIX EDITORS

TEXT EDITING

14.1 Introduction

This chapter contains basic information about *text editing*, the process of creating, adding information to, modifying, and saving files. A *text editor* creates and modifies files. The word *text* refers to the ASCII data in a file, that is, the keyboard symbols you enter. The word *edit* refers to the process of entering or modifying ASCII data. In Section 7.3 we provided an introduction to the **pico** text editor, which is used with the **pine** mail program. There you learned about cursor movement, cutting and pasting text, saving and inserting files, and other editing commands. It is a good idea to review that section before reading this material.

In this chapter we introduce you to basic text-editing functions and principles. Text editing is an individualized process with different people having a wide range of preferences and styles; there are generally many ways of accomplishing the same thing. Thus, there usually is not a single preferred way or right way of achieving a given editing task. On the other hand, there are often very efficient ways of accomplishing an editing goal and more roundabout ways of accomplishing the same thing. Since editing is really a way of inputting information into a computer, you will want to spend as little time on this as possible, so you can devote more time to the actual development of the material itself. This point deserves further clarification, as the following sample scenario demonstrates.

Consider two computer science majors, Detlef and Eugene, who need to develop a C program on scratch paper. Next, they need to enter the program into the computer, so they can compile and run it. Furthermore, suppose Detlef and Eugene are each given 50 minutes to accomplish this task. In order to enter their code into a file, they will need to be able to create a file, type in the program making corrections as they go, and save the file. To enter the program efficiently, they will need to be familiar with the computer keyboard and basic editing commands.

Detlef, who is very familiar with editing, can spend 45 minutes (or 90% of his time) on developing the program and 5 minutes (or 10% of his time) on editing, whereas Eugene, who is less experienced with editing and typing, may need to spend 25 minutes (or 50% of his time) on developing the program and a full 25 minutes (or 50% of his time) on editing. If Detlef and Eugene are equally good programmers, we see that within the allotted time it is very likely that Detlef will be able to develop a superior program. This is because most of his time can go into program development. In other words, because Detlef is competent with editing, he can spend his time on program development rather than fumbling around with the editor. In contrast, Eugene spends as much time working with the computer tools themselves, in this case the text editor, as he does on the development of his program.

The scenario we have just presented highlights the importance of becoming fluent in using a text editor. Hopefully, after reading this chapter and either Chapter 15 about the **emacs** text editor or Chapter 16 about the **vi** text editor, you will find yourself in Detlef's place rather than Eugene's. If so, you can spend most of your time concentrating on your main task.

The goals for the remainder of this chapter are

❑ to discuss editors from a general point of view. We describe how to learn one and how to choose one.

❑ to take a quick look at creating and saving a file in **emacs** and in **vi**.

❑ to describe basic principles of editing.

❑ to present some helpful editing hints.

14.2 Editors—Learning and Selecting One

There are essentially three general-purpose text editors available on Unix systems. They are **pico**, **emacs**, and **vi**. The basics of the **pico** editor were covered in Section 7.3. **Pico** is an easy-to-use editor, but it is not nearly as powerful as **emacs** or **vi**. We strongly recommend learning either **emacs** or **vi** if you plan to do much serious editing. For simple editing tasks, **pico** may suit your needs just fine.

In the succeeding two chapters we cover the fundamentals of the two most popular Unix-based text editors. In Chapter 15 we present the **emacs** text editor, and in Chapter 16 we present the **vi** text editor. It is a good idea to learn the basics of both of these editors. Several reasons for learning about both of these editors are as follows:

❑ you may at some point be working with another person who uses a different editor from you. When looking over this person's shoulder while a file is being edited, it helps to know the basic editing commands. If you do, you will be able to communicate more effectively with the person doing the editing and guide the person as changes are entered. For example, you might say "Do a **Control-E**, then two **Control-D**'s, then an **Escape-D**" in order to have the person accomplish a given editing task. If you are not at all familiar with the editor the person is using, it will be more difficult to follow what is happening and communicate clearly.

❑ you can make a more informed decision about which editor to use.

❑ if you take over someone else's terminal who was in the middle of an editing session using the opposite editor from you, it is helpful if you can gracefully exit from the editor.

❑ you may find yourself on a system which has only one of the two editors on it.[1] If your favorite editor is missing, you will not be able to do any editing.

We recommend that you read either Chapter 15 or Chapter 16 thoroughly and carefully to learn about either **emacs** or **vi**, respectively, and then skim over the other chapter, learning the basic editing commands for the second editor. The two chapters cover essentially the same material, but for the separate editors. You will see that **emacs** commands are very similar to **pico** commands; you will see that **emacs** has many more capabilities than **pico**.

Both **emacs** and **vi** are complex editors. You will need to devote a considerable amount of time in order to learn either one of them. We recommend learning the basics of both of these editors initially before deciding which one to make your primary editor. Some Unix users swear by **emacs**, while others swear by **vi**. Once a user has invested a significant amount of time to learning either one of these editors and becomes comfortable with it, it is not likely that the user will switch over to the other editor. Thus, it is very important which editor you learn first, since in all likelihood it will be the editor you will use permanently.

Once you have decided on an editor, we recommend practicing with the editor online. It is fine to read about commands in a manual, but most users are able to assimilate better when they are actually executing the commands. Initially, focus on only those commands you need. That is, the basic commands such as those for cursor movement, text deletion, saving files, and exiting the editor. Once you are confident with these fundamental commands, you can learn more advanced commands.

---

1. Actually, nearly all Unix systems have **vi** on them.

Exercises

1. Provide references for three books that are devoted entirely to **emacs**.
2. Provide references for three books that are devoted entirely to **vi**.
3. Write a one-page article for *The Wall Street Journal* explaining the differences between email programs, operating systems, and editors.
4. Compare and contrast learning to use an email program with learning to use an editor.
5. Compare and contrast learning to use an operating system with learning to use an editor.

14.3 Example Using Emacs and Vi

Learning to use an editor is not easy. Both **emacs** and **vi** have a vast (read overwhelming) number of commands. Most of these commands are difficult for a beginning user to remember. It is a good idea to create a scratch directory where you can practice editing. In this way, if something goes wrong, you do not end up destroying an important file. In this section we consider the process of creating a file called **oneliner.txt** containing the single line of text

```
My first file created with a Unix editor.
```

We first illustrate how to generate the file using **emacs** and then examine how to create the identical file using **vi**. To produce the file **oneliner.txt** using **emacs**, simply type

```
%emacs oneliner.txt
```

This command will open a window such as that shown in Figure 14.1. The double underscore characters (_ _) shown near the top of the figure denote the flashing cursor you will see. We will explain the various items in Figure 14.1 in Chapter 15. For now, we are interested only in adding a line of text to the file **oneliner.txt** and saving the file. You can enter the line of text to the **emacs** editor by simply typing it in on the screen. That is, just type in

```
My first file created with a Unix editor.
```

```
Buffers Files Tools Edit Search Mule TeX Help
_ _




--11:---F1 oneliner.txt     (Text)--L1--All---------
(New File)
```

Figure 14.1—Sample **Emacs** Window

To exit **emacs** and save the file, you can enter **Control-X Control-C**. **Emacs** will ask if you would like to save the file. You type in **y** for "yes." This example illustrates that creating and saving a file with a single line of text in it is trivial in **emacs**. (Of course, if you made a typo, you would need to use some other editing commands to correct it.)

Now we consider creating the file **oneliner.txt** using **vi**. We assume this file does not currently exist. To create the file using **vi**, simply type

```
%vi oneliner.txt
```

The result of this will be the appearance of a window such as that shown in Figure 14.2. The double underscore characters (_ _) shown at the top of the figure denote the flashing cursor you will see. The **vi** editor marks blank lines with the ~ character. Type **i** to enter **insert** mode. Now you can enter the line of text to the **vi** editor by typing it in on the screen; that is, just type in

```
My first file created with a Unix editor.
```

```
 _ _
~
~
~
~
~
~
~
~
~
~
~
~
"oneliner.txt"  [New File]
```

Figure 14.2—Sample **Vi** Window

To exit **vi** and save the file, you press **Esc** followed by **:x** (type the colon character and the **x** character). This example illustrates that creating and saving a file with a single line of text in it is also trivial in **vi**. (Of course, if you made a typo you would need to use some other editing commands to correct it.)

Even this simple example of file creation illustrates that **emacs** and **vi** are very different programs. Their appearance is different and they behave differently. In Chapters 15 and 16 you will see that there are many other distinguishing features between the editors as well. In fact, it's arguable that knowing the specifics of one of these editors does little, if anything, to help you learn the other.

We have stressed the importance of choosing one editor to concentrate on learning and in doing this fairly early on in your study of editors. You may want to talk to some other users to see which editor they prefer and why. The decision you make will probably be a permanent one, so give it some thought. There is no right choice other than the choice that is right for you.

Exercises

1. Create the file **oneliner.txt** using **emacs**. Create the file **oneliner.txt** using **vi**. Did you have any problems with either editor? If so, which editor was more difficult for you to use? Why?

2. Read the **man page** for **emacs**. Report three interesting facts you learned.

3. Read the **man page** for **vi**. Report three interesting facts you learned.

14.4 Basic Principles of Editing

In this section we make several general comments about text editing that will apply regardless of which text editor you use. These are just a few of the considerations you will want to take into account when editing. As you gain more experience, you will develop your own editing strategies.

One of the most important principles of editing is to save your work often. The mechanics of how you save your work will depend on the specific text editor you are using. The important point is that you do not want to get in a situation where you lose work. Thus, it is a good idea to save the file you are editing very regularly. Some users save their file after 500 keystrokes have been entered. Others save their file after typing in a new paragraph. It is especially important to save your work regularly if you are making "on the fly" edits. That is, you are jumping all around the file tweaking things here and there. It will be very difficult to re-enter such edits (especially if there is no paper trail), and so you should periodically save your file during such an editing session.

Another important principle is to reuse work when possible. This can save you lots of typing time. For example, suppose you need to code two 50-line C programs that are nearly identical. It makes sense to generate the file for the first program, say **prog1.c**, and then to copy that file and generate the second program by editing the copy of **prog1.c**. That is, you can enter the command

```
%cp prog1.c prog2.c
```

and then edit the file **prog2.c**. If **prog1.c** and **prog2.c** are very similar, the time you save by not typing in **prog2.c** from scratch can be significant. In general, try to reuse sections of your own work when you need to produce a similar portion of text.

A third principle is to remember the trade-off between the time you devote to editing versus the time you devote to the real task at hand. The more accurately and efficiently you can perform your editing, the more time you have to devote to your real project. Do not get lazy while editing. Always look for shortcuts and try to enter your data quickly. Make sure you concentrate on what you are doing. Many users spend far too long entering information into the computer, even experienced users. The trap many people fall into is that they always do things the same way—the comfortable way. A little time spent here and there trying to become more efficient will end up saving you many weeks' time over the course of several years.

Finally, it is a good idea to take short breaks every 45 minutes or so while editing. (You may need to build up to 45 minutes initially.) This will give your eyes and hands a rest. Additionally, it will let you recharge yourself mentally so that you can concentrate fully while editing. You will probably get more accomplished by working hard for 45 minutes out of an hour rather than coasting for the full hour. In addition, you will find that you are able to work longer and more efficiently when you are well rested. Many students fall into the trap of having to "work all of the time." In many cases the reason for this is because they are working very inefficiently. If you learn to be efficient, you will have more free time.

Exercises

1. Have you ever lost any work while editing? If so, describe your experience.
2. Describe why it is important to save your work periodically, even if the system administrator routinely backs up the system.

3. Suppose you need to type in a 1,000-word handwritten essay. Assume you type 15 words per minute while tired and 40 words per minute while rested. How much time savings will you realize if you type in the essay when rested?

4. Belinda and Honey type 10 and 80 words per minute respectively. Belinda is twice as good a programmer as Honey in the sense that Belinda can develop code on paper twice as fast as Honey. Other than this difference, assume the two always produce identical code. Belinda takes 15 hours to develop a program that consists of 2,000 words. How long does it take Honey to get her program into the computer, including development time? Who can complete the assignment of developing and entering this program into the computer sooner?

5. Suppose you have the endurance to work four hours nonstop on the computer, but then you cannot touch a machine for 20 hours. Alternately, you can work up to 12 hours consecutively as long as you take 15 minute breaks every hour. However, after working these 12 hours with breaks, you need 12 hours sleep. Assume you have put off a large project that needs to be completed in a one-week time period. What is the maximum number of hours you can work in a week given the assumptions just stated?

14.5 Helpful Editing Hints

Regardless of the editor you choose, the editing hints provided in this section can help you work more efficiently. The items presented here are by no means an exhaustive list. In the exercises, we ask you to provide several other useful editing hints. You will find some of these hints to be of greater value to you than others, and perhaps some of them will not apply to you at all. However, each one is worth considering, as they come from years of experience.

14.5.1 Editing Style

It is important to develop a consistent editing style. By this we mean it is important that similar elements in a file be laid out the same way throughout the file. For example, suppose you are writing a paper on the animals of Africa. Figures 14.3 and 14.4 show two sample files containing the same text for the paper. The text in Figure 14.3 is presented in a consistent manner, whereas that in Figure 14.4 is not. In Figure 14.3 the section headings Buffalo, Elephant, Leopard, Lion, and Rhino are spaced equally and the text associated with each heading follows in a consistent manner. By looking at the file, it is easy to see which text goes with which animal. Contrast this with the text shown in Figure 14.4, where a lot of the material runs together. It is harder to see which text belongs to which animal.

```
Animals of Africa

Introduction

The buffalo, elephant, leopard, lion, and rhino are collectively
called the "Big Five" of African Animals. Each of these animals
is beautiful to watch in its native environment. In this brief
paper we mentioned a few words about each.

Buffalo

The buffalo is a dark, massive animal with interesting shaped horns.

Elephant

The elephant is a gray giant with enormous ears.

Leopard

The leopard is a large, elusive cat.

Lion

The lion is a large, lazy cat.

Rhino

The rhino is a massive animal distinguishable by its huge,
frontal horn.
```

Figure 14.3—Consistent Style: Draft of Animals of Africa

Another important thing to notice about the files is that in Figure 14.3 the lines are divided at natural break points. In Figure 14.4, the lines are choppy and appear to be divided at random. For example, consider the four lines

```
is
beautiful to
                          watch
in its native environment.
```

Notice that the word **watch** is placed towards the middle of the line rather than at the beginning. It is a good idea to consistently begin lines at the left margin, as is illustrated in Figure 14.3.

The main point here is that with a consistent style you will be able to find material in the file that needs to be edited more quickly. This point is easy to illustrate using our two sample drafts. The section headings for the animals stand out in Figure 14.3, so it would be easy to move the cursor to the section pertaining to any specific animal. In Figure 14.4 one needs to stare at the file for a while before picking up on all the animal names. For example, visually moving the cursor to the word **Leopard** in the file represented by Figure 14.4 is not as easy as it would be in the file represented by Figure 14.3.

```
Animals of Africa

Introduction

The buffalo,
elephant, leopard, lion,
and
rhino are collectively called the "Big Five" of African Animals.
          Each of these animals
is
beautiful to
                              watch
in its native environment.
In
this brief paper we mentioned a few words about each. Buffalo
The buffalo is
a dark, massive animal
with interesting shaped
horns.
Elephant

The elephant is a gray giant with enormous ears.
Leopard
The leopard is a large, elusive cat.
Lion

The lion is a large, lazy cat.
Rhino
The
rhino is a massive
animal
distinguishable by its huge, frontal horn.
```

Figure 14.4—Inconsistent Style: Draft of Animals of Africa

We believe that developing a consistent style such as that illustrated in Figure 14.3 will help to make you a more efficient user of a text editor. If you ever need to collaborate on a project where you are sharing files with other users, it will be very important for you to use a consistent style in your work. If you do, your collaborators will know what to expect from you.

14.5.2 Layout of Text within a File

The layout of the text shown in Figure 14.3 versus Figure 14.4 illustrates some of the advantages of using white space and a consistent style within a file. However, in some cases you may want to take this even further for more efficiency. In Figure 14.5 we show a small portion of the file depicted in Figure 14.3 but reformatted.

```
Animals of Africa

Introduction

The
buffalo,
elephant,
leopard,
lion,
and
rhino
are collectively called the "Big Five" of African Animals.
Each of these animals is beautiful to watch in its native
environment. In this brief paper we mentioned a few words
about each.
```

Figure 14.5—Visual Layout of a List in a File

In the figure we have spaced the list of animals differently, giving each animal its own separate line. The advantage of doing this is seen if we need to modify the list. For example, it is now easy to add another animal to the list and maintain the alphabetical order using only a quick visual inspection. We do not really have to search *within a line* for the new animal's position in order. Some people feel the giraffe should be in the "Big Six" Animals of Africa because the giraffe is such an unusual animal. Notice how easy it is to see that **giraffe** belongs after **elephant** in the list. It would be straightforward to insert a new line with the word **giraffe** on it after the line containing the word **elephant**.

There is another advantage to listing items from lists on their own separate lines. If, when you first produce the list, you are unable to complete it because you do not yet have all the information you need, you can leave yourself some sort of indicator in the file that the list still needs updating. For example, you could simply leave an extra blank line or a line with a double question mark (**??**) on it, as shown below.

```
buffalo,
elephant,
??,
```

```
leopard,
lion,
and
rhino
```

Once you have the complete information, it will be very easy to see where it needs to be inserted, as indicated by the double question mark. In addition, the double question mark serves as a reminder that you still need to insert an item into the list.

There are many other elements for which a visual layout will help you with editing. For example, figures and tables are two obvious candidates for visual formatting. In general, you will want to develop your own set of consistent layout rules.

14.5.3 Line Width

For typical text writing in a paragraph, it is a good idea to use a consistent line width of between 70 and 80 characters. Standard terminals usually display 80 characters. In using 70 to 80 characters per line, you will be able to display a large amount of information on the screen. It will also be easy to move the cursor to any location within the line even using just simple editing commands. Finally, a line width of about 80 characters achieves a nice balance between the two possible extremes. That is, consider writing only a single word of a file per line. In this case very little information will be displayed on the screen. You will find yourself having to constantly page up and down. At the other end of the spectrum, imagine you put the entire contents of a file on a single line. Your access to various parts of the file will be more difficult than if you had displayed the file over a number lines. In addition, it will be more difficult to locate items within the file.

14.5.4 Cutting and Pasting

All general-purpose editors provide a mechanism for selecting a region of text, cutting it, and then pasting it in somewhere else within a file. It is a good idea to reuse as much of your work as a situation merits. To demonstrate the utility of this concept, we consider a simple scenario.

Suppose you are formatting several tables using the LaTeX document preparation system. The LaTeX template code required for formatting a table is shown in Figure 14.6. It makes sense to cut and paste this template for each new table you are going to format rather than retyping it. For one, it would be very easy to make a mistake in typing this template over and over again. Notice also that the code involves some special characters such as \, {, and }. These symbols are hard to type in quickly.

```
\begin{table}[htb]
\begin{center}
\begin{tabular}{}
rows and columns go here
\end{tabular}
\end{center}
\caption{}
\label{}
\end{table}
```

Figure 14.6—LATEX Code for Formatting a Table

By cutting and pasting text, you can often save yourself time and maintain a higher degree of accuracy in your work. Of course, cutting and pasting will proliferate errors, so before cutting and pasting on a large scale, it is worth spending an extra minute double-checking that the text items to be cut and pasted are correct.

14.5.5 Using Markers within a File

All general-purpose text editors provide sophisticated searching mechanisms so that you can locate various patterns of text within a file. However, there will be times when the pattern you are searching for occurs many times in a given file. Thus, simply searching for the pattern is not a powerful enough technique to bring you directly to the location you want to be editing in a file. You can, however, place your own unique marker in a file to help you get back to a particular location. We consider one scenario to illustrate the utility of this idea.

Suppose you are working on a large C program, say 10,000 lines of code, that has a nasty bug in it. You believe you have narrowed down the possible locations of the bug to two places in the file. You could mark the first place with a C comment such as

```
/* Bugaboo1 */
```

and the second location with the comment

```
/* Bugaboo2 */
```

Since the pieces of text **Bugaboo1** and **Bugaboo2** do not occur anywhere else in the file, by searching for these strings, you can immediately move to the first or second possible location for the bug. Once at either location, you can try to fix the code and recompile it. If the bug has not been fixed, you can easily return to the same location again and again as necessary. Once you have corrected the code, you can delete your special markers.

You will find many other uses for this marking technique in your work.

14.5.6 Adding Comments to a File

With most types of files you work on, there is a way to include comments in the file that do not affect the function of the file. The `/*` and `*/` pair can be used to include a comment in a C program. A comment included between these delimiters in a C program will not have any effect on the program itself. Similar commenting mechanisms exist for other types of files, and you should learn them as needed.

Comments are useful for leaving yourself notes in the file. For example, you might want to leave a note to yourself that a particular section is not yet completed or needs more work. You might want to leave a note indicating you need to cut and paste another piece of text at a particular location. If you are collaborating with another user on a given program, you might want to leave your collaborator a note in the file. For example, Marcus might leave a comment such as follows in a file he is working on with Jill.

```
        Jill---Please complete this section.
    I am lost here. Marcus
```

You will find many other uses for comments in your files as well, and not just as they relate to editing.

Exercises

1. Matilda has a file that contains 1,000 different lists, each one containing between 30 and 40 items. She uses a different layout for each list. Explain why her inconsistent format makes it more difficult for another user to update each of her lists rather than if Matilda had originally used a consistent format.

2. Suppose you were given two lists containing the same 100 words, where the words appear in alphabetical order on list A and in random order on list B. Now suppose you are given a specific word and you need to determine if it is contained in the list or not. Which list is easier to check? Why? How could alphabetizing a list help you edit more efficiently? Is there any trade-off?

3. Suppose there is a text editor that displays very long horizontal lines of text completely using a scroll bar. Assume you have two copies of a file consisting of 3,200 words. In the first copy, **first**, there are 80 characters per line and in the second copy, **second**, the entire file is written on one line. Furthermore, suppose your terminal screen is 80 characters wide and displays 50 lines. What percentage of first and **second** would be displayed on your screen? Is there an editing advantage to using a layout like that in **first** versus that in **second**? Explain.

4. Give two examples of where cutting and pasting text makes sense and saves the typist a great deal of time.

5. You have inherited the task of porting a 1 million–line C program to another system. For the sake of this exercise, suppose the entire program resides in a single file. It turns out that you need to change only three lines of code to make the port successfully. Explain why it makes sense to comment and/or mark these changes in the file.

6. A sudden lightning storm strikes in the location where you are working on your computer. You are in the middle of editing a large file. You decide it is best to log out and unplug your machine, since you do not have a surge protector and are afraid that the machine may get damaged if lightning strikes nearby. What can you do before saving the file for the last time, so that after the storm goes past, you can quickly return to the location in it where you were working last?

7. Provide three additional editing hints that you feel are general enough to benefit a wide range of users.

BASICS OF THE EMACS TEXT EDITOR

In this chapter we introduce the following commands:

Unix Command	DOS Command	Description
emacs	EDIT	invoke the emacs text editor

15.1 Introduction

This chapter provides an introduction to the powerful, general-purpose Unix text editor called **emacs**. In fact, **emacs** is more than just an editor, it provides you with an entire computing environment. Our purpose here, though, is to acquaint you with the basic editing functions of **emacs**. Keep in mind that **emacs** has many more features than it makes sense to describe in a book about Unix. There are many reference books about **emacs** where you can learn more about it. Section 15.4 mentions several ways of getting online help about **emacs**.

In the remainder of this chapter you will learn about

- ❏ **emacs** commands and special keys.
- ❏ **emacs** windows and modes.
- ❏ an **emacs** tutorial and how to obtain online help about **emacs**.
- ❏ creating and saving a file using **emacs**.
- ❏ basic cursor movement commands.
- ❏ cutting and pasting text.
- ❏ text searching.
- ❏ miscellaneous **emacs** commands.

15.2 Emacs Commands and Special Keys

We begin by explaining a bit about **emacs** commands. The commands in **emacs** are entered by specifying certain patterns of characters from the keyboard. There are two important keys that are involved in nearly all **emacs** commands. They are the **Control** key and the **Meta** key. We visit each of these keys in turn.

The **Control** key is labeled **Ctrl** or **Ctl** on most keyboards. The key is typically located in the lower left-hand corner of the keyboard. Many **emacs** commands involve using a key sequence involving the **Control** key. Most **emacs** documentation uses the letter **C** to denote the **Control** key. When talking about **emacs**; we will follow this convention. (Recall that the **pine** mailer uses the symbol ^ to denote the **Control** key. This is the same **Control** key, but various programs have different conventions for writing it.)

We consider a sample **emacs** command to illustrate how the **Control** key is used. The key sequence

```
C-x C-c
```

is used to exit the **emacs** editor. The sequence means hold down the **Control** key and press **x**, and then hold down the **Control** key and press **c**. Many of the **emacs** commands you will use have this flavor. Once you get used to such key sequences, they are very easy to type.

The **Meta** key is labeled **Meta**, **Alt**, **Edit**, or **Esc** on most keyboards. One of these keys is typically located in the upper left-hand corner of the keyboard or near the spacebar. Many keyboards have both an **Alt** key and an **Esc** key. Many **emacs** commands involve using a key sequence involving the **Meta** key. On our keyboard the **Meta** key is the **Esc** key. On your keyboard it could be a different key. Most **emacs** documentation uses the letter **M** to denote the **Meta** key, and when talking about **emacs**, we will follow this convention.

We consider a sample **emacs** command to illustrate how the **Meta** key is used. The key sequence

```
M-x
```

is used to move back one screen in the editor. (You can think of **M-x** as accomplishing the opposite of spacebar in the **more** command.) The key sequence **M-x** means hold down the **Meta** key and press **x**. Many of the **emacs** commands you will use involve the **Meta** key. Once you get used to such key sequences, they are very easy to type.

We will see that the **Meta** key often does "one step" more than the **Control** key. For example,

```
C-f
```

means move the cursor forward one space, whereas

```
M-f
```

means move the cursor forward one word. It is helpful to keep the relationship between the **Control** key and the **Meta** key in mind when using **emacs**. Now that you have learned the basic format of **emacs** commands, we can delve into the specifics of the editor.

15.3 Emacs Windows and Modes

In this section we start by describing **emacs** windows. There are several useful terms for discussing editors, and it is worth clarifying those terms here. They are *screen*, *window*, and *buffer*. It is difficult to give precise definitions of these terms because they are used in so many different contexts in computer science. Nevertheless, we provide some intuition as to how the terms are often used. The term *screen* refers to your computer's display area. That is, your viewing area on the monitor. Your screen may be divided into several *windows*. In this context a *window* refers to a subdivision of the screen. In Figure 15.1, we show two computer screens. The first screen shows a single window and the second one shows two windows. A *buffer* is a storage area where **emacs** maintains information. A file you are editing is stored by **emacs** in a *buffer;* the buffer can be loaded into a window. So, when you go to edit a file, **emacs** maintains a buffer associated with the file. Even if you change a buffer, the file itself is not altered on disk unless you save the corresponding modified buffer. Subsequent examples will help to make these concepts clear.

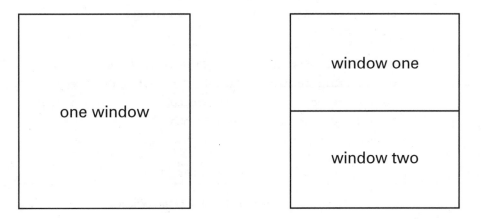

Figure 15.1—A Computer Screen Divided into One and Two Windows

In Figure 15.2, we display the result of typing the command

```
%emacs
```

on our system. In our case, the screen is filled with a single window containing the information shown. The underlining of the first character **W** indicates the position of the cursor in the window; **emacs** displays the cursor as a flashing underscore.

Notice that we are running GNU Emacs. Several of the most important **emacs** commands are mentioned in this window. We see that **C-h** can be used to obtain help, **C-x u** can be used to undo your last edit, **C-x C-c** can be used to exit **emacs**, **C-h t** can be used to run the **emacs** tutorial, and so on.

```
Buffers Files Tools Edit Search Mule TeX Help

Welcome to GNU Emacs, one component of a Linux-based GNU
system.

Get help           C-h            (Hold down CTRL and \= press h)
Undo changes       C-x u          Exit Emacs      C-x C-c
Get a tutorial     C-h t          Use Info to read docsC-h i
Activate menubar   F10 or ESC     ` or M-`
(`C-' means use the CTRL key. `M-' means use the Meta
(or Alt) key. If you have no Meta key, you may instead
type ESC followed by the character.)

If an Emacs session crashed recently, type M-x recover-session
RET to recover the files you were editing.

GNU Emacs 20.4.1 (i386-redhat-linux-gnu, X toolkit)
Cof Sat Sep 25 1999 on porky.devel.redhat.com
Copyright (C) 1999 Free Software Foundation, Inc.

GNU Emacs comes with ABSOLUTELY NO WARRANTY; type
C-h C-w for full details. Emacs is Free Software--Free as
in Freedom--so you can redistribute copies of Emacs and modify
it; type C-h C-c to see the conditions.
Type C-h C-d for information on getting the latest version.

--11:---F1 *scratch*       (Lisp Interaction)--L1--All--
```

Figure 15.2—Initial **Emacs** Window

In addition to all of these important **emacs** commands, there is some information about the version of **emacs** being run, copyright information, and a disclaimer. There are two other lines that are particularly important and merit further discussion. They are the last two lines in Figure 15.2. The second one is shown as a blank line in the figure; it is where **emacs** will display messages to the user. We now describe their meanings and purpose.

The line

```
--11:---F1 *scratch*       (Lisp Interaction)--L1--All--
```

is called the *mode line*. The **emacs** editor has a wide range of modes. The mode **emacs** is in depends on the type of file you are editing. For example, if you are editing a C program, a file with a **c** extension, **emacs** will run in **C mode**. If you are editing a LaTeX file, a file with a **tex** extension, **emacs** will run in LaTeX mode.[1] If you are editing a text file, a file with a **txt** extension, **emacs** will run in **text mode**. There are many other modes as well.

When **emacs** is in a certain mode, it has information programmed into it that is pertinent to the particular type of file you are editing. For example, in the programming language C each **{** (open curly brace) symbol must be closed with a corresponding **}** (closed curly brace) symbol. When you type in a **}** symbol in **C mode**, **emacs** flashes the cursor on the previous **{** symbol if there is one. This highlights the most recent pair of open and closed curly braces. This feature is helpful to C programmers who need to make sure that the curly braces match up properly. The other modes that **emacs** runs in have a wide variety and large number of similar helpful features.

We will not delve into the specifics of **emacs** modes here. You can get help about the various **emacs** modes by typing

```
%emacs
```

and then entering

```
C-h m
```

We should point out that **emacs** specifies which mode it is in via the mode line. The mode line

```
--11:---F1 *scratch*    (Lisp Interaction)--L1--All--
```

indicates that **emacs** is in **Lisp Interaction mode**. (Lisp is the name of a programming language; in fact, **emacs** is programmed in Lisp.) The parentheses show the mode **emacs** is in.

There are a couple of other tidbits of information in the mode line worth mentioning. From left to right, we discuss them.

❑ The two characters after the colon (:) indicate the status of the buffer. If these characters are -- (as in the example in Figure 15.2), the buffer for the file has not been modified. A double star (******) is used to indicate the buffer has been modified. This means the buffer has been edited. Finally, a double percent (**%%**) is used to indicate the file is read-only.

❑ The string following the blank space after the **F1** (in Figure 15.2 the string is ***scratch***) indicates the name of the buffer corresponding to a given window.

---

1. It will actually usually run in TeX mode.

❑ Following the double dash after the buffer name is the line number that the cursor is currently positioned on. The line number is from the beginning of the file, with the first line numbered 1. In Figure 15.2 the **L1** indicates the cursor is on the first line.

❑ The line number is followed by two dashes that in turn are followed by a percentage value. This value indicates the percentage of the file that is above the top line of the screen. The percentage is similar to the percentage as displayed by the **more** command.

There are three special cases when a percentage is not displayed. If the entire buffer contents is displayed, you will see the word **All**. This is the situation in Figure 15.2. If the cursor is located on the first line of the buffer, you will see the word **Top**. If the cursor is located on the last line of the buffer, you will see **Bot**.

The line directly beneath the mode line is called the *echo line*. This is the area where **emacs** displays important user-directed messages. For example, when you save the file **/home/connie/work/boat.txt**, **emacs** will display the message

```
Wrote /home/connie/work/boat.txt
```

in the echo line. This is an indicator that the file was actually saved to the disk.

As we noted earlier, many **emacs** commands require two sets of keystrokes. For example, the command to exit **emacs** is

```
C-x C-c
```

If you type in the **C-x** and hesitate for about two seconds, **emacs** will display

```
C-x-
```

in the echo line. This serves to remind you what you have already typed. If you are interrupted as you are entering a command, this reminder proves useful when you return to the terminal.

In any event, it is a good idea to read the messages **emacs** puts in the echo line. From time to time you will need to respond to questions **emacs** poses to you in the echo line.

You are probably already getting the correct sense that **emacs** is a complex program. In the next section, we describe a simple strategy for learning **emacs** and explain how to use the **emacs** tutorial.

Exercises

1. Enter the command **emacs file.txt**. Now type in **C-n** five times. Print out the mode line and explain the meaning of the items listed in it. (To exit **emacs**, you may enter **C-x C-c**.)

2. Enter the command **emacs test.c**. Print out the mode line and explain the meaning of the items listed in it. (To exit **emacs**, you may enter **C-x C-c**.)

3. Can you see any reason for having multiple **emacs** windows open at the same time? Explain.

15.4 Emacs Tutorial

For any piece of complex software containing dozens and dozens of features, it is generally true that the vast majority of users know and use only a tiny fraction of the available features. Users who actually learn a piece of software inside out are known as *power users*. You will need to devote a considerable amount of time to studying **emacs** in order to become an **emacs** power user. This is an admirable goal. If you become an **emacs** power user, you will be very efficient at editing. In reality, very few users become **emacs** power users.

Our goal in this chapter is to get you started to becoming a power user, but, more importantly, to bring you to the point where you can function on a day-to-day basis with **emacs**. To this end, we follow the school of thought that says you will use and retain only the commands that you use daily. The more you practice a given command, the longer you will retain it. We will cover the basic **emacs** commands in this chapter. If you ever require more specialized commands, you can look them up on an as-needed basis.

A natural place to begin learning **emacs** is the **emacs** tutorial. In Figure 15.3 we depict the first part of the **emacs** tutorial. The tutorial begins by explaining the **Control** and **Meta** keys and how to enter **emacs** commands. It also explains how to exit the tutorial by entering

```
C-x C-c
```

```
Buffers Files Tools Edit Search Mule TeX Help

You are looking at the Emacs tutorial.

Emacs commands generally involve the CONTROL key (sometimes
labeled CTRL or CTL) or the META key (sometimes labeled EDIT
or ALT). Rather than write that in full each time, we'll use
the following abbreviations:

C-<chr>     means hold the CONTROL key while
            typing the character <chr>. Thus, C-f would be:
            hold the CONTROL key and type f.

M-<chr>     means hold the META or EDIT or ALT key down
            while typing <chr>. If there is no META, EDIT or
```

```
          ALT key, instead press and release the ESC key and
          then type <chr>. We write <ESC> for the ESC key.

Important note: to end the Emacs session, type C-x C-c.
(Two characters.) The characters ">>" at the left margin
indicate directions for you to try using a command.
For instance:

>>   Now type C-v (View next screen) to move to the
     next screen. Go ahead, do it by holding down the
     control key while typing v). From now on, you should
     do this again whenever you finish reading the screen.


--:---F1 TUTORIAL    (Fundamental)--L1--Top--------
```

Figure 15.3—First Part of **Emacs** Tutorial

To bring the tutorial up on your screen, enter the command

%emacs

Then type

C-h t

This will invoke the **emacs** tutorial. Notice that many of the key strokes in **emacs** commands have a mnemonic meaning. In bringing up the tutorial, the **h** stands for "help" and the **t** for "tutorial."

The **emacs** tutorial is an excellent way to learn the basics of **emacs**. You can walk through it at your own pace, trying out the various elements described in the tutorial. If you get hung up, you can type

C-g

which cancels a command that you have begun to enter. If you have had enough of the tutorial, you can exit it by entering

C-x C-c

You can always return to the tutorial later.

In addition to the tutorial, **emacs** comes with a built-in help facility. You can invoke the **emacs** help facility by typing

C-h ?

You will be given a list of possible options to explore. There is an extensive **man page** for **emacs** as well. To learn more about **emacs**, enter the command

%man emacs

Table 15.1 summarizes the commands described in this section.

Emacs Command	Function
C-h t	bring up the **emacs** tutorial
C-h ?	bring up the **emacs** help facility
C-g	cancel a command
C-x C-c	exit **emacs**

Table 15.1—Summary of **Emacs** Commands Described in Section 15.4

Exercises

1. Invoke the **emacs** tutorial and read through it trying out the various commands as you go. Was anything confusing to you? How long did it take you to go through the tutorial?

2. Invoke the **emacs** help facility. Describe how to get help about a specific command.

3. Read the **man page** for **emacs**. Describe three interesting facts you learned.

15.5 Creating and Saving a File

Having read the last section on the **emacs** tutorial and how to obtain help about **emacs**, you are now in a position to learn **emacs** on your own (if you want). However, in each of the next few sections we walk through the most important **emacs** commands.

Many Unix users spend a great deal of time doing file manipulation; that is, creating, editing, and saving files. All of these operations are straightforward to perform using **emacs**. To invoke the **emacs** editor and create the file called **story**, you can enter the command

```
%emacs story
```

You will notice the message

```
New File
```

on the echo line. Once **emacs** is running, you can type in text as you desire. By hitting the **Enter** or **Return** key, you can move to a new line. Text will be inserted where the cursor is flashing. The cursor moves to the right as you type. The **Backspace** key will move the cursor back one space, deleting the character to the left of its original position. The **Delete** key deletes the character in the position where the cursor is flashing. After you have typed in some text, you may save it by typing

```
C-x C-s
```

You will see a message in the echo line indicating that the file **story** was written. This is the point at which the file **story** is actually written to the disk and saved.

Suppose you want to save a version of the file called **story.1** at some point. You can enter the command

```
C-x C-w
```

The **w** in this command stands for "write." In the echo line you will be prompted for the name of the file in which you want the contents of the **story** buffer written. If you enter

```
story.1
```

and press **Enter**, you will have created a new file called **story.1**. If the file **story.1** already exists, **emacs** will query you as to whether or not the original file should be overwritten. If you do overwrite the original file, its contents will be permanently lost.

Emacs has an *autosave* feature. The default on many systems is that a file is automatically saved after every 500 keystrokes you type. **Emacs** systems also generate automatic backup copies of files in some cases. You may find such files in the same directory as the original file. For the file **story**, **emacs** might create backups with one or more of the following names: **#story#**, **story.bak**, or **story~**. The name of the backup file will depend on your system. Sometimes these automatic backup files come in handy if you accidentally destroy a file, so check your system to see what naming convention is in use.

Once you are done editing, as usual you can enter the command

```
C-x C-c
```

to exit **emacs**.

Table 15.2 summarizes the commands described in this section.

Emacs Command	Function
Backspace	delete the character to the left of the cursor
Delete	delete the character above the cursor
C-x C-c	exit **emacs**
C-x C-s	save a file
C-x C-w	write out the current buffer

Table 15.2—Summary of **Emacs** Commands Described in Section 15.5

Exercises

1. Create the file **numbers** with nine lines, each line containing its line number. How many bytes long is the file?

2. Create a file containing the words used in this exercise. How many bytes long is the file?

3. What happens if the cursor is at the end of a line and you press the **Delete** key? How about at the beginning of a line?

4. What happens if the cursor is at the beginning of a line and you press the **Backspace** key? How about at the end of a line?

5. Carefully explain the difference in **emacs** between the **Backspace** and **Delete** keys.

6. Does your **emacs** autosave? If so, explain when.

7. Does your **emacs** have automatic backups? If so, explain the naming convention and when such backups are generated.

15.6 Cursor Movement Commands

We have seen that when you load **emacs**, you can immediately begin inserting text into the buffer. So far, we have only talked about how to move the cursor backwards one space using the **Backspace** key. **Emacs** provides many different commands for moving the cursor around the screen. Remember, when you type things into **emacs**, they are inserted at the current location of the cursor. In order to be an efficient editor, you need to be able to reposition the cursor to any location on the screen very quickly. In this section we go over many of the **emacs** cursor movement commands.

The most common cursor movements are forward one character and backward one character (there is no deletion here, as opposed to the **Delete** key). To move the cursor forward one space, you can enter

    C-f

Note that the **f** in the command stands for "forward." To move the cursor backward one space, you can enter

    C-b

Note the **b** in the command stands for "back" or "backward."

It is tedious to move to the center of a line from the beginning of it by using a series of **C-f**s. **Emacs** provides commands so that you can jump one word forward at a time or one word backward at a time. As expected, due to the relationship between the **Control** key and the **Meta** key that we mentioned previously, the command for moving forward over a word is

```
M-f
```

and the command for moving backward over a word is

```
M-b
```

Using the commands **C-f**, **C-b**, **M-f**, and **M-b**, you can comfortably move around within a line. To move to the beginning of a line, you can enter the command

```
C-a
```

(Note that **b** was already taken to move back one space, so **a** was chosen to move to the beginning of a line.) To move to the end of a line, you can enter the command

```
C-e
```

Note that the **e** stands for "end."

Two useful but perhaps lesser used commands are

```
M-a
```

to move back to the beginning of a sentence and

```
M-e
```

to move forward to the end of sentence.

To move to the line beneath the one the cursor is currently flashing on, you can enter the command

```
C-n
```

Note that the **n** stands for "next." To move to the line above the one that the cursor is currently flashing on, you can enter the command

```
C-p
```

Note that the **p** stands for "previous."

We have now seen a variety of commands that are useful for moving around a buffer in small steps. You can also use the arrow keys ➡, ⬅, ⬆, and ⬇ to reposition the cursor. To move to the next screen, you can enter the command

```
C-v
```

The command

```
M-v
```

moves you back one screen. One final interesting command is the command

    C-1

which re-centers the screen on the line where the cursor resides. This is very useful when you are editing near the very top or the very bottom of the screen, since it allows you to obtain the surrounding context quickly.

Table 15.3 summarizes the commands described in this section.

Emacs Command	Function
C-a	move to the beginning of a line
C-b	move backward one character
C-e	move to the end of a line
C-f	move forward one character
C-1	redisplay the window moving the text around the cursor to the center of the screen
C-n	move to the next line
C-p	move to the previous line
C-v	move forward one screen
M-a	move backward to the beginning of a sentence
M-b	move backward one word
M-e	move forward to end of a sentence
M-f	move forward one word
M-v	move backward one screen

Table 15.3—Summary of **Emacs** Commands Described in Section 15.6

Exercises

1. Suppose a line is 80 characters wide and the cursor is located on the first character of the line. What is the minimum number of **emacs** commands needed to move the cursor to the middle of the line? Use only the commands discussed in this section and explain your answer.

2. You are at the top of a buffer, as indicated by the mode line, which says **Top**. You enter the command **C-v** and notice a percentage of

seven in the mode line. How many more **C-vs** will you need to execute until the mode line says **Bot**?

3. Explain the difference between **C-a** and **M-a**. Can you make any general statements about which command moves the cursor farther?

4. We noted that the commands **M-a** and **M-e** were used to move to the beginning and end of a sentence, respectively. Define the word "sentence" precisely in this context.

5. Describe any special cases for the **C-l** command, for example, what happens if the cursor is near the actual bottom of the buffer?

15.7 Cutting and Pasting Text

Computer scientists are generally people who do not like to waste any effort. If they can reuse something, such as a portion of program or a section of text, they usually will. In this section we illustrate how to cut and paste text in **emacs**. Using this technique, you will be able to save yourself lots of typing time through reuse.

Emacs maintains a special buffer known as the *kill buffer*. When you cut some text, the text is stored in the kill buffer. You can think of the kill buffer as a special temporary storage area. To capture a line of text, which means place it in the kill buffer, you can enter the command

```
C-k
```

Note that the **k** stands for "kill." When you type **C-k**, the text to the right of the cursor will disappear. To capture an entire line of text, position the cursor at the beginning of the line and type **C-k**. To paste the text back, you can enter the command

```
C-y
```

Note that the **y** stands for "yank." So, in **emacs** jargon "cut and paste" is "kill and yank." A yanked piece of text will be placed at the position of the cursor. So to move a line, you simply kill the line, move the cursor, and then yank it. For example, to move the line the cursor is currently on after the succeeding three lines, you would enter the commands

```
C-a C-k C-n C-n C-n C-e Enter C-y
```

The **C-a** moves the cursor to the beginning of the line, **C-k** kills the line, the three **C-ns** move you down three lines, the **C-e** moves you to the end of the third line, the **Enter** inserts a blank line, and the **C-y** yanks the line. With some experimentation, you will quickly adapt to the kill and yank procedure. In the event you make a mistake, you can undo your last edit by entering the command

```
C-x u
```

Note that the **u** stands for "undo." You can undo only your last edit. If you need to reverse a change, do it immediately.

In general, you may want to kill more than just a single line of text. For example, you may want to move a large paragraph. If you enter a series of *n* **C-k**s, you will kill *n* lines. All *n* of the lines will be placed in the kill buffer. You can then move the cursor to the location you want to drop the *n* lines into and yank the lines back out of the kill buffer.

Once some text is in the kill buffer, you can yank it out any number of times. So, to produce five regions with the contents of the kill buffer, you can enter five **C-y**s. The phase "kill some other text" is commonly used when talking about editing in **emacs**. This phrase means you killed some text originally and then executed another command before killing some more text. Once you kill some other text, the original content of the kill buffer is gone. In other words, the kill buffer can only have one set of killed text in it at a given time.

Suppose you have a large region of text that you want to move. Here, by large we mean several screens worth. It would become tedious to type several hundred **C-k**s. Instead, **emacs** allows you to set a marker, a starting kill position, and then move the cursor to the ending kill position. Once you execute the kill command, you place the text between the marker and the cursor in the kill buffer. To set a marker, you enter the command

```
C-@
```

Then move the cursor downward until the text you want to cut is encapsulated between the marker and the cursor. Now execute the command

```
C-w
```

Think of the **w** as standing for "wipe out." All of the text you have wiped out will disappear from the window and will be placed in the kill buffer. You can bring the text back by entering the command

```
C-y
```

To move a single word, you can kill it using the command

```
M-d
```

move the cursor to the desired new location for the word, and then enter

```
C-y
```

Note that in doing this, you replace the contents of the kill buffer with the word you cut. It is usually a good idea to paste shortly after cutting so you do not accidentally lose the contents of the kill buffer when cutting again.

By cutting and pasting in appropriate situations, you will save yourself lots of typing time.

Table 15.4 summarizes the commands described in this section.

Emacs Command	Function
C-@	set a marker
C-k	cut some text to the kill buffer
C-w	wipe out some text to the kill buffer
C-x u	undo the last edit
C-y	paste the text from the kill buffer
M-d	cut a word to the kill buffer

Table 15.4—Summary of **Emacs** Commands Described in Section 15.7

Exercises

1. Kill a line of text using the **C-k** command. Describe exactly what happens to the window you are viewing.
2. Suppose you have the numbers 1, 2, 3, 4, and 5 occurring in reverse order on the first five lines of a file, one number per line. Assume you can only use the commands **C-n**, **C-p**, **C-k**, and **C-y**. What is the minimum number of **C-ks** and **C-ys** you need to use to sort the numbers in increasing order?
3. Can **M-d** be used to delete more than a single word? If so, explain the technique and how to put the words back into the file.
4. Iman realizes she killed the wrong three lines during a cut and paste operation. What should she do to move the correct three lines to location **A** without making any other changes to the original file?

15.8 Text Searching

There will be many times you want to search for a particular string in a buffer. For example, perhaps you realize you were misusing the words *effect* and *affect* and need to swap their uses around. One way to correct this problem is as follows:

1. move to the beginning of the buffer
2. search sequentially through the buffer for the word **effect**
3. replace each occurrence of **effect** you find with the string **aaaaa**

4. move to the beginning of the buffer
5. search sequentially through the buffer for the word **affect**
6. replace each occurrence of **affect** you find with the word **effect**
7. move to the beginning of the buffer
8. search sequentially through the buffer for the string **aaaaa**
9. replace each occurrence of the string **aaaaa** you find with the word **affect**

The placeholder string **aaaaa** is a string that does not occur elsewhere in the buffer.

Below we will see a more efficient way of carrying out the same operation. First we demonstrate how to carry out this more lengthy procedure using **emacs** since it illustrates a number of important commands. To move to the beginning of a buffer, you can enter the command

```
M-<
```

Incidentally, to move to the end of a buffer, you can enter the command

```
M->
```

To search for a string, you can enter the command

```
C-s
```

Note that the **s** stands for "search." In the echo line, **emacs** will respond with

```
I-search:
```

The **I** stands for "interactive." Now, type in your search query. In our example, we would type in the word **effect**. As you are typing your query, **emacs** moves the cursor to the nearest location matching your query. That is, even as you type in "eff" **emacs** is doing the pattern matching. The pattern matching is "on the fly." When you finish typing the word **effect**, **emacs** will position the cursor after the first occurrence of **effect** in the buffer. A second **C-s** will move the cursor to the next occurrence of **effect**, and so on. (If you execute some other command in the interim, two **C-ss** can be used to look for the most recently searched for pattern.) If the pattern **effect** is not found, **emacs** will respond with

```
Failing I-search:
```

in the echo line. If you are searching and locate something, you can enter the command

```
C-g
```

to abort the search and return to the location from where the search was initiated.

From time to time this technique will come in handy; for example, when you just want to peek ahead a bit. By the way, the command

```
C-r
```

is used to do a backward search through the buffer.

Continuing with our procedure for swapping **effect**s and **affect**s, we can type

```
M-b
```

to move back over an occurrence of **effect**. The command

```
M-d
```

can be used to delete the word **effect**. Next, we type in the string **aaaaa** to replace the word **effect**. We can repeat this same process until we end up with

```
Failing I-search:
```

Now to return to the top of the buffer, we can enter the command

```
M-<
```

Using a process similar to that just described, we can carry out the remaining steps of our procedure completing the swap of **effect** and **affect**.

As you can see, this process gets a bit cumbersome, especially when there are a lot of occurrences of a word to be replaced. **Emacs** provides another command that is very useful for replacing a large number of patterns with another user-specified pattern. The command is known as *query replace* and is executed by typing

```
M-%
```

In response to this command, **emacs** will display

```
Query replace:
```

in the echo line. You can now enter the string that you would like **emacs** to find. Suppose you entered the word **effect**. That is, you typed in the word **effect** and pressed the **Enter** key. In the echo line, **emacs** will next prompt you with

```
Query replace effect with:
```

Here you respond with the string to replace occurrences of **effect**. Suppose you typed in **aaaaa**. **Emacs** would then locate the next occurrence of **effect** in the file and display the message

```
Query replacing effect with aaaaa: (? for help)
```

in the echo line. If you type **y** (standing for "yes"), this occurrence of **effect** will be replaced by **aaaaa**, and then the cursor will be moved to the next occurrence of **effect**, where you will be prompted with the same query, and so on. If you type **n** (standing for "no"), this occurrence of **effect** will not be replaced, and the process will continue as in the case of a **y** response. Upon completion of the query replace command, you will see a display such as

```
Replaced 5 occurrence
```

in the echo line, if five **effect**s were replaced. In general, **emacs** will display the number of occurrences replaced. By performing three query replace operations, it should be clear how to swap all the **effect**s and **affect**s.

Care must be taken when using query replace, since it is easy to make a mistake from which it is hard to recover. Before carrying out any query replace operation, be sure to think through all the ramifications.

Table 15.5 summarizes the commands described in this section.

Emacs Command	Function
C-r	reverse search
C-s	forward search
M->	move to the bottom of a buffer
M-<	move to the top of a buffer
M-%	query replace

Table 15.5—Summary of **Emacs** Commands Described in Section 15.8

Exercises

1. Explain why it was necessary to introduce the string **aaaaa** in order to exchange the **effect**s and **affect**s in the example in this section.
2. Suppose you have a buffer that contains exactly one occurrence of the word **toad**. What happens if you search for **toad** and repeatedly press **C-s**?
3. Is the query replace operation case sensitive? That is, are upper- and lowercase letters treated differently?
4. Pete labeled items of lists in his term paper **a**, **ab**, **abc**, and **abcd**. His professor says he needs to change these labels to **1**, **2**, **3**, and **4**, respectively. How can Pete do this using query replace operations?
5. Suppose a line of text consists of seven words, each of length 10, and that the cursor is positioned in the middle of the line. What is the quickest way to move to the beginning of the sixth word,

where "quickest" means using the fewest key strokes? Explain your answer.

15.9 Miscellaneous Emacs Commands

At the beginning of this chapter, we mentioned that **emacs** is an extremely powerful editor. We have touched on a variety of **emacs** commands up to this point. However, many other **emacs** commands exist that we have not explained. In this section we mention a couple of others that we find useful. In particular, we describe commands for

❑ repeating a command an arbitrary number of times.
❑ file insertion.
❑ using multiple editing windows.

15.9.1 Command Repetition

There will be many times you want to execute the same command over and over again. For example, perhaps you are at the top of a file and want to move to line 47. It would get a bit tedious typing **C-n** 46 times. You could type **C-v** to skip a screen, and then type a bunch of **C-n**s, but again this is cumbersome. A more efficient way to move to line 47 is to enter the command

```
C-u 46 C-n
```

In general, you enter **C-u** followed by a number *n* followed by a command in order to execute the command *n* times. In our example above, the effect of the command is to execute 46 **C-n**s.

You will find many other uses for the repetition command, and as a result become more efficient with your editing.

15.9.2 File Insertion

Occasionally, you will want to insert the contents of a file into the buffer you are editing. To insert a file at the location of the cursor, simply enter the command

```
C-x C-i
```

In the echo line you will be prompted for the name of a file. You can enter the name of a file that is located in the same directory as the file you are editing and press **Enter** to insert the file. To insert a file that is not in the same directory as the file you are editing, specify its full pathname.

15.9.3 Multiple Windows

We would be remiss not to mention the utility of working on multiple buffers at once. At times, it is very useful to be editing two or more files simultaneously. For example, you may need to move portions of text between two files. **Emacs** provides a convenient mechanism for doing this. We touch on the essentials of editing multiple buffers here. Our description is by no means complete but provides you with a good starting point.

To split a window you are editing into two windows, you can enter the command

```
C-x 2
```

After executing this command, your screen will be divided into two windows as shown in Figure 15.4. The contents of the buffer you were working on will be loaded into both windows. You can load another file into the window where the cursor is located by entering the command

```
C-x C-f
```

and then typing in the name of a file. Note that the **f** stands for "find." This command can be used to load a file into a window at any time. After "finding" another file, you have two separate files—one in the upper window and one in the lower window. Each window has its associated buffer and behaves essentially independently.

```
Buffers Files Tools Edit Search Mule TeX Help

This is window 1.




--:**-F1 window1.tex            (TeX)--L1--Top---------
This is window 1.




--:**-F1 window1.tex            (TeX)--L1--Top---------
```

Figure 15.4—Two Identical Editing Windows—Cursor Is in Top Window

The window that contains the cursor is called the *active window*. To make the other window the active window, you can enter the command

  C-o

Note that the **o** stands for "other." That is, you can switch to the other window using this command. A window without the cursor in it is called an *inactive window*.

When you are in the active window, you can cut text using the

  C-k

command in the usual way. You can switch to the other window using the command

  C-o

and then paste the cut text there using the

  C-y

command. That is, the kill buffer is shared among the windows. This gives you a very easy way to move text between two different files.

To return to a single window, you can enter the command

  C-x 1

The active window will remain, and other windows will disappear. It is useful to return to a single window if it is necessary to view a large portion of a buffer at one time.

When you use multiple windows, be careful to make sure you save the changes you desire. If there are modified buffers that have not been saved, **emacs** will prompt you to see if you want to save them as you exit. You can respond with **y** (standing for "yes") to save a buffer or **n** (standing for "no") to discard the changes.

There are many other more specialized uses of buffers that we will not delve into here. You may pursue these through other references.

Table 15.6 summarizes the commands described in this section.

Emacs Command	Function
C-x C-f	load a file into a buffer
C-x i	insert a file
C-o	switch to the other window
C-x 1	display only the active window on the screen

C-x 2	divide the active window into two windows
C-u *n* **ZZ**	execute command **ZZ** *n* times

Table 15.6—Summary of **Emacs** Commands Described in Section 15.9

Exercises

1. Explain how you can move to any column within a line using the **C-u** command.
2. Give three instances where command repetition would be useful.
3. What happens if you try to insert a file in the middle of a line?
4. Create a sample file called **test** that is 80 lines long. Move the cursor to line 40. Write down the contents of the mode line. Insert the file test into itself at this location. Compare and contrast the new mode line with the old one.
5. How can you divide a single window into three windows? What effect does **C-o** have now?
6. Explain why dividing a window into 10 separate windows is not a useful editing practice.
7. Explore the **C-x C-b** command and explain what its function is.

15.10 A Word of Caution

A closing word of caution is in order regarding **emacs**. There are many different versions of **emacs** in use today. Not all versions are going to behave exactly the same way. In particular, not all of the keystroke commands will be identical over different versions. However, all versions of **emacs** do include the same basic functionality. Thus, if you try out a command discussed in this chapter and it does not seem to behave properly for you, it may be that on your system a different set of keystrokes is required to execute the command. Using the help facility accompanying your version of **emacs**, you can learn what all of your keystroke commands are.

To learn more about **emacs**, you can consult any of the online references mentioned in this chapter or purchase a book on **emacs**. A complete summary of the **emacs** commands described in this book is provided in Appendix F.

BASICS OF THE VI TEXT EDITOR

In this chapter we introduce the following command:

Unix Command	DOS Command	Description
vi	EDIT	invoke the vi text editor

16.1 Introduction

This chapter provides an introduction to the powerful, general-purpose, full-screen Unix text editor called **vi**. The name **vi** stands for "visual editor." This is in contrast to earlier editors that were line-based. Our goal here is to acquaint you with the basic editing functions of **vi**. Keep in mind that **vi** has many more features than it makes sense to describe in a book about Unix. There are many reference books about **vi** where you can learn more about it. We will mention several ways of obtaining online help information about **vi** in Section 16.4.

In the remainder of this chapter you will learn about

- ❑ **vi** commands and special keys.
- ❑ **vi** windows and modes.
- ❑ a **vi** tutorial and how to obtain online help about **vi**.
- ❑ creating and saving a file using **vi**.
- ❑ basic cursor movement commands.
- ❑ cutting and pasting text.
- ❑ text searching.
- ❑ miscellaneous **vi** commands.

16.2 Vi Commands and Special Keys

We begin by explaining a bit about **vi** commands. The commands in **vi** are entered by specifying certain patterns of characters from the keyboard. There are two important special keys that are involved in **vi** commands. They are the **Control** key and the **Escape** key. We visit each of these keys in turn.

The **Control** key is labeled **Ctrl** or **Ctl** on most keyboards. The key is typically located in the lower left-hand corner of the keyboard. Several **vi** commands involve using a key sequence involving the **Control** key. Most **vi** documentation uses the caret symbol (**^**) to denote the **Control** key and when talking about **vi**, we will follow this convention. (The **emacs** editor uses the symbol **C** to denote the **Control** key. This is the same **Control** key, but various programs have different conventions for writing it.)

We consider a sample **vi** command to illustrate how the **Control** key is used. The key sequence

     `^F`

is used to move forward one screenful in the file you are editing. The sequence means hold down the **Control** key and press **f**. Note that **vi** commands incorporating the **Control** key are described using capital letters; however, it is not necessary to type these keys in as capital letters, as we illustrated with the lowercase **f** above. (For **vi** commands that do not use the **Control** key, case is significant.) A number of the **vi** commands you will use consist of the **Control** key and a lowercase letter.

The **Escape** key is labeled **Esc** on most keyboards. It is typically located in the upper left-hand corner of the keyboard or near the spacebar. In typing the **Escape** key, you enter **vi**'s **command mode**. Once in **command mode**, you can type in **vi** commands. Most **vi** commands consist of a single character. For example,

     `j`

is used to move the cursor down one line. There are a number of commands that consist of more than a single character. For example, the three-key sequence

     `:wq`

is used to write the file out that you are currently editing and exit the editor. Note that **w** stands for "write" and **q** for "quit." Once you get used to such key sequences, they are very easy to type.

Now that you have learned the basic format of **vi** commands and the special keys involved, we can delve into the specifics of the editor.

16.3 Vi Windows and Modes

In this section we start by describing **vi** windows. There are several terms that we will use when discussing editors, and it is worth clarifying our use of them here. They are *screen*, *window*, and *buffer*. It is difficult to give precise definitions of these terms because they are used in so many different contexts in computer science. Nevertheless, we provide some intuition as to how the terms are often used. The term *screen* refers to your computer's display area. That is, the viewing area on the monitor. Your screen may be divided into several *windows*. In this context, a window refers to a subdivision of the screen. In Figure 16.1 we show two computer screens. The first screen consists of a single window, and the second one consists of two windows. A *buffer* is a storage area where **vi** maintains information. A file that you are editing is stored by **vi** in a buffer; the buffer can be loaded into a window. So, when you go to edit a file, **vi** maintains a buffer (called the *editing buffer*) associated with the file. Even if you change a buffer, the file itself is not altered on disk unless you save the corresponding modified buffer. Subsequent examples will help to make these concepts clear.

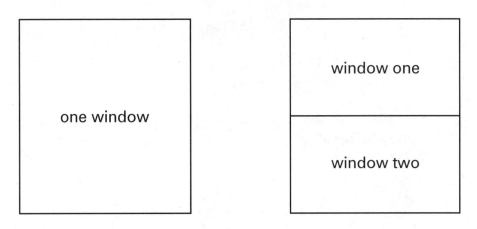

Figure 16.1—A Computer Screen Divided into One and Two Windows

In Figure 16.2 we display the result of typing the command

```
%vi
```

on our system. In our case, the screen is filled with a single window containing the information shown. The underlining of the first character indicates the position of the cursor in the window; **vi** displays the cursor as a flashing underscore. Notice that we are running **VIM**—Vi IMproved. We will refer to **vim** as **vi** throughout. In addition to **vim**, there are several other versions of **vi** commonly in use. They are **elvis** (named after the king), **nvi** (new **vi**), and **vile** (vi like **emacs**). The version of **vi** you are running will depend on who set up your system and on which version of Unix you are using. Most of the various versions of **vi** have the same basic functionality. Occasionally, you will notice a difference.

Several of the most important **vi** commands are mentioned in the initial **vi** window. We see that **:q** followed by **Enter** can be used to exit **vi**, **:help** followed by **Enter** or just pressing the **F1** key obtains online help, and **:help version5** followed by **Enter** can be used to obtain information about this version of **vi**.

```
___
~
~
~
~
~                      VIM - Vi Improved
~
~                         version 5.4
~                     by Bram Moolenaar et al.
~
~              Vim is freely distributable
~       type  :help uganda <Enter>     if you like Vim
~
~       type  :q<Enter>    to exit
~       type  :help<Enter> or <F1>     for on-line help
~       type  :help version5<Enter>    for version info
~
~
~
~
~
```

Figure 16.2—Initial **Vi** Window

Another important thing to notice about the **vi** window shown in Figure 16.2 is that all but the first and last lines begin with a ~ character. When lines extending beyond the end of a file are displayed in a **vi** window, the editor marks the beginning of each of them with a ~ character. These tilde symbols give you a visual context in which to edit. This is helpful because rather than working with a window whose latter portion is devoid of symbols, you can use the tilde characters to count off a number of lines.

The last line in Figure 16.2 is shown as a blank line. This line is called the *echo line* or *command line*. This is the area where **vi** displays important user-directed messages. For example, when you go to save the file **boat.txt** in your current working directory, you can type in the **vi** command

    :wq

The editor will display the command you are typing in the echo line. Once you enter the command, **vi** will display a message such as

```
"boat.txt" 75L, 392C written
```

in the echo line. This is an indicator that the file was actually saved to the disk. It tells us that 75 lines (L) consisting of 392 characters (C) were written.

It is a good idea to read the messages **vi** puts in the echo line. From time to time you will need to respond to questions **vi** poses to you there.

The **vi** editor has two modes. They are **command mode** and **input mode**. (Note that **command mode** is called **all powerful beep mode** by some users, and **input mode** is called **insert mode** or **text entry mode** by some users.) When you start up the **vi** editor, you are automatically placed in **command mode**. This is the jargon often employed by Unix users; we say *you* are in **command mode** rather than that the **vi** editor itself is in **command mode**. As the name suggests, in **command mode** you can enter **vi** commands. Most of the remainder of this chapter will be spent describing the various **vi** commands. Among other things, in **command mode**, you can enter commands to reposition the cursor, search for a pattern, save a file, and exit the editor.

When you are in **input mode**, all of the characters that you type are inserted into the file you are editing. The file you are editing is not modified on the disk until you actually save it. The editor uses an *editing buffer,* and the contents of the editing buffer are what you see displayed on your screen. Until you write the buffer out, no changes are made on disk. This is a useful feature, since to discard your edits all you have to do is not save the file. In **vi**, you can enter **:q!** to exit without saving.

Many beginning users often get hung up by **vi**. That is, they get themselves into a position where **vi** seems stuck. The key to avoiding this situation is to understand how to switch between **command mode** and **input mode**. Since you are initially placed in **command mode** by the editor, we will first examine how to switch to **input mode**.

Vi provides a number of commands for going from **command mode** to **input mode**. Each such command puts you into **input mode** and specifies a different location where you can begin inserting text. In order to describe these commands, it is necessary to understand the notion of *current line,* which simply refers to the line where the cursor is located. The basic commands to change to **input mode** are

❑ **a**—insert text after the current cursor position. The **a** is an abbreviation for "append."

❑ **i**—insert text before the current cursor position. The **i** is an abbreviation for "insert."

- ❑ **A**—insert text at the end of the current line. The **A** is an abbreviation for "append."
- ❑ **I**—insert text at the beginning of the current line. The **I** is an abbreviation for "insert."
- ❑ **o**—create a new line below the current line and place the cursor at the beginning of this line. The **o** is an abbreviation for "open."
- ❑ **O**—create a new line above the current line and place the cursor at the beginning of this line. The **O** is an abbreviation for "open."

Note that all you need to do is type a single character to enter **input mode**. It is not necessary to press **Enter**.

We will use Figure 16.3 to illustrate the various commands to switch to **input mode**. In the figure, we have not shown a cursor position. In each example we will describe where the cursor is assumed to be located. Note that in **vi** the cursor is usually displayed as a flashing underscore character or a solid rectangle. Throughout this chapter, we will use the underscore character to denote the cursor. For each example we assume the original file shown in Figure 16.3 is being edited. Furthermore, each example begins with the user in **command mode**. In the echo line in Figure 16.3, **vi** is displaying the message

```
-- INSERT --
```

indicating that the user is in (in our case, just switched over) **input mode**. At this point, any characters you type in will be inserted into the editing buffer.

```
Tuckerman Ravine Trail on Mount Washington
is considered steep and rocky by some people.
However, for the great mountaineers of the
world, it is neither steep nor rocky.
~
~
~
~
~
~
~
~
-- INSERT --
```

Figure 16.3—Working in **Input Mode**

If the cursor had been on the **T** in **Tuckerman** when you entered **input mode**, using the **a** command, any text you next type in would follow the **T**. For example, if you typed

```
he T
```

the current line would have the following appearance:

```
The Tuckerman Ravine Trail on Mount Washington
```

Note that when you enter **input mode** the echo line goes from being blank to containing the message

```
-- INSERT --
```

(or -- **APPEND** -- or -- **OPEN** -- depending on how you entered **input mode**, and on which version of **vi** you are running). Suppose you were editing the file shown in Figure 16.3 again. If the cursor had been on the **T** in **Tuckerman** when you entered **input mode** using the **i** command, any text you next type in would be inserted before the **T**. For example, if you typed

```
The ⊔
```

(**The** followed by a blank space), the current line would have the following appearance:

```
The Tuckerman Ravine Trail on Mount Washington
```

The examples of switching to **input mode** using **a** and **i** illustrate two different ways of accomplishing the same task. In general, there are many ways of reaching the same goal in **vi**. This makes the editor very flexible. Once you become comfortable with **vi**, you will learn which commands are most efficient for your editing style.

Suppose you were editing the file shown in Figure 16.3 again, and the cursor were located on the **R**. If you typed **I** to enter **input mode**, the cursor would be moved to the **T** in **Tuckerman**, and the text you typed in next would be inserted at the beginning of the current line. For example, if you typed

```
The ⊔
```

(The followed by a blank space), the current line would have the .following appearance:

```
The Tuckerman Ravine Trail on Mount Washington
```

Suppose you were editing the file shown in Figure 16.3 again, and the cursor were located on the **R**. If you typed **A** to enter **input mode**, the cursor would be moved to the space following the **n** in **Washington**, and the text you typed in next would be inserted at the end of the current line. For example, if you typed

```
in the Whites
```

the current line would have the following appearance:

```
Tuckerman Ravine Trail on Mount Washington in the Whites
```

Suppose you were editing the file shown in Figure 16.3 again, and the cursor were located on the **R**. If you typed **o** to enter **input mode**, the cursor would be moved to the beginning of a blank line inserted by **vi** below the current line. The text you typed in next would be inserted at beginning of this new line. For example, if you typed

```
in the Whites
```

the first two lines would have the following appearance:

```
Tuckerman Ravine Trail on Mount Washington
in the Whites
```

Suppose you were editing the file shown in Figure 16.3 again, and the cursor were located on the **y** in **rocky**. If you typed **O** to enter **input mode**, the cursor would be moved to the beginning of a blank line inserted by **vi** above the current line. The text you typed in next would be inserted at beginning of this new line. For example, if you typed

```
in the Whites
```

the first two lines would have the following appearance:

```
Tuckerman Ravine Trail on Mount Washington
in the Whites
```

We have seen that there are a variety of ways to switch from **command mode** to **input mode**. The choice for which command to use will depend on where you need to insert new text.

There is only one way to switch from **input mode** to **command mode**. Remember, when you are in **input mode** everything you type is inserted into the file you are editing. Therefore, to switch modes, we need to get a command "through to **vi**." Thus, we need to use a special character. The **Escape** key is used to switch to **command mode**. Once you have pressed the **Escape** key, you will be in **command mode** and can begin entering **vi** commands.

Many **vi** editors will display a message such as -- **INSERT** -- (or -- **APPEND** -- or -- **OPEN** --) in the echo line to indicate that you are in **input mode**. However, when you are in **command mode**, no message is displayed in the echo area. If your editor does not give an indication that you are in **input mode**, then it is possible that you might forget which mode you are actually using. At any time by pressing the **Escape** key, you can bring the editor to **command mode**. If you hear a beep, this means you were already in **command mode** and no harm is done. If you do not hear a beep (assuming you have good hearing), this means you were in **input mode**.

In summary,

❏ to switch from **command mode** to **input mode**, you can enter one of these commands: **a**, **i**, **A**, **I**, **o**, or **O**, depending on where you want to begin inserting text.

❏ to switch from input mode to command mode, you can press the **Escape** key.

❏ if you are not sure what mode **vi** is in, you can press the **Escape** key to enter command mode.

Throughout this chapter, when we talk about entering a given command, we will assume that you are already in **command mode**.

You are probably already getting the correct sense that **vi** is a complex program. In the next section, we describe a simple strategy for learning **vi** and explain how to use the **vi** tutorial.

Table 16.2 summarizes the commands described in this section.

Vi Command	Function
A	switch to **input mode** and be positioned to insert text at the end of the current line
a	switch to **input mode** and be positioned to insert text after the current cursor position
I	switch to **input mode** and be positioned to insert text at the beginning of the current line
i	switch to **input mode** and be positioned to insert text before the current cursor position
O	switch to **input mode**, open a new line above the current line, and be positioned to insert text at the beginning of the newly inserted line
o	switch to **input mode**, open a new line below the current line, and be positioned to insert text at the beginning of the newly inserted line
Escape	switch to **command mode**

Table 16.1—Summary of **Vi** Commands Described in Section 16.3

Exercises

1. Enter the command **vi birds**. Is any message displayed in the echo line? Now enter **input mode** using a command of your choice. Is any message displayed in the echo line? Now enter **command mode**. Is any message displayed in the echo line? Summarize your findings. (To exit **vi** without saving the file, you can enter **:q!** from **command mode**.)

2. (Recall that to save a file in **vi** you can enter the command **:wq**.) Suppose you were given a file **lastname** consisting only of your last name. Assume you have just entered the command **vi lastname**. Describe in detail two ways to accomplish each of the following editing goals:

   a. Assume the cursor is positioned on the first letter of your last name. Generate a file containing your first name followed by a space, followed by your last name.

   b. Assume the cursor is positioned on the last letter of your last name. Generate a file containing your first name followed by a space, followed by your last name.

   c. Assume the cursor is positioned on the last letter of your last name. Generate a file containing your first name on line 1 and your last name on line 2.

3. Is it ever necessary to type more than one **Escape** character to enter **command mode**? Carefully explain your answer.

16.4 Vi Tutorial

For any piece of complex software containing dozens and dozens of features, it is generally true that the vast majority of users know and use only a tiny fraction of the available features. Users who actually learn a piece of software inside out are known as *power users*. You will need to devote a considerable amount of time to studying **vi** in order to become a **vi** power user. This is an admirable goal. If you become a **vi** power user, you will be very efficient at editing. In reality, very few users become **vi** power users.

Our goal in this chapter is to get you started becoming a power user but, more importantly, to bring you to the point where you can function on a day-to-day basis with **vi**. To this end, we follow the school of thought that says you will use and retain only the commands that you use daily. The more you practice a given command, the longer you will retain it. We will cover the basic **vi** commands in this chapter. If you ever require more specialized commands, you can look them up on an as-needed basis.

A natural place to begin learning **vi** is the **vi** tutorial. In Figure 16.4 we depict the first part of the **vi** tutorial. We are actually running the VIM Tutor and your tutorial may look slightly different. *In fact, your version of **vi** may not even come with a tutorial.* If you do not have a vi tutorial, you may want to skim the remainder of this section.

The tutorial shown in Figure 16.4 begins with a description of itself and an indication that about one half hour will be required to complete the tutorial. The first lesson contains a description of how to move the cursor keys. Other lessons describe additional fundamental **vi** commands.

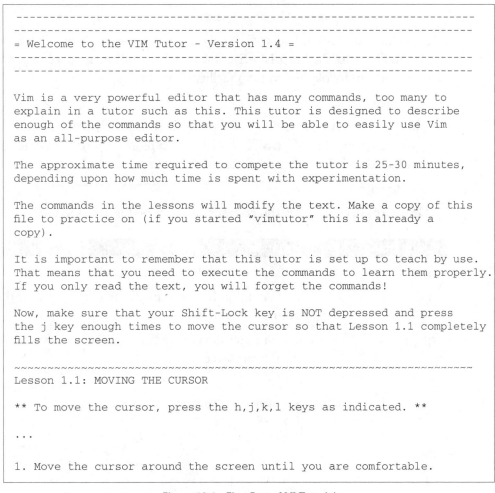

Figure 16.4—First Part of **Vi** Tutorial

To bring the tutorial up on your screen, simply enter the command

```
%vimtutor
```

This will place you in the tutor. If you are not running **vim**, your command will be different from ours. Your system administrator can help you load the appropriate **vi** tutorial for your system.

The **vi** tutorial is an excellent way to learn the basics of **vi**. You can walk through it at your own pace, trying out the various elements that are described in the tutorial. If you get hung up or want to exit the tutorial, you can type

```
:q
```

If you have modified the editing buffer, **vi** may ask you to type **:q!** to exit without saving the file. You will see a message such as

```
No write since last change use ! to override.
```

in the echo line. Remember, you can always return to the tutorial later.

In addition to the tutorial, **vi** comes with a built-in help facility. On many systems you can invoke the **vi** help facility by typing

```
:help
```

followed by the **Enter** key. You can type **:quit** to exit **help** and return to editing. You will be given a list of possible options to explore. There is an extensive **man page** for **vi** as well. To learn more about **vi**, enter the command

```
%man vi
```

Table 16.2 summarizes the commands described in this section.

Vi Command	Function
:help	obtain online help information about **vi**
:q	exit **vi**; if you have modified the editing buffer the editor will not exit
:q!	exit **vi** regardless of whether or not the last changes have been saved

Table 16.2—Summary of **Vi** Commands Described in Section 16.4

Exercises

1. Invoke the **vi** tutorial and read through it trying out the various commands as you go. Was anything confusing to you? How long did it take you to go through the tutorial?
2. Invoke the **vi** help facility. Describe how to get help about a specific command.
3. Read the **man page** for **vi**. Describe three interesting facts you learned.

16.5 Creating and Saving a File

Having read the last section on the **vi** tutorial and how to obtain help about **vi**, you are now in a position to learn **vi** on your own (if you want). However, in each of the next few sections, we walk through the most important **vi** commands.

Many Unix users spend a great deal of time doing file manipulation; that is, creating, editing, and saving files. All of these operations are straightforward to perform using **vi**. To invoke the **vi** editor and create the file called **story**, you can enter the command

```
%vi story
```

You will notice the message

```
"story" [New File]
```

on the echo line. Once **vi** is running, you can enter commands as desired. To insert text, you will need to switch to **input mode**. Text will be inserted where the cursor is flashing. The cursor moves to the right as you type, as does any text appearing to the right of the cursor. Usually, in **command mode** the **Delete** key removes the character at the cursor location. The **Backspace** key will delete the character in front of the cursor and move the cursor back one space in **command mode**. In **input mode** the **Backspace** key moves you back one space on your first press and beeps on the second press. After you have typed some text, you may save it by entering **command mode** and typing

```
:w
```

The **w** stands for "write." You will see a message in the echo line indicating that the file **story** was written, along with a notation indicating how many lines and characters were actually saved. This is the point at which the file **story** is actually written to the disk and saved.

Suppose you want to save a version of the file called **story.1** at some point. You can enter the command

```
:w story.1
```

If this is a new file, the echo line will indicate this to you as the file is written. In this case you will have just created a new file. If the file **story.1** already exits, you will see a message such as

```
File exists (use ! to override)
```

By entering the command,

```
:w! story.1
```

you can overwrite the existing **story.1** file. The content of the original file is gone for good, so be careful. Notice how the exclamation mark (!) was used for overriding the **write** operation (as it was earlier for overriding the **exit** operation). This override is a way to protect the user from accidentally losing edits to a file or from destroying an existing file. It is unlikely you would type an exclamation mark by mistake.

Once you are done editing the file **story**, as usual, you can enter the command

```
:wq
```

to write the file and exit **vi**.

Table 16.3 summarizes the commands described in this section.

Vi Command	Function
Backspace	in **command mode**, delete the character in front of the cursor and move the cursor one character to the left
Delete	in **command mode**, delete the character above the cursor
:w	write out the contents of the editing buffer
:w!	write out the contents of the editing buffer even if this means overwriting another file

Table 16.3—Summary of **Vi** Commands Described in Section 16.5

Exercises

1. Describe the effect of pressing the **Enter** or **Return** key when you are in **input mode**. Consider all possible cases.

2. Create the file numbers having nine lines, with each line containing its line number. How many bytes long is the file?

3. Create a file containing the words used in this exercise. How many bytes long is the file?

4. For both modes, what happens if the cursor is at the end of a line and you press the **Delete** key? How about at the beginning of a line?

5. For both modes, what happens if the cursor is at the beginning of a line and you press the **Backspace** key? How about at the end of a line?

6. Carefully explain the difference in vi between the **Backspace** and **Delete** keys. Do these keys have any effect in the echo area? Explain.

7. Does your vi autosave? That is, will vi save the editing buffer automatically after so many keystrokes? If so, explain when.

8. Does your vi have automatic backups? If so, explain the naming convention and when such backups are generated.

9. Suppose you are in the middle of editing a file using vi and the system crashes. Is there a way to recover the file you were editing, even if you had not saved the last changes? Explain.

16.6 Cursor Movement Commands

We have seen that when you load **vi** and switch to **input mode** you can begin inserting text into the editing buffer. So far, we have only talked about how to move the cursor backwards one space in **command mode** using the **Backspace** key, but **vi** provides many different commands for moving the cursor around the screen. Remember, when you type characters into **vi** while in **input mode**, they are inserted either before or after the current location of the cursor depending on how you entered **input mode**. In order to be an efficient editor, you need to be able to reposition the cursor to any location on the screen very quickly. In this section we go over many of **vi** cursor movement commands.

For the discussion of cursor movement commands that follows, we assume you are in **command mode**. The most common cursor movements are forward one character and backward one character (there is no deletion here, as opposed to the **Delete** key). To move the cursor forward (to the right) one space, you can enter

l

This is the letter "ell," not the number one. To move the cursor backward (to the left) one space, you can enter **h** or **Backspace**.

It is tedious to move to the center of a line from the beginning of it by using a series of **l**s. **Vi** provides commands so that you can jump forward over the next word or jump backward one word at a time. (We ask for precise definitions of *next* and *word* in the exercises.) The command for moving forward to the first character of the next word is

w

and the command for moving backward to the first character of the previous word is

b

A series of alternating **w**s and **b**s will take you back and forth between the first characters of two adjacent words. Note that many **vi** commands that perform entirely different functions look similar. For example, **w** moves the cursor forward to the first character of the next word but **:w** is used to write out a file. Initially, you will need to use caution when typing **vi** commands. The command

e

can be used to move forward to the last character of the next word.

Using the commands **l**, **h**, **w**, **b**, and **e**, you can comfortably move around within a line. To move to the beginning of the current line, you can enter the command

0

This is the zero character, not a capital letter. To move to the end of a line, you can enter the command

$

Two useful but perhaps lesser used commands are

-

to move backward to the beginning of the previous line and

+

to move forward to the beginning of the next line. The **Enter** key has the same effect as **+**.

To move to the line beneath the one the cursor is currently flashing on, you can enter the command

j

To move to the line above the one the cursor is currently flashing on, you can enter the command

k

Notice that the keys for moving the cursor **h** (left), **j** (down), **k** (up), and **l** (right) are adjacent on a standard keyboard. For a touch typist these keys appear to the left of the right index finger, under the right index finger, under the right middle finger, and under the right ring finger, respectively. Once you get familiar with this layout, you can move around the screen very quickly.

We have seen a variety of commands that are useful for moving around a buffer in small steps. You can also use the arrow keys ➡, ⬅, ⬆, and ⬇ to reposition the cursor. To move to the next screen, you can enter the command

^F

The **F** stands for "forward." The command

^B

moves you back one screen. The **B** stands for "backward." To move forward half a screenful, you can enter the command

^D

The **D** stands for "down." The command

^U

moves you up half a screenful. The **U** stands for "up."

There are many other more specialized cursor movement commands in **vi** as well. We ask for an explanation of several of these in the exercises.

Table 16.4 summarizes the commands described in this section.

Vi Command	Function
^B	move backward one screen
^D	move forward half a screen
^F	move forward one screen

^U	move backward half a screen
b	move backward to the first character of the previous word
e	move forward to the last character of the next word
h	move backward one character
j	move down to the next line
k	move up to the previous line
l	move forward one character
w	move forward to the first character of the next word
0	move to the beginning of the current line
-	move backward to the beginning of the previous line
+	move forward to the beginning of the next line
$	move to the end of the current line

Table 16.4—Summary of **Vi** Commands Described in Section 16.6

Exercises

1. Define "next" and "word" as used in this section to describe cursor movement commands.
2. Suppose a line is 80 characters wide and the cursor is located on the first character of the line. What is the minimum number of **vi** commands needed to move the cursor to the middle of the line? Use only the commands discussed in this section and explain your answer.
3. Explain the difference between – and **0**. Can you make any general statements about which command moves the cursor farther?
4. What are the functions of the (and) commands?
5. What are the functions of the { and } commands?
6. What are the functions of the **W**, **E**, and **B** commands? How do they differ from the lowercase versions of the same commands?

16.7 Cutting and Pasting Text

Computer scientists are generally people who do not like to waste any effort. If they can reuse something, such as a portion of program or a section of text, they usually will. In this section we illustrate how to cut and paste text in **vi**. Using this technique, you will be able to save yourself lots of typing time through reuse.

Vi maintains a special buffer that holds the last item you deleted. For our purpose, this buffer will be referred to as the *delete buffer*. This buffer is sometimes called the *edit buffer* or the *cut and paste buffer*. We refer to the process of deleting something as cutting text. When you cut some text, it is stored in the delete buffer until other text is cut. You can think of the delete buffer as a special temporary storage area. To capture a line of text, which means place it in the delete buffer, you can enter the command

        dd

The **d** stands for "delete." When you type **dd**, the line the cursor is currently on will disappear. To paste the line back, you can enter the command

        p

The **p** stands for "put." That is, you put the text back. So, in **vi** jargon "cut and paste" is "delete and put." A deleted line will be placed after the current line, so to move a line, you delete it, move the cursor to the line you would like the deleted line to be inserted after, and then put it. For example, to move the line the cursor is currently on after the succeeding three lines of the file, you would enter the commands

        dd j + p

in succession. The **dd** deletes the line, the **j** moves you down a line, the **+** moves you to the beginning of the next line, and the **p** puts the line in after the current line. Note that the sequence **dd jj p** would also suffice.

With some experimentation, you will quickly adapt to the delete and put procedure. In the event you make a mistake, you can undo your last edit by entering the command

        u

The **u** stands for "undo." You can undo only your last edit. If you need to reverse a change, do it immediately.

In general, you may want to delete and move more than just a single line of text. For example, you may want to move a large portion of a paragraph. On our system, if you enter a series of *n* **dd**s, you will delete *n* lines but only the last line will be stored in the delete buffer. Thus, using **dd** in this manner, you will not be able to achieve your goal. The **d** command can be used for this. The general syntax for the **d** command is

```
d cursor move
```

When you type such a command, you type **d** and the cursor movement command. There are no spaces in the command. Here **cursor move** denotes any cursor movement command, including backward movements. The semantics of this command is that the text from the current position of the cursor to the position specified by the move will be deleted and stored in the delete buffer. You can put the text back by using the **p** command as before. We will see an example of this shortly.

In **vi** it is possible to repeat commands a specified number of times by prefacing them with a number. For example, to move the cursor forward seven spaces, you can type the command

```
7l
```

If the cursor is less than seven spaces away from the end of a line, it will stop at the last character in the line.

So, to delete four lines of text from the current cursor position and deposit them three lines later, you could enter the command sequence

```
d3j 2j p
```

or equivalently,

```
4dd j + p
```

The first three commands are parsed as follows: the **d** command is used to delete four lines by moving the cursor ahead three lines; the **2j** command has the effect of **j j**, so the cursor is moved ahead two lines; and the **p** command puts the text after the current line. The second four commands are parsed as follows: the **dd** command is repeated four times and is used to delete four lines, the **j** command moves the cursor forward one line, the **+** command moves the cursor to the beginning of the next line, and the **p** command puts the text after the current line.

Once some text is in the delete buffer, you can put it any number of times, so to produce five regions that all have the contents of the delete buffer, you can simply enter **5p**. Once you delete something else, the original contents of the delete buffer is gone. In other words, the delete buffer can have only one set of deleted text in it at a given time.

Suppose you have a large region of text that you want to move. Here, by large we mean several screens worth. It would become tedious to type several hundred

dds. One option you have is to turn on **vi**'s line numbering. To do this, enter the command

    `:set number`

The result of this command is that all lines in the file are numbered consecutively starting from one. The numbers are not actually part of the file, but are useful for reference. To delete a large region of text, you can simply determine the line number of the last line you would like to delete. Call this number **ee**. Then move the cursor to the line where you want to be begin deleting. Call this number **bb**. Let **r** = **ee** − **bb**. That is, **r** is the number that is the difference between **ee** and **bb**. By entering the command

    `drj`

you can delete the desired region, or equivalently, you could enter the command

    `( r + 1 )dd`

(the number **r + 1** followed directly by **dd**). The **p** command, along with the standard cursor movement commands, can be used to put the region back where desired.

So far, we have addressed moving lines of text or regions of text. Suppose you want to move a smaller amount of text. To move a single word, you can delete it by placing the cursor on its first letter and then entering the command

    `de`

Next, move the cursor to the desired new location for the word, and then enter

    `p`

as usual. Note that in doing this, you replace the contents of the delete buffer with the word you deleted. It is usually a good idea to put shortly after deleting so you do not accidentally lose the contents of the delete buffer when deleting again. Remember, you can always undo one edit using the **u** command.

There are a number of other **vi** commands relating to deleting and putting. Several of them are addressed in the exercises, as are a number of **vi** delete and put idioms. By deleting and putting in appropriate situations, you will save yourself lots of typing time.

Table 16.5 summarizes the commands described in this section.

Vi Command	Function
d cursor move	delete from the current cursor location to the location specified by the cursor movement command; the deleted text is placed in the delete buffer
dd	delete the current line of text; the deleted text is placed in the delete buffer
*n***command**	repeat the **command** *n* times
p	put the text from the delete buffer into the editing buffer
:set number	turn on line numbering

Table 16.5—Summary of **Vi** Commands Described in Section 16.7

Exercises

1. Delete a line of text using the **dd** command. Describe exactly what happens to the window you are viewing. Does the position of the cursor on the line matter?
2. Suppose you have the numbers **1, 2, 3, 4,** and **5** occurring in reverse order on the first five lines of a file, one number per line. Assume you can only use the commands **j, k, d cursor move,** and **p**. What is the minimum number of **d cursor move**s and **p**s you need to use to sort the numbers in increasing order?
3. Specify a command to delete three words.
4. What are the functions of the **D, X,** and **x** commands?
5. What are the functions of the **r** and **R** commands?
6. Latresia realizes she deleted the wrong three lines during a delete and put operation. What should she do to move the right three lines to location **A** without making any other changes to the original file?
7. What is the function of the **P** command? Compare and contrast it with the **p** command.
8. Describe what each of the following commands accomplishes:
   a. **d23k**
   b. **dw**
   c. **d4)**
   d. **dG**

16.8 Text Searching

There will be many times you want to search for a particular string in a buffer. For example, perhaps you realize you were misusing the words *effect* and *affect* and need to swap their uses around. One way to correct this problem is as follows:

1. move to the beginning of the buffer
2. search sequentially through the buffer for the word **effect**
3. replace each occurrence of **effect** you find with the string **aaaaa**
4. move to the beginning of the buffer
5. search sequentially through the buffer for the word **affect**
6. replace each occurrence of **affect** you find with the word **effect**
7. move to the beginning of the buffer
8. search sequentially through the buffer for the string **aaaaa**
9. replace each occurrence of the string **aaaaa** you find with the word **affect**

The placeholder string **aaaaa** is a string that does not occur elsewhere in the buffer.

Below we will see a more efficient way of carrying out the same operation. First we demonstrate how to carry out this more lengthy procedure using **vi** since it illustrates a number of important commands. To move to the beginning of a buffer, you can enter the command

```
1G
```

The **G** command jumps to the line number that prefaces it. So, **1G** says "jump to line 1." Incidentally, to move to the end of a buffer, you can enter the command

```
G
```

That is, with no number preceding it, the **G** command takes you to the end of the buffer. You can enter

```
:value
```

to go to the line numbered **value**. To search for a string, you can enter the command

```
/
```

followed by the string you want to find. This is similar to searching with the **more** command. In our example, we would type in the word **effect**. If the complete pattern you typed in is matched, **vi** will move the cursor to the first character in your pattern at the nearest location below the cursor matching your query. A second / with no argument will move the cursor to the next occurrence of **effect**, and so on. (If you execute some other command in the interim, a single / with no argument can still be used to look for the most recently searched for pattern.) If the pattern **effect** is not found, **vi** will respond with

```
Pattern not found: effect
```

in the echo line. If you are searching and locate something, you can enter the command

```
u
```

to abort the search and return to the location from which the search was initiated. From time to time this technique will come in handy; for example, when you just want to peek ahead a bit. By the way, the command

```
?
```

is used to do a backward search through the buffer. On most systems / and ? will wrap around automatically.

The command

```
dw
```

can be used to delete the word **effect**. Next we can simply type in the string **aaaaa** to replace the word **effect**. We can repeat this same process until we end up with

```
Pattern not found: effect
```

Now to return to the top of the buffer, we can enter the command

```
1G
```

Using a process similar to that just described, we can carry out the remaining steps of our procedure completing the swap of **effect** and **affect**.

As you can see, this process gets a bit cumbersome, especially when there are a lot of occurrences of a word to be replaced. **Vi** provides another command that is very useful for replacing a large number of patterns with another user-specified pattern. The command is known as *search and replace,* and its syntax is

```
:%s/oldpattern/newpattern/c
```

The **%** tells **vi** to perform the command on all the lines in the editing buffer, **s** stands for "substitute," **oldpattern** is the original pattern that is being replaced, **newpattern** is the pattern that you want to be substituted for the old pattern, and **c** stands for "confirm," indicating that you want **vi** to ask you for each occurrence whether or not you want it replaced. To replace an occurrence, you simply enter **y**, standing for "yes"; otherwise, enter **n**, standing for "no."

In our example we could enter the command

```
:%s/effect/aaaaa/c
```

to get things started. As each new occurrence of **effect** is found, if you type **y**, the occurrence of **effect** will be replaced by **aaaaa**. Then the cursor will be moved to the next occurrence of **effect**, where you will be prompted with the same query and so on. If you type **n**, the occurrence of **effect** will not be replaced, and again the process will continue as in the case of a **y** response.

By performing three search-and-replace operations, it should be clear how to swap all the **effect**s and **affect**s. This process is much more efficient than the brute force approach described at the beginning of this section.

Care must be taken when using search and replace since it is easy to make a mistake from which it is hard to recover. Before carrying out any search-and-replace operation, be sure to think through all the ramifications. For example, imagine what could happen to a sentence such as

```
Can I have the Canteen Dad?
```

if you were not careful in replacing **Can**.

Table 16.6 summarizes the commands described in this section.

Vi Command	Function
?	reverse search
/	forward search
1G	move to the top of a buffer
G	move to the bottom of a buffer
:%s/oldpattern/newpattern/c	search and replace with confirmation

Table 16.6—Summary of **Vi** Commands Described in Section 16.8

Exercises

1. Explain why it was necessary to introduce the string **aaaaa** in order to exchange the **effect**s and **affect**s in the example in this section.
2. Suppose you have a buffer that contains exactly one occurrence of the word "toad." What happens if you search for **toad** and repeatedly enter **/**?
3. Is the search-and-replace operation case sensitive? That is, are upper- and lowercase letters treated differently?

4. Pete labeled items on lists in his term paper **a**, **ab**, **abc**, and **abcd**. His professor says he needs to change these labels to **1**, **2**, **3**, and **4**, respectively. How can Pete do this using search-and-replace operations?

5. Suppose a line of text consists of seven words, each of length 10, and that the cursor is positioned in the middle of the line. What is the quickest way to move to the beginning of the sixth word, where "quickest" means using the fewest keystrokes? Explain your answer.

6. Is there a way to perform a search-and-replace operation in **vi** within a certain range of lines? For example, how would you replace each pattern of **Stallion** occurring between lines 20 and 1,000 with the pattern **horse**, yet have no effect on occurrences of the word **Stallion** outside this range?

16.9 Miscellaneous Vi Commands

At the beginning of this chapter, we mentioned that **vi** is an extremely powerful editor. We have touched on a variety of **vi** commands up to this point. However, many other **vi** commands exist that we have not explained. In this section, we mention a couple of others that we find useful. In particular, we describe commands for

❑ repeating a command an arbitrary number of times.
❑ file insertion.
❑ using multiple editing windows.

16.9.1 Command Repetition

We briefly touched on command repetition in Section 16.7. Here we will examine this concept more generally. There will be many times you want to execute the same command over and over again. For example, perhaps you are at the top of a file and want to move to line 47. It would get a bit tedious typing **j** 46 times. You could type **^F** to skip a screen, and then type a bunch of **js**, but again this is cumbersome. A more efficient way to move to line 47 is to enter the command

    46j

You can also enter **:47** or **47G**, and you can type **^G** to locate the line where the cursor resides. Many commands allow you to preface them with a number *n*. The effect is then to have the command executed *n* times. In our example above, the effect of the command is to execute 46 **js**.

You will find many other uses for the repetition command, and as a result become more efficient with your editing.

16.9.2 File Insertion

Occasionally, you will want to insert the contents of a file into the buffer you are editing. Suppose the file **reunion** is located in the directory where you are working. To insert the file **reunion** after line **T**, simply move the cursor to line **T** and enter the command

```
:r reunion
```

Think of **r** as standing for "read in a file." To insert a file that is not in the same directory as you are working, specify its full pathname.

16.9.3 Multiple Windows

We would be remiss not to mention the utility of working on multiple buffers at once. At times, it is very useful to be editing two or more files simultaneously. For example, you may need to move portions of text between two files. **Vi** provides a convenient mechanism for doing this.[1] We touch on the essentials of editing multiple buffers here. Our description is by no means complete, but provides you with a good starting point.

To split a window you are editing into two windows, you can enter the command

```
:split
```

After executing this command, your screen will be divided into two windows, as shown in Figure 16.5. The contents of the buffer you were working on will be loaded into both windows. In this case, we were working on a file called **test**. To divide the screen into two windows and load a different file from your current working directory (say **storm**) into one of them, you can enter the command

```
:new storm
```

from the original buffer containing the file **test**. If you wanted to have the file **test** in one buffer and no file in the other buffer, the command

```
:new
```

without an argument could be used. Each different window you create has its associated buffer and behaves essentially independently.

---

1. We describe the **vim** commands for doing this. The commands for working with multiple buffers are less standard than some of the basic **vi** commands, and so they may be different on your system. The functionality will be the same, though.

```
This is window 1.
~
~
~
~
test
This is window 1.
~
~
~
~
test
:split
```

Figure 16.5—Two Identical Editing Windows—Cursor Is in Top Window

The window that contains the cursor is called the *active window*. To make the other window the active window, you can enter the command

    `^W p`

The **p** stands for "previous." That is, you can switch to the other window using this command. A window not having the cursor in it is called an *inactive window*. The different buffers share a single echo line. The commands you enter are applied to the active window.

When you are in the active window, you can delete text using the

    `d cursor move`

command in the usual way. You can switch to the other window using the command

    `^W p`

and then put the deleted text there using the

    `p`

command. That is, the delete buffer is shared among the windows. This gives you a very easy way to move text between two different files.

To return to a single window, you can enter the command

    `:q!`

Doing this will quit the active window without saving, and it will disappear. It is useful to return to a single window if it is necessary to view a large portion of a buffer at one time.

When you use multiple windows, be careful to save the changes you desire. If there are modified buffers that have not been saved, **vi** will warn you to quit with **:q!**. You can enter **:wq** to save and quit the active buffer.

There are many other more specialized uses of buffers that we will not delve into here. You may pursue these through other references.

Table 16.7 summarizes the commands described in this section.

Vi Command	Function
^W p	switch to the other window
:new file	split the window and load file into the new buffer
:r file	insert file into the editing buffer
:split	divide the active window into two windows
*n***ZZ**	execute command **ZZ** *n* times

Table 16.7—Summary of **Vi** Commands Described in Section 16.9

Exercises

1. Starting from the beginning of a line, explain how you can move to any column within it using the **l** command.
2. Give three instances where command repetition would be useful. Can negative numbers be used for command repetition?
3. What happens if you try to insert a file in the middle of a line?
4. Create a sample file called **test** that is 80 lines long and save it. Reopen the file for editing with **vi**. Move the cursor to line 40. Insert the file **test** into itself at this location and save it. Compare the sizes of the two files. Are the results as anticipated?
5. How can you divide a single window into three windows? What effect does **^W p** have now?
6. Explain why dividing a window into 10 separate windows is not a useful editing practice.
7. Explore the **:only** command and explain what its function is.

16.10 A Word of Caution

A closing word of caution is in order regarding **vi**. There are many different versions of **vi** in use today. Not all versions are going to behave exactly the same way. In particular, not all of the keystroke commands will be identical over different versions. However, all versions of **vi** do include the same basic functionality. Thus, if you try out a command discussed in this chapter and it does not seem to behave properly for you, it may be that on your system a different set of keystrokes is required to execute the command. Using the help facility accompanying your version of **vi**, you can learn what all of your keystroke commands are.

To learn more about **vi**, you can consult any of the online references mentioned in this chapter or purchase a book on **vi**. A complete summary of the **vi** commands described in this book is provided in Appendix G.

UNIX SHELLS,
PIPES AND JOBS

BASICS OF THE C-SHELL

chapter 17

In this chapter we introduce the following commands:

Unix Command	DOS Command	Description
chsh	—	change your login shell
echo	ECHO	display a line of text
history	—	print a listing of recently executed commands
printenv	—	print information about your current working environment
set	SET	display shell variables; turn on a shell variable
setenv	PATH	display environment variables; change the value of an environment variable
umask	—	set file creation mask
unset	—	turn off a shell variable

17.1 Introduction

Whenever you use Unix, you type in commands to the Unix *shell*. The shell processes your commands; the shell is the Unix *command interpreter*. The shell also has its own interpreted programming language in which you can code general programs. The word "interpreted" means that the code is not compiled but executed "on the fly." There are a number of different Unix shells that are popular. We summarize the more popular ones in Table 17.1.

Shell Name	Program Name	Brief Description
Bash	**bash**	extended version of the Bourne shell developed as part of the GNU project; Bash stands for "*Bourne again shell*"
Bourne shell	**sh**	original Unix shell developed by Steven Bourne at Bell Labs
-shell	**csh**	shell developed by William Joy for BSD Unix
Korn shell	**ksh**	extended version of the Bourne shell developed by David Korn
Tcsh	**tcsh**	extended version of the C-shell developed by Ken Greer and others

Table 17.1—A List of Unix Shells

The two most popular shells are the *C-shell* and the *Bourne shell*. The default *prompt* used by the C-shell is the percent symbol (%), whereas the default prompt used by the Bourne shell is the dollar sign ($). Thus, it is easy to guess which shell you are running. The shell that starts up automatically each time you log in is called your *login shell*. You can try out other shells that are available on your system by entering their program name. You can type the command

```
%exit
```

to return to the previous shell you were using.

In this chapter, we will examine a number of facets of the C-shell. The basic features of many of the shells are the same. When we use the word "shell" in this chapter, we will be referring to the C-shell, unless otherwise noted. Our goal is to touch on the features of the shell that you will find most useful and interesting. The material we cover here will suffice for an intermediate Unix user. We should note that the shell programs are very complex and large. It would be worthwhile for you to scroll through the documentation for some of the shells to get a better sense of how sophisticated the shell programs are. The documentation can be read by entering the command

```
%man shell
```

where **shell** stands for the name of the any of the shells shown in Table 17.1.

A comprehensive treatment of the shell would require a couple of hundred pages. Many long-time Unix users know surprisingly little about the shell and can still complete their work efficiently. If you learn the material in this chapter, you will be adequately prepared to work with the shell. In this chapter we cover the following key topics:

❑ an explanation of environment variables and shell variables.

❑ a description of shell initialization files.

❑ techniques for efficiently entering shell commands.

❑ an introduction to shell scripts.

❑ a comparison of the C-shell and the Bourne shell.

❑ a discussion of how to change your login shell.

17.2 Environment and Shell Variables

In this section we discuss environment and shell variables, and how to manipulate them.

17.2.1 Environment Variables

The Unix operating system maintains a set of global variables that allow you to customize your work environment. These variables are called *environment variables*. They are global in the sense that the entire Unix operating system has access to their values. You can get a listing of your environment variables and their corresponding values by entering the command

```
%printenv
```

A selected portion of the output from this command is depicted in Figure 17.1. For our purposes, it is not important to understand each and every one of these variables. Two things to notice, though, are that the names of the environment variables are displayed in capital letters, and each variable name is followed by an equals sign (=), which in turn is followed by the value that the variable is assigned.

```
EDITOR=/usr/dt/bin/dtpad
HOME=/home/jones
LANG=C
LOGNAME=jones
MAIL=/var/spool/mail/jones
OPENWINHOME=/usr/openwin
PATH=/usr/local/bin:/bin:/usr/bin:/usr/X11/bin:/home/jones/bin
TERM=sund-cmd
SHELL=/bin/csh
TZ=US/Eastern

USER=jones
```

Figure 17.1—Selected Global Environment Variables

The **setenv** command can be used to change the value of an environment variable for your current login session. Permanent changes should be made in the initialization files that are described in Section 17.3. For example, to change the value of variable **X** to value **Y**, you can enter the command

    %setenv X Y

By entering the **setenv** command with no arguments, you can display the variables and their values, similar to the **printenv** command.

17.2.2 Shell Variables

The global environment variables pertain to your entire environment. You also have the option to set *shell variables*. A shell variable is an item that you can set a value for, allowing you to customize the shell. If you are running multiple shells, they can be customized individually. You can obtain a listing of your shell variables and their corresponding values by entering the command

    %set

A selected portion of the output from this command is depicted in Figure 17.2. For our purposes it is not important that you understand each and every one of these variables. Two things to notice, though, are that the names of the shell variables are displayed in lowercase letters, and each name is followed by the value that the variable is assigned. You will see a number of similarities between Figures 17.1 and 17.2, and it is a good exercise to compare and contrast the two.

```
argv ()
cshdepth 2
cshx 3
cwd /home/jones/papers/biology/eggplant
filec
history 100
home /home/jones
path (/usr/local /usr/sbin /usr/bin /home/jones/programs)
prompt >>>
savehist 100
shell /bin/csh
status 0
term sun-cmd
user jones
```

Figure 17.2—Selected Shell Variables

The **set** command can be used to change the value of a shell variable for your current session. Permanent changes should be made in the initialization files that are described in Section 17.3. For example, to change the value of variable **x** to value **y**, you can enter the command

```
%set x = y
```

Note that there is an equals sign (=) required between the two values. The spaces around the equals sign are optional; they help to improve readability. If the value you are setting a variable to includes spaces, you should put single quote marks (') around the value.

17.2.3 Setting and Unsetting On/Off Shell Variables

Some shell variables are either "on" or "off." These variables are not set to a specific value per se. For example, the **filec** variable is used for *file completion*. A simple example will clarify the use of this variable. Then we will show how to set it and how to set such variables in general. Suppose you want to edit the file called

```
laugavegurinn.middle.iceland
```

Since this file name is so long and hard to spell, it is difficult to type. If **filec** is set, you can type

```
%emacs laug
```

and then press the **Escape** key to have the shell complete the file name. If no other file name in the current working directory begins with **laug**, the shell can fill out the entire name of the file for you. This feature can save a lot of typing time. In general, the shell will fill out as much of the file name as is unambiguous. If the name cannot be completed, the system will beep. For example, if you had another file called **laughing**, the shell could not distinguish the two files from only the prefix **laug**. In this case, you need to fill out more of the name, so that a single file can be identified. Here, typing in an **a** would allow the system to distinguish between these two file names. So, by typing **a** and pressing **Escape**, the name of the desired file could be completed.

If **filec** is not on, you can set it by entering the command

```
%set filec
```

Let **command** denote any shell variable that takes a value of on or off. In general, if you enter the command

```
%set command
```

you will turn **command** on. To turn **command** off, you can use the following command

```
%unset command
```

Some of the most important shell variables are depicted in Table 17.2, along with a brief explanation of each. For example, the *prompt* is the string of characters that the shell displays when it is ready for user input. The default prompt for the C-shell is the percent sign (**%**). To change the value of the prompt to the string **abc>**, you can enter the command

```
%set prompt = abc>
```

Shell Variable	Description
history	a number indicating how many of your most recently executed commands are to be remembered by the shell
home	the name of your home directory. When you log in initially, this directory is your current working directory. A **cd** with no argument will deposit you in this directory.
mail	the location of your mailbox
path	a list of directories where the system is to look for the commands that you execute

prompt	the value of your command line prompt
shell	the location of the shell program that you are using
term	the name of the type of terminal that you are using
user	the userid of the currently logged in user

Table 17.2—Important Shell Variables

17.2.4 Printing Variables

The **echo** command can be used to print a line of text. The command

```
%echo Hello, world!
```

simply responds with

```
Hello, world!
```

So, it is easy to see how the command got its name. The **echo** command would not be too useful if this were all it could do. **Echo** can also be used to print the value of a shell or environment variable. For example, the command

```
%echo $TERM
```

prints the value of the variable **TERM**. Notice that the variable name needs to be preceded by the dollar sign (**$**).

17.2.5 Environment and Shell Variables that Overlap

In comparing Figures 17.1 and 17.2, you have probably noticed that some of the global environment variables and some of the shell variables have the same names. The only difference in the names is that the environment variables are written in uppercase letters. Here, it suffices to say that some of these variables are in fact linked and allow the shell to coordinate as necessary with the global system. To learn more about environment or shell variables, you should consult the **man page** for the shell.

Exercises

1. Print out a list of your system's global environment variables and their corresponding values.
2. Print out a list of your system's shell variables and their corresponding values.
3. If you ignore case, how many global environment and shell variables have the same name on your system? What are they? Do they have

the same values assigned? Are the values expressed in the exact same syntax?

4. What command would you issue to set your terminal type to **Linux**?
5. What command would you issue to set your prompt to **yes dear,**?
6. Some users set their prompt so that it responds with the name of the machine that they are working on, followed by the greater than symbol (>). How is this accomplished?

17.3 Shell Initialization Files

There are two initialization files that are processed each time you log into the system. They are both hidden files, namely **.cshrc** and **.login**.[1] The file **.cshrc** is processed first, followed by the execution of the **.login** file. The **.cshrc** file is also executed each time you start a new shell. A number of important initializations go into the **.cshrc** and **.login** files. We will cover the most important features of these files in this section.

Your system administrator will set up your Unix account with default **.cshrc** and **.login** files. These files will provide values for certain shell variables, as well as set up your environment with some standard features. It is a good idea not to modify the initialization files until you are sure you understand what you are doing. Even when you do decide to edit these files, it is a very good idea to keep a backup copy of them. Once you are comfortable with the shell, you will probably want to customize some of the items in the initialization files.

17.3.1 .cshrc File

In Figure 17.3 we show a simple **.cshrc** file. It is customary to set shell variables and define aliases in this file. We explain the key items in the initialization file shown in Figure 17.3. The first line of the file

```
#!/bin/csh
```

has a special meaning. It says to use the program **/bin/csh** to interpret the script. In general, the program to interpret the script is specified in the first line of the script following the characters **#!**. Any line after the first line that begins with the pound sign character (**#**) is a comment and is not executed by the shell. This comment tells us that this file is for the C-shell.

---

1. The names of these files may be different for other shells, for example, **.profile** is used by the Bourne shell.

```
#!/bin/csh

umask 077
set path=(/bin /usr/bin /usr/ucb /etc .)
set history=50
alias rm 'rm -i'
```

Figure 17.3—A Sample **.cshrc** File

The next line of the file

umask 077

defines how the default file protections are to be set on any new file you create. That is, if you edit a new file and save it, the protections specified in the **umask** command are the protections that the file will be assigned. In this case, the argument **077** specifies that the file is to have the permissions

-rwx------

These grant the user read, write, and execute permissions; the group no permissions; and others no permissions. This is a typical default permissions setting.

The question arises as to how the numbers following the **umask** command are interpreted. We now describe their meaning. The **umask** command takes as an argument three numbers concatenated together; the numbers are between 0 and 7 inclusive. In Table 17.3 we show the corresponding binary numbers expanded to three bits for these decimal values. Remember, a bit is either a 0 or a 1. To *complement* a binary number, you simply change 0's to 1's and vice versa. For example, the complement of 000 is 111, and the complement of 101 is 010. To interpret the **umask** argument, first convert the three decimal numbers to binary numbers using Table 17.3. In the example at hand, this results in

077 → 000 111 111

Decimal Value	Binary Value
0	000
1	001
2	010
3	011
4	100

5	101
6	110
7	111

Table 17.3—Decimal to Binary Conversion Displaying Three Bits

where we have inserted a space between the binary equivalents for readability. Next, simply complement the binary values. This results in

```
111 000 000
```

Notice that there are nine values here. These values correspond to the nine permissions settings for a file or a directory; the values correspond positionally as well. A value of 1 indicates the permission is "on" and a value of 0 indicates the permission is "off." So, this permission setting means the user has read permission (the first 1), write permission (the second 1), and execute permission (the third 1); the group does not have read permission (the first 0), write permission (the second 0), nor execute permission (the third 0); and others do not have read permission (the fourth 0), write permission (the fifth 0), nor execute permission (the sixth 0). All permissions settings specified by the **umask** command are interpreted in a similar manner. Thus, it is straightforward to set any desired default file creation permissions with the **umask** command.

The next line of the **.cshrc** file shown in Figure 17.3 is

```
set path=(/bin /usr/bin /usr/ucb /etc .)
```

This line defines your search *path*. These are the directories where the system will look for commands that you try to execute. In general, when you type a command to the shell, the shell walks sequentially through the sequence of directories listed in your path in search of the command. The shell will execute the first command it finds in one of these directories that matches your request. For example, if you enter the **ls** command, and it is in the directory **/bin**, then this particular **ls** command will be executed regardless of whether **ls** appears in some of the subsequent directories. Remember, the **which** command described in Section 9.5.1 can be used to determine which version of a particular command you are executing.

It is important to order the directories in your path so that the most frequently used commands occur early in the path. (This was especially important when computers were slower.) The system administrator will supply a default path for you that should include essentially all the commands you will initially need. From time to time, you may find it necessary to add directories to your path. Permanent changes to your path should be made in the shell initialization files.

It is worth pointing out that when . occurs in your path, it means to search the current working directory. It is generally not considered a good idea to include . in your path. The following scenario illustrates why. Suppose you did include . at the beginning of your path. Furthermore, suppose some hacker gained access to your account (presumably, this might be easier than breaking into the entire system) and included an **ls** command in your home directory that really was the command **rm**. If you entered the command

```
%ls *.*
```

from your home directory, the search for this command would use the bogus **ls** command and delete all your files having a file extension. As this example suggests, it is probably not a good idea to include . in your path.

The next line of the **.cshrc** file shown in Figure 17.3 is

```
set history=50
```

The shell provides a history mechanism for remembering the commands you execute. We will examine the history facility in detail in Section 17.4. History is a feature that allows you to be more efficient in entering commands to the shell. The **set** command used here in the initialization file says to remember 50 commands. That is, the shell will keep track of the previous 50 commands you executed.

The final line of the **.cshrc** file shown in Figure 17.3 is

```
alias rm 'rm -i'
```

This sets **rm** as an alias for the command **rm –i**, which means delete with inquiry. Thus, when you go to remove a file using the **rm** command, the system will prompt you to make sure you really want to delete the file. This is a good security measure to help prevent you from deleting files that you really do want to keep.

The sample **.cshrc** file shown in Figure 17.3 illustrates many of the basic features that should be included in such an initialization file. As you learn more about the shell, you will want to customize this file.

17.3.2 .login File

In Figure 17.4 we show a sample **.login** file that is a modified version of the **.login** file distributed with Solaris. This initialization file illustrates many of the basic items that a typical **.login** file should contain. Such a file usually includes information for opening up your windowing environment (assuming you are running one), setting various shell variables, and performing standard initializations. The example shown in Figure 17.4 begins with a line indicating that the program **/bin/csh** is to be used to interpret the script, includes some code to set up the **OpenWindows** windowing environment assuming the user is logged in at the console, clears the screen, and closes the initial console window. The details of this code are not important for our purposes, although you will probably recognize most of the commands included in the file. In Section 17.5 we will take a look at shell scripts in general, and there we will explain some of the elements of this code.

```
#!/bin/csh

if ( 'tty' == "/dev/console" ) then

    if ( $TERM == "sun" || $TERM == "AT386" ) then

        if ( $ {?OPENWINHOME } == 0 ) then
                setenv OPENWINHOME /usr/openwin
        endif

        echo ""
        echo -n "OpenWindows in 5 (use Control-C to stop)"
        sleep 5
        echo ""
        $OPENWINHOME/bin/openwin
        clear  # clear screen
        logout # close console

    endif

endif
```

Figure 17.4—A Sample **.login** File

You may be wondering what to include in your **.cshrc** file versus what to include in your **.login** file. Typically, the system administrator will set up these files for you, so you really do not need to worry about such issues. In most cases, it will not make much of a difference which of these files you include your initializations in, since both files are run when you log in. If you follow the guidelines we presented in the past two subsections, you should not run into any problems. For assistance with these initialization files, you should consult a Unix guru or your system administrator.

17.3.3 .logout File

The shell also provides a termination file called **.logout**. The commands in this file are executed as you log out of the system. Many users include the **fortune** command in this file. This command prints a random saying on your screen.

Exercises

1. Print your **.login** file. Explain the elements it contains.
2. Are there any aliases set up in your **.cshrc** file? How about in your **.login** file?
3. What are the default file permissions on a new file that you create? Where and how are these default permissions specified?
4. Create a **.logout** file and include the **fortune** command in it. Describe what happens when you log out.
5. Include the **date** command in your **.logout** file. Describe what happens when you log out.
6. Create an experiment to prove which order your **.cshrc** and **.login** files are executed. Explain your experiment and your findings. (*Hint:* Make backup copies of any files you plan to modify.)

17.4 Entering Shell Commands Efficiently

The shell is your command interpreter. As we have seen, the shell can be customized to meet an individual user's needs. The shell includes many different features that can help you work more efficiently. In this section we cover the shell's *history mechanism*, some special characters that can be entered to the shell, and the concept of "single quoting" a string. We saw earlier in this chapter that you can initialize a shell variable called **history** in your **.login** file. If you set **history** to a value of n, the shell will remember the last n commands that you executed. We now illustrate how this feature can help you work more efficiently.

17.4.1 History Mechanism

It is very easy to get a listing of the previous commands you have executed by entering the command

```
%history
```

Figure 17.5 displays some sample output from this command. In the figure, eight previously executed commands are listed. The commands are each preceded by a number. The initial numbering starts at 1 each time you log in. Thus, higher numbered commands were executed more recently.

```
994      dvips -f main.dvi > main.ps
995      emacs -nw unixsummary.tex
996      latex main
997      dvips -f main.dvi > main.ps
998      date
999      fg
1000     emacs shell.tex
1001     history
```

Figure 17.5—Output from the **History** Command

The utility of the history mechanism derives from the various ways you can execute one of the previous commands or execute a modified command. To execute the previous command again, you simply enter

%!!

That is, two exclamations points (!!). The exclamation point is read "bang" by Unix users. If the example shown in Figure 17.5 indicated the last commands executed by a user, then typing **!!** would result in the execution of the command

%history

Commands can also be referred to with a bang followed by their number. For example,

%!994

would mean execute the command

%dvips -f main.dvi > main.ps

You can also abbreviate a command by specifying a prefix of it. Prefixes are matched with the most recently executed commands first. For example,

%!d

would result in the command (998, if executed right after the commands shown in Figure 17.5)

%date

being executed, whereas

%!dv

would result in the command (997, if executed right after the commands shown in Figure 17.5)

%dvips -f main.dvi > main.ps

There is one more feature of the history mechanism involving substitution that we would like to point out. The following scenario illustrates the utility of this form of substitution. Suppose you are in the process of copying three files from one directory to another and you just copied the first file by entering the command

```
%cp ../../public_html/images/GIF/house1.gif .
```

This command means copy the file **house1.gif** from the specified directory to the current working directory and give it the same name, **house1.gif**. Suppose the second file to copy is located in the same directory and has the name **house2.gif**. You could simply enter the command

```
%cp ../../public_html/images/GIF/house2.gif .
```

which is rather cumbersome to type, or, using substitution, you could type

```
%^1^2
```

to accomplish the same goal. The syntax for using the double wedge (^^) is as follows. The command

```
%^match^replace
```

says find the first occurrence from left to right of the pattern **match** in the previous command, and replace **match** with the string **replace**, leaving the rest of the command as it was originally. If **match** is a string occurring in the original command, the modified command is automatically executed after you press **Enter**. If **match** is not found, you will receive a message such as

```
modifier failed
```

If the third file to copy is called **house3.gif**, we can enter the command

```
%^2^3
```

to copy it. Again, this substitution is very efficient.

You will find many uses for double wedge substitutions. Occasionally, you will have to get creative to make a good substitution because the first pattern you think of matching may occur two or more times in the original command, and the pattern you need to replace is not the first one.

17.4.2 Special Characters for Command Line Editing

There are three important key combinations that you will find helpful while you are entering shell commands. The first is the **Delete** key, which you have already been using to correct a single typo. Suppose you mistype an entire word. You can type **Control-W** to erase a word. For example, suppose you begin to enter the command

```
%rm junk tape.old databank
```

and just after you type **databank** realize that you should delete the file **beta** instead of **databank**. If you type **Control-W**, the shell will delete the word **databank** and reposition the cursor where the **d** character was. You can now enter the correct file to delete, namely **beta**.

If you mistype an entire line, you can type **Control-U** to delete it. For example, suppose you type

```
%lpr -dhp finalversion.poem
```

to print the file **finalversion.poem**. However, before hitting **Enter** you realize that you are not in the directory where this file is located. If you type **Control-U**, you can delete the entire line. There will be times you begin to type in a command and then decide to enter a completely different command. In situations such as these, **Control-U** comes in handy.

We should point out that some shells provide a whole host of special key combinations you can enter, thereby virtually turning the command line into a full-screen editor.

17.4.3 Single Quoting

There are a number of characters that have a special meaning when entered to the shell; for example, **#**, **^**, **&**, and **$**, among others. In order to have these symbols interpreted literally by the shell, you need to *single quote* them. That is, place the string they occur in within single quotation marks. We consider an example to illustrate how this is done.

Suppose you have a file whose name is **$test**. To remove the file you need to enter the command

```
%rm '$test'
```

Single quotes are needed around the file name in order to delete it. Otherwise, the $ sign is interpreted differently. You will find several other uses for single quoting. If you are not sure about whether the shell will interpret a character literally, and you would like the character to be interpreted literally, it is a good idea to single quote the string containing the character.

Exercises

1. How many commands does your shell currently store in your **history**? Is this enough? Discuss a value that is appropriate for your usage and explain why it is the right number for you.

2. Print out the last 20 commands you executed. Were any of the commands repeated two or more times? If so, when they were repeated, did you retype the commands or did you use the history mechanism to enter them more efficiently?

3. Suppose the last three commands you entered from most recent to least recent were **file lookout**, **find lookout**, and **finger lookout**. If each of the following commands is executed immediately after these three commands, what command results?

   a. **%!!**
   b. **%!fi**
   c. **%!fin**
   d. **%!find**
   e. **%^l^n**
   f. **%^le^nd**
   g. **%^o^i**
   h. **%^file lookout^ls**

4. Report on three interesting flags to the **history** command. Include a description of the **r** flag in your answer.

5. You just typed in the command

   ```
   %ls -l moody.blues
   ```

   However, you meant to type in

   ```
   %ls -l airplane
   ```

   What is the fewest possible number of keystrokes you need to type in to make this change?

6. You typed in

   ```
   %rvup yjod od trs;;u jpy ersyjrt gpt Sihidy om Vjo;r
   ```

   but meant to type in

   ```
   %echo This is really hot weather for August in Chile
   ```

   What is the fastest way to make the correction? How could you possibly have typed in the first line when attempting to type in the second one?

7. Create a file called **$foo**. Try to delete the file without single quoting the file name. Explain what happens.

17.5 Shell Scripts

The shell has its own programming language. In this section, we mention a few points about the shell scripting language. A program written in the shell language is called a *shell script*. Such programs are interpreted by the shell. That is, when you run a shell script, it is executed line by line as opposed to being a compiled program.

You have already seen two shell scripts. The initialization files contained in Figures 17.3 and 17.4 are shell scripts. In discussing those scripts, you learned that the pound sign (#) prefaces comments and that Unix commands can be included in a shell script. A shell script can be executed by typing its name at the command line. Before executing a shell script, you will first need to add execute permission to the script. On some systems, you will need to preface the name of the script with a . in order to execute it. For example, to run **myscript**, you would type

```
%. myscript
```

The first line of a script should include information indicating the shell scripting language in which the program is written. This is necessary because the various scripting languages are different. An appropriate line for a C-shell script is

```
#!/bin/csh
```

The syntax of the shell programming language is similar to that of the C programming language, which we discuss in Chapter 23. Among other things, the shell scripting language contains an **if-then** statement, an **if-then-else** statement, and a **foreach** loop. The **echo** command can be used within a shell script to print output to standard output. As noted earlier, shell scripts can also include Unix commands.

A shell script is a good vehicle for grouping together a series of Unix commands that you frequently use in combination. In Figure 17.6, we show a script for processing the file **main.tex** with LaTeX, and then having the output sent to the printer. The script first compiles the file **main.tex** with LaTeX. Next, it runs the bibliography processor **bibtex** on the file. The script then executes the **makeindex** command to produce an index for the document. LaTeX is then run twice on the file so that all of the LaTeX labels are filled in properly. Finally, the **dvi** file is converted to a PostScript file and sent to the printer named **hp**. You can develop similar time-saving scripts in this manner.

```
#!/bin/csh
# C-shell script to process a file in LaTeX
# and then print the file.

latex main
bibtex main
makeindex -s index.isty main
latex main
latex main
dvips -f main.dvi | lp -dhp
```

Figure 17.6—Shell Script Grouping Together Several Unix Commands

It is a good idea to set up a test directory in order to experiment with shell scripts. This way you do not accidentally wipe out some important work. If you borrow shell scripts from some other user or a repository, be certain to exercise caution while using them. It is very easy to delete files that you intended to keep.

If you are interested in programming, it would be a good idea to examine the **man page** for the shell. In addition, you can pursue the references provided at the back of this book.

Exercises

1. Write a shell script to print the message

   My first shell script!

   Run your script. Did you need to make the file executable?
2. Write a shell script that groups together a series of three or more Unix commands that you often use in combination.
3. Report three interesting facts about shell scripts.
4. What is the difference between a shell script and a CGI (Common Gateway Interface) script?

17.6 Comparison of the C- and Bourne Shells

Our focus in this chapter has been on the C-shell. In this section we highlight some of the main differences between the C-shell and the Bourne shell.

We have already noted that the default prompt for the Bourne shell is the dollar sign (**$**), as opposed to the percent sign (**%**) used by the C-shell. The program name for the Bourne shell is **bsh**, and it typically resides in the **bin** directory. The initialization files for the Bourne shell are slightly different, too. The **.profile**

file corresponds to the **.login** file for the C-shell, and the **.bshrc** file corresponds to the **.cshrc** file. Like the C-shell, the Bourne shell also has a **.logout** file.

The shell variables for the Bourne shell differ slightly from those used by the C-shell, but you will likely not find any significant differences. The Bourne shell has a history mechanism that is similar to that employed by the C-shell, although its syntax is slightly different. Finally, the Bourne shell has a different scripting language, but many of the basic constructs look and function similarly.

In summary, a novice user who is primarily entering basic Unix commands to the shell will likely not notice a large difference between the Bourne shell and the C-shell. A more experienced programmer, who is performing more sophisticated commands, will notice some difference.

Exercises

1. Can you access both the C-shell and the Bourne shell? If so, which is a larger program? Which has better documentation?
2. Compare and contrast the shell variables for the Bourne shell and the C-shell.
3. Decribe any differences you can determine between how the Bourne shell history mechanism works and how the C-shell history mechanism works.
4. How many Unix shells can you name? What are they?

17.7 Changing Your Shell—chsh Command

We saw in Figure 10.4 that a user's login shell is specified in the system password file—**/etc/passwd**. The **chsh** command can be used for changing the information in this password file, and hence, your login shell. The syntax for the **chsh** command varies from system to system, so you will want to execute the command

```
%man chsh
```

to find out how to change your login shell on your system. On some systems, you simply enter the command

```
%chsh
```

The system will respond with a message such as

```
changing shell for userid.
Password:
```

Here **userid** denotes your account name. After typing in your password, you will be prompted to enter your new shell as follows:

```
New Shell [/bin/csh]:
```

Your old shell is shown in square brackets. To this prompt, you simply enter the full pathname of the shell you would like to become your login shell.

The file

```
/etc/shells
```

contains a listing of the shells that are available and full pathnames to them. Once you have entered the full pathname for the new shell, the change is complete. The next time you log in, you will notice the change in your login shell. As you can see, if you decide to change shells, it is fairly straightforward. We should note that not all shells are available on all systems. If the shell you prefer is not available on your system, you will need to contact your system administrator.

Exercises

1. Are you allowed to use the **chsh** command on your system? If so, what is the syntax of the command?
2. What shells are available on your system? What are their relative sizes? Is the documentation for each shell available online at your installation?

REDIRECTION, PIPES, AND FILTERS

18.1 Introduction

You have acquired a great deal of knowledge about Unix to this point, but there are still a number of important items that we have not yet discussed. To some extent, you have already been using the techniques we will describe in this chapter. However, here we present the items in more detail. The material described in this chapter is very important, and you will likely use much of it in your day-to-day work. We have delayed presenting it to this point because of its technical and abstract nature.

In this chapter we cover the following items:

- ❑ standard input, standard output, and standard error.
- ❑ redirection of input and output.
- ❑ pipes.
- ❑ filters.

18.2 Standard Input and Standard Output

Throughout this book, you have been working with input and output. For example, you are familiar with input to a program or to the Unix operating system, and output to a computer terminal or a printer. The concepts of input and output in Unix are defined very generally; in this section we explore them. We begin with a few preliminaries.

Input is data produced by some source and handed off to another entity for processing. For example, input can be generated by a user typing at the keyboard, a program that is run, a file containing information, a medical device hooked to a machine, an athlete pedaling a bicycle that has a sensor connected to a computer, and so on. The *source* of the input is the item from which the input comes. The sources for the inputs in our previous examples are the keyboard, the program, the file, the medical device, and the sensor, respectively. In Unix, a program is the entity that does the processing of the input.

Output is processed data that is generated by some entity for display on a device, or input for another program. For example, output can be generated by a user typing at the keyboard, a program that is run, a file containing information, a medical device hooked to a machine, an athlete pedaling a bicycle that has a sensor connected to a computer, and so on, so we see that input and output can be generated in the same way. The *target* of the output is the device where the output is to be displayed. Such a device could be a physical device such as a screen, a printer, or an oscilloscope; or a logical device such as another program or a file. The key difference between input and output is that output is data which has already been processed and is ready for display, whereas input is unprocessed data.

In Unix, a *stream* is defined as a logical path over which data flows. If you run a Unix program, it is automatically opened with three associated streams:

❑ one for input called *standard input*.
❑ one for output called *standard output*.
❑ one for diagnostic messages called *standard error*.

One of the things that makes Unix so powerful is that various input sources can be connected to standard input, and various output targets can be connected to standard output. In Sections 18.3 and 18.4, we will show you how to connect a program to different inputs and outputs. Fortunately, the Unix shell takes care of the details for connecting different input sources and output targets in the appropriate manner while hiding the details from the user.

When a programmer writes a Unix program to process input, the source of the input to the program is not specified. The program is written so that input can be taken from essentially any source. As long as the information is presented to the program in the correct manner, it does not matter how the input was generated. For example, the program does not know if its input comes from the keyboard or from a file.

The shell takes care of connecting the input source to a program in the correct way. Initially, the shell sets the default input to come from the keyboard. The default input source is often called *standard input*. In most circumstances, when someone says the input is from standard input, the person means the input comes from the keyboard. Some users identify the keyboard itself with standard input although standard input is really just an abstraction—an input data stream.

Analogously, when a programmer writes a Unix program to display output, the target of the output of the program is not specified. The program is written so that its output can be sent to any target. For example, the program does not know if its output is going to be displayed on the screen or a printer.

The shell takes care of connecting program output in the appropriate manner to its target device. Initially, the shell sets the default output to be displayed on your screen. The default output target is often called *standard output*. In most circumstances, when someone says the output is to standard output, the person means the output is going to the screen. Some users identify the terminal screen itself with standard output although standard output is really just an abstraction—an output data stream.

We should point out that the term *standard IO* is used to talk collectively about standard input and standard output. As noted earlier, Unix also has the notion of *standard error*. The screen is the default location where error messages are written. For example, if you run a Unix command and it results in an error, the diagnostic message will be displayed on your screen. Some users identify the terminal screen itself with standard error, although standard error is really just an abstraction—a diagnostic data stream.

In summary, Unix provides very flexible input and output conventions for programs. The input to a program can come from many different sources; the output of a program may be sent to many different targets. The shell takes care of the programming details behind the scenes so the user is sheltered from any complexities that need to be addressed.

Exercises

1. Compare and contrast the concepts of input and output.
2. Compare and contrast the Unix concepts of standard input and standard output.
3. Enter the command **man –k stream**. What **man pages** were returned? Write a paragraph about streams based on the information you learned from these **man pages**.
4. What are **stdin**, **stdout**, and **stderr**?

18.3 Redirection

In the last section we explained how the input to a Unix program can come from many difference sources. We explained how standard input is initially set up to come from the keyboard. It is very easy to have standard input come from a file instead. When we change the source of the input, we say we *redirect* standard input.

The Unix **sort** command sorts its input. Suppose you have a file **values** consisting of data. To sort this data, you can enter the command

```
%sort < values
```

In general, input can be redirected to any program, not just a Unix command. We consider another example of this in what follows.

Suppose you have a program called **summation** that adds 10 numbers together, and which when run prompts you to enter 10 numbers from the keyboard. Instead of having the values typed from the keyboard, it would be very easy to have the numbers input from a file instead. If the file **numbers** contained 10 numbers, then the command

```
%summation < numbers
```

could be used to input the values contained in the file **numbers** to the program **summation**. That is, the less than sign (<) is used to redirect standard input. The less than sign looks like a left arrow, suggesting input and movement of data from right to left.

Suppose the program **summation** normally sends its output to the screen, the default for standard output. We can redirect standard output to a file as follows:

```
%summation > answer
```

In this case, after the user has entered ten numbers to the program **summation**, its output will be written to the file **answer**. We say that standard output has been redirected. The greater than sign (>) is used to perform the redirection of standard output. The greater than sign looks like a right arrow, suggesting output and movement of data from left to right. If you redirect standard output, be careful that you do not destroy an existing file by overwriting it.

We can redirect standard input and standard output in the same command. For example, the command

```
%summation < numbers > answer
```

says to take the input for the program **summation** from the file **numbers**, and write the output of the program in the file **answer**.

A very common use of redirecting standard input occurs while using the Unix **mail** program. Suppose you want to send a message to the user **gerri**. You can first compose the message using your favorite editor in a file called **letter**, and then send it using the following redirection command:

```
%mail gerri < letter
```

This command will email the file **letter** to the user **gerri**. The concise syntax for redirection is elegant.

Note that when < and > are used for redirection, they affect standard input and standard output only for the command in which they occur. That is, they have only a temporary effect.

There may be times you are collecting data in a particular file and need to keep adding new information to the bottom of the file. That is, you need to keep appending information to the file. Suppose you have a file called **planet.data** and the information in this file is produced by a program called **planets**. Every few weeks, **planets** needs to be run to generate more data that in turn needs to be appended to the file **planet.data**. You can accomplish this very easily with the following command:

```
%planets >> planet.data
```

The double greater than sign (>>) redirects standard output to a file and appends data to the end of the file. Notice how efficient this command is; you do not even need to explicitly open the file **planet.data**. The system takes care of everything for you.

We have touched on a number of practical uses for redirecting input and output. You will find many other uses for input and output redirection as you continue to work with Unix.

Exercises

1. Run the **who** command and redirect standard output to a file called **who**. What are the characteristics of the file you created?
2. Create a file containing 52 lines, each having a distinct lowercase or uppercase letter on it. Using redirection of standard input, sort the lines of the file using the **sort** command. Create a file called **alphasorted** that contains the sorted alphabet.
3. How can you copy a file using redirection of standard output?
4. Describe three practical situations where you would find it useful to redirect standard input.
5. Describe three practical situations where you would find it useful to redirect standard output.
6. What are the meanings of the following redirection commands?
   a. **%>!**
   b. **%>>!**

18.4 Pipes

In the last section we saw how to redirect the output of a program to a file. This was accomplished using the greater than sign (>). Unix also allows you to send the output of a program to another program. The vertical bar (|) is used for this purpose. The following example illustrates the idea.

```
%grep executable *.tex | more
```

This command says to send the output of the command

```
%grep executable *.tex
```

to the **more** command, instead of to standard output. The outcome is to have the results of the **grep** command displayed using the **more** command. If the results are longer than one screenful, this is helpful so that the initial matches do not scroll off the screen. The Unix jargon to describe this command uses the word *pipe*. We say "pipe the output of **grep** to **more**." The notion of pipe symbolizes the bridge created between the two commands so that information can flow from one to the other.

Another common practice is to pipe the output of a command to a printer. For example,

```
%dvips -f main.dvi | lp -dhp
```

says to send the output of the **dvips** command to the command **lp –dhp** rather than to standard output. This has the effect of printing the output of the **dvips** command on the printer named **hp** rather than sending it to the screen.

It is possible to use multiple pipes in the same command. Such a construct is called a *pipeline*. The analogy with a water pipeline is clear. Multiple pipes connected together allow for a longer flow. Here is an example:

```
%cat names1 names2 | sort | more
```

In the example, two files, **names1** and **names2**, are arguments to the **cat** command. Rather than sending the output of **cat** to standard output, it has been piped to the **sort** command. The **sort** command sorts the lines from **cat**'s output. The sorted lines are then input to the **more** command rather than being output to standard output. The results can then be paged through in alphabetical order using **more**.

We have described several examples involving pipes. You will find many other uses for pipes. In doing so, you can use the power of Unix to combine many different commands.

Exercises

1. Which direction does information flow in a pipe? Explain.
2. Give an example of how **spell** can be used as part of a pipe.
3. Explain what the following command does and what the results of the sorting mean:

   ```
   %wc *.* | sort | more
   ```

4. Explain what the following command does:

```
%who | sort | grep cervino | lpr -D laser
```

5. Write a Unix command involving three pipes.

18.5 Filters

Many Unix commands can be classified as *filters*. These are programs that take their input from standard input, process that input, and then produce some output that is sent to standard output. In other words, such programs filter their input somehow by manipulating it. This is analogous to the common use of the word "filter." For example, we filter water during a camping trip to remove impurities from the water. Similarly, we filter data to perform some type of operation on the data. Perhaps we remove unwanted information. Filters can be used as parts of pipelines.

We consider an example to make the concept of filters clear. Suppose a sales manager has a very large file, called **carsales**, containing records of car sales. Specifically, suppose each line of her file has the form

```
model, salesperson
```

where **model** is the type of car sold and **salesperson** is the last name of the person who sold the car. To determine how many cars **Thompson** sold, the sales manager could enter the command

```
%cat carsales | grep Thompson | wc -l
```

Here the **grep** command is used as a filter. Think of it as filtering out all names except Thompson. Notice that the **wc** command is also used as filter here. This compact command accomplishes a lot of processing very efficiently and provides valuable information for the sales manager. She could enter many similar commands to find out more information; for example, how many Jaguars were sold.

As you learn more about Unix, you will find that by using filters you can expand the capabilities of the operating system greatly. That is, by combining Unix commands and using them as filters, you can essentially generate an entire entourage of "new" commands.

Exercises

1. Give examples of pipelines where the following commands are used as filters:
   a. **cat**
   b. **grep**
   c. **spell**
   d. **sort**
   e. **sort** and **spell**
   f. **grep** and **sort**
   g. **grep**, **sort**, and **spell**

2. What is a shorter command for achieving the same output as the following command?

   ```
   %cat carsales | grep Thompson | wc -1
   ```

3. Write a command to help the sales manager mentioned in this section determine how many Jaguars were sold.

4. Give an example of a Unix command that cannot be used as a filter. Explain your answer.

5. Describe the **colrm**, **fmt**, and **paste** commands. Give an example that uses these commands as filters.

chapter 19

PROCESS AND JOB CONTROL

In this chapter we introduce the following commands:

Unix Command	DOS Command	Description
bg	—	move a process into the background
fg	—	move a process into the foreground
jobs	—	obtain a listing of suspended jobs
kill	PAUSE	terminate a Unix process
nice	—	change the priority of a job
ps	—	check the status of processes

19.1 Introduction

There are several additional Unix system commands that are worth describing in this introductory book. These commands will help you become more knowledgeable about your system and perhaps give you enough ammunition to get yourself out of some jams.

In this chapter we cover commands that permit you to

❑ determine which processes you are running.
❑ terminate a process.
❑ suspend a process.
❑ restart a process.
❑ execute a process in the background.
❑ list suspended processes.
❑ change the scheduling priority of a Unix process.

19.2 Checking Process Status—ps Command

Most computers have a single *central processing unit (CPU)*. The CPU, or *processor* for short, is the part of the computer hardware that executes your instructions. The Unix operating system creates *processes* to carry out specific user requests. You can consider a process as any program that is running. A process is also commonly referred to as a *job*. A large number of processes that belong to a group of users can be run on a single processor by time-sharing.

The **ps** command can be used to display a list of your processes that are running. The command **ps** is an abbreviation for "process status." It is helpful to think of a process as a task that you are having the operating system perform. For example, if you decide to run a user-developed program, Unix creates a process to run the program. When you run a Unix command, a process is created to execute the command. Some processes spawn other processes, so the computer's processor is the hardware used for executing instructions, whereas a process is a software entity used for performing a user request. Our goal in this section is to learn the basics of the **ps** command. Understanding this command will help you to gain insight into Unix processes.

If we enter the **ps** command with no arguments, the result is a list of the processes that are currently running on the terminal. For example, on our system entering

```
%ps
```

results in the following display:

```
PID  TTY          TIME CMD
 665 pts/2    00:00:00 bash
1184 pts/2    00:10:07 latex
1187 pts/2    00:00:00 man
1188 pts/2    00:03:01 sh
1189 pts/2    01:43:20 sh
1193 pts/2    00:00:00 less
1202 pts/2    00:00:00 ps
```

This display indicates that there are seven different processes we are running. The processes are for **bash**, **latex**, **man**, **ps**, **less**, and two for **sh**. At this point, it is not particularly important what specific processes we are running, other than to note that the last process listed in the display was the one that carried out the **ps** command for us.

The **ps** command without any arguments displays four different columns of information, as we just saw. The first column (PID) shows the process identification number, the second column (TTY) shows the terminal where the process is running, the third column (TIME) shows how long the process has been running, and the last column (CMD) shows the command name.

In this case, the cumulative execution time of the **latex** process is 10 minutes and 7 seconds, that of the first **sh** process is 3 minutes and 1 second, and that of the second **sh** process is 1 hour, 43 minutes, and 20 seconds. All of the other processes have been running a negligible amount of time. There may be times you run a program that takes a *very* long time to execute. By performing a **ps** command, you can determine if the process executing the program is still running, and if so, how much cumulative CPU time has been devoted to the process running the program.

We executed a second **ps** command on our system. The result this time was

```
 PID TTY          TIME CMD
 665 pts/2    00:00:00 bash
1184 pts/2    00:10:07 latex
1187 pts/2    00:00:00 man
1188 pts/2    00:03:01 sh
1189 pts/2    01:43:20 sh
1193 pts/2    00:00:00 less
1203 pts/2    00:00:00 ps
```

Notice that all the PIDs are the same as before, except for the **ps** command process. Each process is given a unique identification number by the Unix operating system. Notice that the identification numbers assigned by the operating system increase by one. That is, the other process for the **ps** command had a PID of 1202, whereas the new process for the **ps** command has a PID of 1203. By looking at the output for the **ps** command we just provided, you can deduce that between the execution of the **bash** process and the **latex** process over 500 other processes were created. (*Note:* PIDs do not grow forever, they eventually start over. So, a process with a high PID could have actually started before a process with a low PID.)

If you decide to become a Unix guru, you will want to learn more about the **ps** command. You can find out more about **ps** by entering the command

```
%man ps
```

In the next section we show how the **ps** command can be used to help delete an unwanted process.

Exercises

1. How many processes are currently running on your system? What are their PIDs?
2. What are the smallest and largest PIDs you have ever seen?
3. Describe the functions of two interesting flags to the **ps** command.

19.3 Killing a Process—kill Command

As we saw in the last section, the **ps** command lists your Unix processes. Occasionally, there will be a problem with one of your processes. For whatever reason, you will decide you need to terminate an errant process. For example, perhaps you were running a test program and realized that it was in an *infinite loop*, and so would never halt on its own. An infinite loop is a portion of a computer program that cycles endlessly. The **kill** command can be used to terminate such a process.

Suppose you executed the **ps** command resulting in the display shown below.

```
PID TTY            TIME CMD
 665 pts/2     00:00:00 bash
1265 pts/2     00:00:00 latex
1266 pts/2     00:00:00 ps
```

To terminate the **latex** process, you enter the command

```
%kill 1265
```

If the process is successfully halted, you obtain a message such as

```
[1]+ Killed                 latex
```

You can then double-check to make sure that the process was killed by executing another **ps** command.

If you are unable to delete a process using the **kill** command without any flags, you can try to terminate the process using the following command

```
%kill -9 PID
```

where **PID** denotes the identification number of the process you are trying to terminate. The –9 flag tells the system to do its best to terminate the process. That is, **9** is the strongest indicator you can provide to the system to tell it to **kill** the process. It is not the case that the higher the value of the flag to **kill**, the greater the indicator to terminate the process. For example, the standard **kill** command with no arguments is equivalent to **kill –15**. Most users will require the **kill** command only rarely.

The **kill** command has several other optional arguments. To investigate these, you can enter the command

```
%man kill
```

Exercises

1. Print out a list of your currently running processes. Try to terminate one of them using the **kill** command. Were you able to terminate the process? Describe what happened.
2. Describe one additional flag to the **kill** command.

19.4 Suspending Jobs—bg, fg, and jobs Commands

Unix provides several useful commands for *job control*. These are commands that allow you to pause, restart, and stop processes. Most processes that are actively running can be stopped by typing **Control-C**. This command sends an interrupt to a program and usually successfully halts it. If you stop a job in this manner, it cannot be resumed. In the last section we saw how to terminate a process using the **kill** command. As with **Control-C**, a process terminated by the **kill** command cannot be restarted.

There are times you will want to be able to temporarily suspend a process. For example, suppose you are editing an article using **emacs** and need to check your email to retrieve some information that you want to insert into the article. On a windowing system, you would find it easy to open another window. However, if you were not on a windowing system, you would find it convenient if you could suspend **emacs** momentarily, open your mailer, read the related email, close up the mailer, and then restart **emacs** exactly where you left off. Unix provides the **Control-Z** command for such situations. By typing **Control-Z**, you can suspend **emacs**. This has the effect of pausing **emacs**. You are returned to the shell and are free to enter whatever commands you would like from the shell. To return to **emacs** in exactly the position where you left off, you simply enter the command

```
%fg
```

The command **fg** is an abbreviation for "foreground." In using the **Control-Z** and **fg** pair, you can suspend any job temporarily and then restart it. In fact, you can then start another job and suspend it. In other words, multiple jobs can be suspended at once. To get a listing of all of the suspended jobs, you can enter the command

```
%jobs
```

A sample listing of the output from the **jobs** command is provided in Figure 19.1. In this case we see that four jobs have been suspended. Each job is assigned a number by the operating system. The jobs shown in Figure 19.1 are as follows: number 1, **emacs**; number 2, **latex**; number 3, **vi**; and number 4, **cc**. The minus sign (−) denotes the previous job, and the plus sign (+) denotes the current job. The word **Stopped** indicates these jobs have all been paused.

```
[1]     Stopped              emacs agenda.tex
[2]     Stopped              latex main
[3]-    Stopped              vi isis.c
[4]+    Stopped              cc isis.c
```

Figure 19.1—Output from the **jobs** Command

To restart the current job, you can enter the command

```
%fg
```

There will be times you will want to start the jobs in a different order than the reverse of the order you stopped them. For example, suppose you wanted to resume job number 2, the **latex** job, first. This could be accomplished by typing the command

```
%fg %2
```

or

```
%fg latex
```

In general, you can use the **fg** command followed by the percent sign (%) and a job number to restart a job, or you can follow the **fg** command with the name of the job.

We have seen that the concept of bringing a job to the foreground means unsuspending it and running it interactively in the shell. When you suspend a job, you also have the option of running it "behind the scenes." This is known as running a job in the *background*. To run the current suspended job in the background, you can use the command

```
%bg
```

To run a different job in the background, you can specify it to the **bg** command, as we did for the **fg** command.

It is convenient to run a job in the background if the job does not write to standard output nor require any user interaction. You can start a job and run it completely in the background as well. For example, suppose you were recompiling the ISIS (intermediate system, intermediate system) networking protocol that was contained in a file called **isis.c**. If this compilation were going to take a long time, you would not want to tie up your terminal during the entire time the file was compiling. You could continue to work on your terminal if you put this job in the background. You could run the compilation entirely in the background by entering the command

```
%cc isis.c &
```

The ampersand character (**&**) instructs Unix to run this job in the background.

When a job in the background is finished running, you will receive a message on the screen such as

```
[2]    Done              cc isis.c
```

This indicates the job completed its operation in the normal manner.

In summary,

❑ **Control-Z** can be used to suspend a job. This is useful if you want to pause a job while you complete some other task.

❑ **fg** can be used to restart a suspended job in the foreground.

❑ **bg** can be used to run a suspended job in the background.

❑ **jobs** can be used to obtain a listing of suspended jobs.

❑ **&** at the end of a command can be used to run a job in the background.

Exercises

1. Describe two practical situations in which you would want to be able to suspend and restart a job.
2. Is there any reason why you would not want to suspend a large number of jobs?
3. Are there any flags to the **fg** and **bg** commands? If so, describe them.
4. What are the characteristics of a job that you would want to start in the background?
5. Describe two interesting flags to the **jobs** command.
6. What happens if you have two suspended jobs with the same name, and you try to start one of them using the **fg** command with the jobs' name?
7. Compare and contrast the **jobs** and **ps** commands.
8. Would you ever want to **kill** a suspended job? If so, describe an example of when.

19.5 Lowering the Priority of a Job—nice Command

Unix provides the **nice** command to allow you to alter the scheduling priority of a job. (*Note:* On some systems you will not be able to increase the priority of your jobs. This privilege may be afforded only to the system administrator.) If you are working on a time-sharing system and have a large job to run whose completion is not time critical, you can enter the command

```
%nice 19 jobname
```

where **jobname** is the name of your job. The 19 indicates the job should be given lowest priority in terms of using CPU cycles. On the other hand, if you have a job that is time critical, the command

```
%nice -20 jobname
```

tells the system to give **jobname** the highest priority possible. Remember, on some systems you will not be able to increase the priority of your job. A typical job has a priority value of 0. The priority numbers vary from system to system, so you will want to consult the **nice man page** on your system.

The name **nice** comes from the fact that you are a nice person if you assign your own job a lower priority. On a time-sharing system, this means you are freeing up some CPU time for other users.

Exercises

1. Can you decrease the priority of one of your own jobs on your system?
2. Can you increase the priority of one of your own jobs on your system?
3. If you **nice** a job and give it lowest priority, is the job guaranteed to complete at some future time? Explain.
4. What number represents the highest scheduling priority for the **nice** command on your system? What number represents the lowest scheduling priority?

THE INTERNET
AND THE WORLD
WIDE WEB

HISTORY OF THE INTERNET

chapter **20**

20.1 Introduction

The Internet is the earth's global system of networked computers coupled with their users and the data that they manipulate. This chapter provides a brief history of the Internet. The Internet provides the infrastructure that allows us to communicate via email and to surf the World Wide Web. The history of the Internet is best explained by considering key events in its development. In this chapter we discuss a number of events that were important to the beginnings of the Internet and to its continued growth and success. Some of these technological breakthroughs required great innovation, but others are included simply because they are interesting tidbits. For each item mentioned we provide a brief synopsis. You will probably find the history of the Internet fascinating both for itself and as a case study of technological innovation. The best place to learn more about the history of the Internet is on the World Wide Web.

20.2 General Comments on the Internet: 1960s

Essential to the early Internet concept was the notion of *packet switching*, where data to be transmitted is divided into small packets of information and labeled to identify the sender and recipient. These packets of information are sent over a network and then reassembled at their destination. If any packet does not arrive or is not intact at its destination, the original sender is requested to re-send the packet. Prior to packet switching, the less efficient *circuit switching* method of data transmission was used. In the early 1960s several papers on packet-switching theory were written that laid the groundwork for computer networking as it exists today.

20.2.1 ARPANET, 1969

In 1969 Bolt, Beranek, and Newman, Inc., (BBN) designed a network called the *Advanced Research Projects Agency Network* (ARPANET) for the United States Department of Defense. The military had created ARPA to enable researchers to share "super-computing" power. Throughout the years, ARPA has flip-flopped between being called ARPA and DARPA (*Defense Advanced Research Projects Agency*). As of 1997, the name is DARPA. It was rumored that the military developed the ARPANET in response to the threat of a nuclear attack destroying the country's communication system.

Initially, only four nodes (or *hosts*) comprised the ARPANET. They were located at the University of California at Los Angeles, the University of California at Santa Barbara, the University of Utah, and the Stanford Research Institute. The ARPANET would later become known as the Internet.

Exercises

1. Select one of the topics highlighted in this section that interests you. Research your topic and write a 1–2 page paper describing your findings. Make sure to cite your references.
2. Locate information about two other interesting Internet-related events that happened during this decade. Write a paragraph or two describing each of them. Make sure to cite your references.

20.3 General Comments on the Internet: 1970s

In this decade the ARPANET was used primarily by the military, some larger companies like IBM, and universities (for email). People were not yet connected in their homes, and very few people were online at work.

The use of local area networks (LANs) became more prevalent during the 1970s. Also during the 1970s the idea of an *open architecture* was promoted—that networks making up the ARPANET could be of any design. In later years, this concept had a tremendous impact on the growth of the ARPANET.

20.3.1 Twenty Plus Nodes, 1972

The ARPANET went international with nodes in Europe at the University College in London, England, and the Royal Radar Establishment in Norway. The number of nodes on the network was up to 23, and the trend would now be for that number to double every year. Ray Tomlinson, who worked at BBN, invented email as a method of exchanging messages over a network.

20.3.2 UUCP, 1976

AT&T Bell Labs developed *Unix to Unix CoPy* (UUCP). In 1977 UUCP was distributed with Unix.

20.3.3 USENET, 1979

User Network (USENET) was started by using UUCP to connect Duke University and the University of North Carolina at Chapel Hill. *Newsgroups* emerged from this early development.

Exercises

1. Select one of the topics highlighted in this section that interests you. Research your topic and write a 1–2 page paper describing your findings. Make sure to cite your references.
2. Locate information about two other interesting Internet-related events that happened during this decade. Write a paragraph or two describing each of them. Make sure to cite your references.

20.4 General Comments on the Internet: 1980s

Transmission Control Protocol/Internet Protocol (TCP/IP), a set of rules governing how networks making up the ARPANET communicate, was established. In this decade, the term "Internet" was used to describe the ARPANET for the first time. Security became a concern during the 1980s, as viruses appeared and electronic break-ins occurred.

The 1980s saw the Internet grow beyond being predominately research-oriented to including business applications and supporting a wide range of users.

As the Internet became larger and larger, the *domain name system* (DNS) was developed to allow the network to expand more easily by assigning names to host computers in a distributed fashion.

20.4.1 CSNET, 1980

The *Computer Science Network* (CSNET) connected all computer science departments in the United States. Computer science departments were relatively new, and only a limited number existed in 1980. CSNET joined the ARPANET in 1981.

20.4.2 BITNET, 1981

Because It's Time Network (BITNET) was formed at the City University of New York and connected to Yale University. Many *mailing lists* originated with BITNET. Today mailing lists are more popular than ever.

20.4.3   Transmission Control Protocol/Internet Protocol, 1983

The United States Defense Communications Agency required that TCP/IP be used for all ARPANET hosts. Since TCP/IP was distributed at no charge, the Internet became what is called an *open system*. This allowed the Internet to grow quickly, as all connected computers were now "speaking the same language." No central administration was necessary to run the network.

20.4.4   NSFNET, 1985

The *National Science Foundation Network* (NSFNET) was formed in order to connect the *National Science Foundation's* (NSF's) five super-computing centers. This allowed researchers to access the most powerful computers in the world at a time when large, powerful, and expensive computers were a rarity and generally inaccessible.

20.4.5   Internet Worm, 1988

The *Internet Worm* (created by Robert Morris while he was a computer science graduate student at Cornell University) was released. This virus infected 10% of all Internet hosts. *Internet Relay Chat* (IRC) was written by Jarkko Oikarinen. Today *chat rooms* are extremely popular.

20.4.6   NSF Assumes Control of ARPANET, 1989

The National Science Foundation took over control of the ARPANET in 1989. This changeover went unnoticed by nearly all users. The number of hosts on the Internet exceeded the 100,000 mark.

Exercises

1. Select one of the topics highlighted in this section that interests you. Research your topic and write a 1–2 page paper describing your findings. Make sure to cite your references.
2. Locate information about two other interesting Internet-related events that happened during this decade. Write a paragraph or two describing each of them. Make sure to cite your references.

20.5 General Comments on the Internet: 1990s

During the 1990s, many commercial organizations started getting online. This stimulated the growth of the Internet like never before. URLs appeared in television advertisements, and for the first time the general public and even children went online in significant numbers.

Graphical browsing tools were developed and the programming language HTML allowed users all over the world to publish on the World Wide Web. Millions of people went online to work, shop, bank, and be entertained. The Internet played a much more significant role in society as many nontechnical users from all walks of life got involved with computers. Computer literacy and Internet courses sprang up all over the country.

20.5.1   Gopher, 1991

Gopher was developed at the University of Minnesota, whose sports team's mascot is the the Golden Gopher. Gopher allowed you to "go for" or fetch files on the Internet using a menu-based system. Many gophers sprang up all over the country, and all types of information could be located on gopher servers. Gopher is still available today and accessible through Web browsers, but its popularity has faded, and for the most part it is only of historical interest.

20.5.2   World Wide Web, 1991

The *World Wide Web* was created by Tim Berners-Lee at CERN (a French acronym for the European Laboratory for Particle Physics) as a simple way to publish information and make it available on the Internet.

20.5.3   WWW Available to Public, 1992

The interesting nature of the Web caused it to spread, and it became available to the public in 1992. Those who first used the system were immediately impressed.

20.5.4   Mosaic, 1993

Mosaic, a graphical browser for the Web, was released by Marc Andreessen and several other graduate students at the University of Illinois, location of one of NSF's super-computing centers. Mosaic was first released under X Window System and graphical Unix. It seemed that each person who used the system loved it and told five friends. Mosaic's use spread rapidly.

20.5.5   Netscape Communications, 1994

Netscape Communications, formed by Marc Andreessen and Jim Clark, released *Netscape Navigator.* This Web browser captured the imagination of everyone who used it. The number of users of this piece of software grew at a phenomenal rate. Netscape made (and still makes) its money largely through displaying advertisements on its Web pages.

20.5.6   Yahoo!, 1994

Stanford graduate students David Filo and Jerry Yang developed their now world-famous Internet search engine and directory called *Yahoo!.* This was the first Internet search tool with a friendly user-interface that became popular world-wide.[1]

20.5.7   Java, 1995

The Internet programming environment, *Java*, was released by Sun Microsystems. This language, originally called Oak, allowed programmers to develop more interactive Web pages.

20.5.8   Microsoft Discovers the Internet, 1995

The software giant Microsoft committed many of its resources to developing its browser (Internet Explorer) and Internet applications.

20.5.9   Internet Courses Offered in Colleges, 1995

Some of the first courses about the Internet were given in 1995. Course development was difficult because of the rapidly changing software.

20.5.10   Internet Telephones, 1996

A number of people began to make their telephone calls over the Internet (with voice communications) rather than paying expensive long-distance rates.

20.5.11   Over 25,000,000 Nodes, 1997

The Internet continued to grow at an astounding rate, and over 25 million host computers were connected.

---

1. Interestingly, this morning's news (June 9, 2000) indicated Yahoo! was the most frequently hit Web site in the world this past week.

20.5.12   Netscape Releases Source Code, 1998

Netscape Communications released the source code for its popular Web browser. As a result, it was easier for developers to create software to interact with it.

20.5.13   NASDAQ Soars over 5,000, 1999

With the explosion of the popularity of the Internet, the so-called **.com** (dot-com) companies drove the NASDAQ stock index to all-time record highs. Initial public stock offerings of **.com**'s sometimes went as high as 10 times the initial asking price in a single day. Many investors gambled on the technology sector of the economy.

20.5.14   Over 55,000,000 Nodes, 1999

The Internet continued to grow, with its size more than doubling in less than two years. There were now over 55 million host computers connected.

Exercises

1. Select one of the topics highlighted in this section that interests you. Research your topic and write a 1–2 page paper describing your findings. Make sure to cite your references.
2. Locate information about two other interesting Internet-related events that happened during this decade. Write a paragraph or two describing each of them. Make sure to cite your references.

20.6   General Comments on the Internet: 2000s

During the early 2000s the Internet continues to grow at an alarming rate. Hundreds of millions of people are online daily to work, shop, trade stocks, and be entertained. The Internet has become a social outlet for many people. Large numbers of people spend many hours per day communicating with other users around the world. Virtually all advertising includes URLs in their campaigns. Many **.com** companies have developed and thrive. A vast number of workers have been and continue to be retrained to enter the high-tech field.

20.6.1   Cisco Becomes World's Largest Company, 2000

Cisco Systems, the world's leading producer of the hardware that powers the Internet, passed Microsoft as the world's largest company in terms of market capitalization.

20.6.2   I Love You Virus, 2000

The "I Love You Virus" spread from the Philippines and infected millions of computers worldwide, causing billions of dollars in damage. The virus was transmitted by PC-based email programs but did not infect Unix systems.

20.6.3   Breakup of Microsoft, 2000?

The United States Justice Department brought Microsoft to trial and ruled that the company be divided into two separate parts due to its monopoly status and unscrupulous business practices, which were deemed detrimental to consumers. Microsoft has appealed. As of this writing, the outcome is pending.

20.6.4   Unix/Linux Popularity Increases, 2001

Many developers continue to use Unix platforms and the number of Unix/Linux users continues to grow quickly.

Exercises

1. Select one of the topics highlighted in this section that interests you. Research your topic and write a 1–2 page paper describing your findings. Make sure to cite your references.
2. Locate information about two other interesting Internet-related events that happened during this decade. Write a paragraph or two describing each of them. Make sure to cite your references.

HTML AND WEB PAGES

21.1 Introduction

Most Web servers are Unix-based. With the ever-increasing interest in the Internet and the World Wide Web, it is important for every Unix user to be able to create and install Web pages on a Unix system. In this chapter, you will become acquainted with the interplay between a number of aspects of the World Wide Web and the Unix operating system. You will also learn about the language of the World Wide Web, namely *Hypertext Markup Language* (*HTML*). HTML is the programming language that nearly all Web pages are developed in.

The goals of this chapter are to

- ❑ explain the concept of *Uniform Resource Locator* (*URL*).
- ❑ provide you with an introduction to HTML.
- ❑ describe how to install Web pages on a Unix-based Web server.
- ❑ teach you the basic elements of HTML.
- ❑ illustrate how to copy and display an image on a Web page.

21.2 Uniform Resource Locator

The address of a Web page is called its *Uniform Resource Locator* or *URL* (pronounced "you-are-ell") for short. This address is used in conjunction with a Web browser, such as Netscape Communicator or Internet Explorer, to access a specific Web page. While browsing the Web, the URL of the current Web page you are viewing will typically be displayed in an area near the top of the screen in the browser window. The area where URLs are displayed by Netscape Communicator is called the "location area," whereas this area is called the "address area" by Internet Explorer. Following Netscape's convention, we will refer to this area as the location area. URLs are the Web-page addresses that you often see displayed in advertisements.

Typing a URL in the location area and pressing the **Enter** key will cause the browser to attempt to retrieve that Web page. If the browser is successful in finding the Web page, the browser will display it. This explanation does not, however, convey any of the details as to how the browser is able to locate a Web page from its URL. To go from a URL to having the Web page displayed, the browser needs to be able to answer questions such as

1. **How** can the Web page be accessed?
2. **Where** can the Web page be found?
3. **What** is the file name corresponding to the Web page?

The URL was designed to incorporate sufficient information to resolve these questions. It is therefore natural that the URL has three parts. We can view the format of a URL as follows:

```
how://where/what
```

The `://` and `/` serve as delimiters to separate the parts of a URL. To make our description more concrete, it is helpful to consider a specific URL:

```
http://www.fbeedle.com/history.html
```

We will split this URL into its three parts and elaborate on each in turn.

❑ **http**—defines the *protocol* or *scheme* by which to access the page. In this case the protocol is *Hypertext Transfer Protocol*. This protocol is the set of rules by which an HTML document is transferred over the Internet.

❑ **www.fbeedle.com**—identifies the domain name of the computer where the Web page resides. The computer is a Web server capable of satisfying user requests for Web pages. The Web server satisfies clients requests by supplying desired Web pages. The name **www.fbeedle.com** tells the browser on which computer to find the Web page. In this case we can deduce that the computer is likely to be located in the state of Oregon, where Franklin, Beedle & Associates, Inc., is headquartered.

❑ **history.html**—provides the local name (usually a file name including the path to the file) uniquely identifying the specific Web page. If no name is specified, the Web server where the page is located may supply a default file. On many systems, the default file is called **index.html** or **index.htm**. In this case, the file to retrieve is **history.html**, which contains a description of the company's evolution. At this point it would be a good idea to load this Web page into your browser window so you can carry out the process we have just described.

This example demonstrates that the URL consists of a protocol, a Web server's domain name, and a file name. Each part is important, and each part needs to be typed accurately.

Barring any problems, entering a URL in the location area of the browser will bring up the designated Web page. If the Web page has moved to another machine or has been deleted, if you type an invalid URL, or if the server you are trying to access is unavailable, an error message will be displayed. Another way to retrieve a Web page is to mouse over and click on a *hyperlink* in a Web page that is currently being displayed. A hyperlink is a string of text or a graphic that points to another Web page. Later in this chapter we will describe how to code hyperlinks into your Web pages.

Exercises

1. Compare and contrast an email address and a URL.
2. Provide valid URLs for five Web pages. Are there any similarities among them? Any obvious differences?

21.3 Rudiments of HTML Programming

Now that you know how to retrieve a Web page, we consider the task of constructing Web pages. *Hypertext Markup Language* (*HTML*) is a programming language that is used to code Web pages. The quickest way to get a handle on HTML is to look at some sample code. In Figure 21.1 we depict a complete HTML program. The output of this program on the Netscape browser is shown in Figure 21.2. You should compare the two figures to see what effects the various snippets of HTML code produce on a Web page. We will go over the different HTML elements in turn, but first a few general remarks are in order.

```
<HTML>
<!-- Updated by Killface on June 3, 2000 -->
<HEAD>
<TITLE>In-line/On-line: Killface's Page </TITLE>
</HEAD>
<BODY BGCOLOR = "white">

<H2 ALIGN = "center">Killface's Page</H2>

<CENTER>
<IMG SRC = "cat.jpg" ALT = "Killface" HEIGHT = "153" WIDTH = "182">
</CENTER>

<HR>
<CENTER>
Thanks for stopping by. <BR>
Yeah, yeah, I know I need to update my photo.<BR>
The good news is I am doing well in Savannah.<BR>
I am still living with <STRONG>Dottie</STRONG> and
<STRONG>Julie</STRONG><BR>
(two German shepherds).
</CENTER>
<HR>

<H5 ALIGN = "center">
```

```
<A HREF = "http://www.cs.armstrong.edu/greenlaw">Ray's Page</A>
</H5>

</BODY>
</HTML>
```

Figure 21.1—HTML Code for Killface's Home Page

Figure 21.2—Killface's Web Page Rendered by Netscape

There are several important things to notice about the HTML program displayed in Figure 21.1. The first is that there are lots of capital letters expressed between opening and closing < (less than) and > (greater than) signs. These items are called HTML tags. HTML consists of many tags. To become proficient in HTML, you will need to learn about 30 of these well. In general, an HTML command has the following syntax:

```
<TAG A1 = "V1" A2 = "V2">item to be formatted</TAG>
```

Here the word **TAG** represents any HTML tag. Many HTML tags have *attributes*. In the abstract form presented above, we have listed two attributes called **A1** and **A2**. The number of attributes varies from tag to tag. As with Unix command flags, some attributes are optional, whereas others are required. For any particular attribute, you typically have a choice of several values. The values an attribute can take are denoted **V1** and **V2** in the expression we gave. Note the placement of the equals sign (=). This is programming syntax for assigning **A1** the value **V1**. Also notice that we put double quotes around **V1** and **V2**.

For all HTML attributes, it is good practice to quote their values in this manner. However, if the value being assigned is a number, it is sometimes not necessary to explicitly quote it. Further observe that we have not left any *white space* (meaning any blank spaces) between the item to be formatted and the surrounding tags. This is a good habit to get into, as otherwise the items you format may be displayed with extra unwanted spaces. This is particularly true in the case of hyperlinks.

TAG has a corresponding *ending* tag (also referred to as a *closing* tag), namely **</TAG>**. The ending tag is the same as the starting tag except for the "**/**" character. Not every tag has an ending tag, but most do. There are some ending tags that are commonly omitted. Ending tags can always be identified by the forward slash preceding the tag name. If you keep these basic rules of syntax in mind while learning new HTML tags, you will have an easier time coding properly.

Now we return to the HTML code depicted in Figure 21.1. We will describe this code from top to bottom. This example uses over 10 of the most important HTML tags. One of the first tags used is the *comment* tag. The beginning and ending pairs for this tag are

```
<!-- and -->
```

In computer science it is always a good idea to comment your code for future reference. Comments are not displayed when the browser renders the code. In this example, Killface has left a date indicating when she last updated her page.

All HTML documents are required to begin and end with the **<HTML>** and **</HTML>** tags. In addition, all HTML documents consist of two main parts: a head and a body. These are specified by the **HEAD** and **BODY** tags. The title of a Web page, which is displayed at the top of the Web page by the browser, is specified within the head of the document inside the **TITLE** tag. It is important to pick a descriptive title for the Web page, as the information contained in the title is usually the information that will be stored along with a *bookmark* for the Web page. A bookmark is simply a URL that you tell the Web browser to save so you can return to a given Web page later. In our example, Killface has chosen a title of

```
In-line/On-line: Killface's Page
```

Following the head of an HTML document is its body. A number of features relating to the display of the Web page can be specified in the **BODY** tag. In this case, Killface has used the **BGCOLOR** attribute of the **BODY** tag to set the background color of the Web page to white. Other background colors may be specified in a similar manner.

Killface next makes use of the **H2** tag to display a large heading on her page. There are seven different sizes for the heading tags: **H1** (the largest) down to **H7** (the smallest). These tags can take, among other attributes, the **ALIGN** attribute. In this case Killface has decided to center her heading by assigning the value "center" to the **ALIGN** attribute. Following this heading is an image of Killface. In Section 21.5 we will go over the code for displaying images on a Web page. Killface has centered the image by enclosing the **IMG** tag inside **CENTER** tags. This centering code illustrates that for various HTML elements there may be different ways to accomplish the same results.

After her picture, a horizontal line is drawn across the browser window by using the **HR** tag. This is followed by some text in the form of a message to readers of the Web page. The browser displays straight text on the screen as it appears in your file. In our example, two additional tags are used before another horizontal line is drawn across the screen. The **BR** indicates a *line break*. That is, the start of a new line. The **STRONG** tag is used on the dogs' names. This displays their names in a dark bold font. The **STRONG** tag should be used on text that needs to be stressed heavily.

Following the second horizontal line is another centered heading. This heading consists of a hyperlink. A hyperlink is specified using the anchor tag. This tag is represented by the pair **<A>** and **</A>**. The text or image between these tags is the clickable item displayed by the browser. The URL that is retrieved when the user clicks on this item is specified in the **HREF** attribute of the anchor tag. In this case, the URL loaded when a user clicks on the hyperlink "Ray's Page" is

```
http://www.cs.armstrong.edu/greenlaw
```

The last part of Killface's Web page consists of the ending tags for the **BODY** and **HTML** tags.

It is important to notice the block structure of the code and how many tags are nested inside of others. The nesting order of tags is important. You should think of them as being peeled off in layers. Thus, it is critical that the last **</HTML>** tag come after the ending **</BODY>** tag. This preserves the nesting allowed by HTML. Notice that Killface wrote her code so that it is easy to read. This style will make it easier for her to maintain the code in the future.

In this section we have provided only an introduction to HTML. You can learn more about HTML by pursuing the references listed at the back of this book, or by searching on the Web for the acronym "HTML." You can also look at the source code for each Web page that you can display in your browser. For example, with Netscape browsers, this can be done by going to the **View** pulldown menu and selecting the **Page Source** option. By studying other people's code, you can learn many additional features of HTML. Remember not to copy another user's code, as everything on the Web is copyrighted by default.

Exercises

1. Locate the source code for Killface's Web page online. Is it actually the same as the source code displayed in this book? If not, what are the differences?
2. Describe the syntax and semantics of three useful HTML tags that were not mentioned in this chapter.
3. Print out the source code for an interesting Web page. Circle all of the HTML tags and underline all of the HTML attributes.
4. Report the URLs of two Web sites useful for learning about HTML.

21.4 Procedure for Web Page Setup

In this section we describe the usual scenario you would go through in setting up your Web page on a Unix-based Web server. Typically, the directory where Web pages are placed on Unix systems is called **public_html**. That is, the word **public**, followed by an underscore, followed by the word **html**. This directory and its subdirectories are the only places you will able to put your Web pages in order for others to access and view them on the Web.

The most important file contained in the **public_html** directory is **index.html**. This is the default file that most Web servers will return if a user requests a Web site without specifying a file name. For example, suppose your userid is **beth** and your Web pages are served from a machine called **pubpages.umontana.edu**. If a user requests the URL

```
http://pubpages.umontana.edu/~beth
```

Beth's **index.html** file will be served. It is a good idea to create **index.html** files in each subdirectory you create for Web pages. This way there will be a default Web page served up when the user does not request a specific page. The default page should contain helpful information for a user who is trying to navigate the site for the first time.

Once you have learned the basics of HTML and URLs, you can begin creating your own Web pages. You will learn HTML very quickly when you are actually developing your own files. The procedure for setting up Web pages involves several steps that you need to follow in order.[1] We describe each step and also give a brief explanation of what the step accomplishes.

---

1. Technically, there are different sequences of commands that would work, but some steps do depend on others.

Procedure for Installing Web Pages

1. **%cd**—change to your home directory.
2. **%chmod og+x ~**—set the permissions on your home directory to be world executable.
3. **%mkdir public_html**—create the directory **public_html**, underneath which all your Web pages will reside.
4. **%chmod og+x public_html**—set the permissions on the directory **public_html** to be world executable. This will allow all users on the Internet[2] to access your **public_html** directory so that they can display your Web pages.
5. **%cd public_html**—change directories to the **public_html** directory.
6. **%edit index.html**—here **edit** stands for your favorite text editor, for example, **pico**, **emacs**, or **vi**. The idea is to create a file called **index.html** and include the appropriate HTML code in it.
7. **%chmod og+r index.html**—set the permissions on the file **index.html** to be world readable. This will allow all users on the Internet to display the file **index.html**.

Once you carry out this sequence of steps, you should be able to view the file **index.html** using your favorite Web browser. Go ahead and execute these steps, and then start up your browser. Enter the URL for your Web page in the location area of the browser. For example, if your Web server is **www.crokie.com** and your account name is **harvey**, your URL would be

```
www.crokie.com/~harvey/index.html
```

Note that it is usually not necessary to type in the **public_html** portion of the pathname.

If your page loads, congratulations; you just published your first Web page. If your page does not load, you need to troubleshoot the situation to find out what went wrong.

Your first option is simply to review all of the steps carefully. Did you execute all steps exactly as outlined without any typos creeping in? If not, you may need to repeat some of the steps. If the careful review of the steps allowed you to catch the problem, great; if not, some techniques follow for determining what the problem is.

The first thing to do is check that you have typed in your URL accurately. Double and even triple check the URL. Make sure that you used the underscore (_) character in the file name **public_html** and not accidently the dash (–). Also, verify that the directory **public_html** was created properly and is in your home directory. Then check that the file **index.html** was created properly and is a

---

2. Assuming there are no *firewalls* preventing access to it.

file contained in the directory **public_html**. If you do not find any problems with the URL, or the name and locations of the **public_html** directory and the **index.html** file, then it is likely you have a problem with the protections being set properly.

If you got an error indicating the protections are not set properly, you have a problem that needs correcting. For example, you may see a message such as

```
File not found
```

There were three steps in which you set permissions. To check the permissions on the file **index.html**, you can execute the command

```
%ls -l index.html
```

The file should be world readable. You should see permissions that display as

```
-rwxr--r--
```

If these are not the permissions that are displayed, you will need to execute the command

```
%chmod og+r index.html
```

Go ahead and verify that the permissions are now set correctly by doing an

```
%ls -l index.html
```

Now try reloading the Web page. If it does not load properly, then continue with the troubleshooting steps that follow. If the permissions were set correctly on the file **index.html**, then this is not the problem. Perhaps you did not set the permissions correctly on the **public_html** directory. You can check your current working directory by typing

```
%pwd
```

If you are not in your home directory, you can type

```
%cd
```

to return to your home directory. By executing the command

```
%ls -ld public_html
```

you can check the permissions on your **public_html** directory. You should see

```
drwx--x--x
```

If the display looks different from this, you need to make the directory **public_html** world executable. This can be accomplished by executing the command

```
%chmod og+x public_html
```

Go ahead and verify that the permissions are now set correctly by performing the command

```
%ls -ld public_html
```

Now try reloading the Web page. If it does not load properly, then continue with the troubleshooting steps that follow. If the permissions were set correctly on the directory **public_html**, then this is not the problem. Perhaps you did not set the permissions correctly on your home directory. You can check the permissions on your home directory by doing a

```
%ls -ld hdpathname
```

where **hdpathname** is the pathname of the directory that your home directory sits in. This directory can easily be determined by using the **pwd** command. You should see the permissions

```
drwx--x--x
```

on your home directory. If the display looks different from this, you need to make your home directory world executable. This can be accomplished by executing the command

```
%chmod og+x ~
```

Go ahead and verify that the permissions are now set correctly by performing the

```
%ls -l hdpathname
```

Now try reloading the Web page. If the page does not load properly, you may want to review the procedure and the troubleshooting steps again. If all else fails, you should consult a local Unix guru. If you have been struggling with this, you will be amazed at how quickly a Unix guru can pinpoint the exact problem you are having. Make sure to note what was going wrong and how the problem was corrected.

As you install new files and subdirectories, you will need to set the permissions on these as you did on the file **index.html** and the directory **public_html**. For example, if you create a file called **mydog.html** in your **public_html** directory, you will need to make it world readable so that other users on the Internet can view it. This is done by executing the command

```
%chmod og+r mydog.html
```

from your **public_html** directory.

As you add more and more Web material, you will find that to stay organized, you need to create some subdirectories of your **public_html** directory. For example, you may decide to create a **GIF** directory to hold all your files that have a **gif** file extension. To create such a directory, simply **cd** to the directory **public_html** and execute the command

```
%mkdir GIF
```

Now you need to make the **GIF** directory world-executable and readable. To do this, enter the command

```
%chmod og+rx GIF
```

Next you can **cd** to the **GIF** directory. As you add files to this directory, make them world readable so they will be accessible to everyone on the Internet.

Exercises

1. Create a file in your home directory called **index.html** and insert some basic HTML code into it. Carry out the procedure described in this chapter for installing Web pages. Bring up your browser and display the Web page on the screen. What is your URL? Estimate how many seconds it took for your browser to display your Web page.
2. Create a second Web page and add hyperlinks between it and your **index.html** file. Give the hyperlinks the labels **home** and **out there**.
3. Design a Web page and add a hyperlink to itself. What happens when you try to click on this hyperlink?

21.5 Copying and Displaying a Graphic

The World Wide Web's popularity has stemmed largely from the fact that it allows for the transmission of visually appealing images. Furthermore, text and images, as well as sound and video, can be combined to create an environment that is more interesting than just plain text. In this section we describe how to copy a graphic from the Web, and then how to display a graphic on a Web page. By tastefully adding images to your Web pages, you can create an interesting and more informative display.

21.5.1 Copying a Graphic from the Web

There are numerous free *clip art collections* available on the Web. These are Web sites that provide free graphics. You can find such a collection by entering a query of "clip art" to any search engine. Make sure to provide a citation for any graphics you copy from the Web and make sure the images you are copying are free; that is, the images are not copyrighted and are in the public domain.

Obtaining a graphic located on another Web page usually involves making a copy of the **.gif** or **.jpg** image file and saving it to one of your world-executable directories. *GIF* stands for *Graphic Interchange Format* and *JPG* stands for *Joint Photographic Expert Group.* GIF and JPG are the two primary image formats used for Web graphics. Once you have saved a **GIF** or **JPG** image, the file needs to be made world-readable in order to be displayed. We describe the procedure to save an image file from a Netscape point of view; that is, assuming the use of a Netscape browser.

One way to copy the image file is to use the **View** menu button to look at the HTML source code of the document. In the source code you will be able to find the URL of the desired image in the **IMG** tag. Typing this URL into the location field and pressing **Enter** will display that image by itself in the document area of the browser window. In order for this to work, the URL needs to be an *absolute URL* consisting of a full pathname, rather than a *relative URL.* A relative URL is a relative pathname for specifying a file within HTML code. If a relative URL is specified in the **SRC** attribute, you will need to "construct" the appropriate absolute URL. (You will need to check if the **BASE** tag is used in the heading of the document when constructing the absolute URL.) Once the image is displayed in the document area, use the **File** menu button to select the **Save As** option. A copy of the image file will be saved in your directory after responding to the prompt to enter a file name.

A second, more direct way to copy an image is to click the right mouse button while mousing over an image. A pop-up menu will appear that offers **View Image**, **Save Image As**, and **Copy Image Location** options. These options may vary depending on the version of the browser you are using. If you select **View Image**, the image will be displayed by itself in the browser window and, as before, you can use the **File** button to select the **Save As** option. Selecting the **Save Image As** is the quickest way to save the image, as it eliminates the need to open the image separately. As in the **Save As** case, you will be prompted for a file name that you would like to call your copy of the image. The **Copy Image Location** option simply copies the URL to a clipboard. You would need to open the image in the browser window if you wanted to save it.

In summary, to copy an image using the Netscape browser:
1. Display the Web page containing the desired image.
2. Mouse over the image and hold down the right mouse button.
3. Select the **Save Image As** option from the pop-up menu.
4. When prompted for a file name, enter the name that you would like your copy of the image file to be called.

Other browsers have similar capabilities. The pull-down menus may have a slightly different look, and menu buttons may have other names, but they all offer the same functionality.

If you save or scan in an image at one computer and then need to move it over to another machine in order to display it on your Web page, you can move it using **ftp** (described in Chapter 22). You should make sure to set the transfer mode to binary when moving images.

21.5.2 Image Tag

You now know how to copy an image to your file space. Once you move the graphic into the appropriate directory and set the permissions, you are ready to display it. The image tag, <IMG>, is used for including images in HTML documents. Here is an example use of the tag:

```
<IMG   SRC = "cat.gif"
       ALT = "Killface's picture"
       HEIGHT = "100"
       WIDTH = "90">
```

We explain the meaning of this code, look at a number of other attributes of the image tag, and discuss some style issues about images in what follows. For a more comprehensive treatment of images and graphics, the reader can pursue the references provided at the end of the book.

The most important attribute of the image tag is **SRC**. This is used to specify the image that is to be displayed. Any type of image can be specified using either a relative or an absolute URL. Relative URLs are relative to the document in which the image appears. To include the image **cat.gif** in a file located in the same directory, you could use the following HTML code snippet:

```
<IMG SRC = "cat.gif">
```

This declaration is the minimum amount of code you can use to include an image.

When a browser retrieves a Web page, it does not automatically get the images that go along with the page. The images each must be retrieved separately. What does this mean in terms of rendering a document on the screen? In order to render a document onscreen, the browser must know what the sizes of the images are. Image dimensions are expressed in *pixels* (picture elements). The browser can obtain these sizes by having you explicitly code them in (as we recommend) or by reading them when the image is brought over. The latter case takes longer because the browser needs to do more work and wait for the dimensions of each image, so a Web page will render more quickly if you include its images' sizes using the **HEIGHT** and **WIDTH** attributes of the image tag.

Suppose the picture **cat.gif** is 100 pixels high and 90 pixels wide. The following code can be used to include it and specify its dimensions to the browser:

```
<IMG   SRC = "cat.gif"
       HEIGHT = "100"
       WIDTH = "90">
```

The order in which you specify the **HEIGHT** and **WIDTH** attributes is not significant. On the other hand, a browser will list image dimensions as $x \times y$, where x is the **WIDTH** of the image and y is the **HEIGHT**. When a browser parses this piece of HTML code, it can determine how much space to leave for the image. Thus, the surrounding text can be rendered immediately. The browser does not have to wait until the image itself arrives. This is why you often see all of the text in a page loaded long before all of the images are rendered.

How can you determine the size of an image? Most browsers have a "Document Info" menu item where you can find the dimensions of an image (in pixels). Of course, if you create the image yourself, you can record its size then.

The **HEIGHT** and **WIDTH** attributes can also take percentages as values. They can be used to scale an image relative to the size of the browser's window. For example, the following code

```
<IMG   SRC = "cat.gif"
       HEIGHT = "50%"
       WIDTH = "50%">
```

produces a version of **cat.gif** that occupies 50% of the browser's window in each dimension. You can create some interesting scaling effects by using percentages. When you scale an image downward, you do not reduce the amount of disk space required to store the image. Therefore, it is not possible to create a reduced size *thumbnail sketch* by using percentage values to the **HEIGHT** and **WIDTH** attributes.

The image tag has another interesting attribute known as **ALT**, which is short for "alternative." The value of **ALT** is a string of text which usually describes the image in words. In our **cat.gif** example, we used the words **Killface's Picture** as a value of the **ALT** attribute. This is because **cat.gif** contains a picture of Killface the cat. If a browser has images turned off or is text-only, the words in the **ALT** attribute will be displayed onscreen where the image would have been. Obviously, there will not be an exact match in terms of the size of the image and the text replacing it. Most Web authors do not worry about this detail, as most of their effort goes into making the pages look good with the images included.

The text in an **ALT** attribute is usually displayed in the form of a *tooltip* when the user mouses over the image. This is usually a light-colored box that is just large enough for the text to fit in. For Web pages that contain a lot of images, the tooltips can become a distraction. This has prompted some users to stop including **ALT**s. Remember, the purpose of including **ALT**s is to serve those users who are unable to display images or who are using text-based browsers. In such cases, the text of an **ALT** can provide the reader with some continuity. In addition, the words in the **ALT** are displayed in place of the image while the user is loading a Web page. This gives the user a preview of what is to follow.

Remember to set the protections on image files similar to what you needed to do for displaying HTML files. You should now have enough background to display images on your Web pages.

Exercises

1. Give the URLs for three Web sites that provide free clip art.
2. Copy a free **GIF** image from the Web using the techniques described in this chapter. Name the file the image is stored in **exercise.gif**. Display the image on your Web page.
3. Research the **GIF** and **JPG** image formats on the Web. Write a one-page summary comparing and contrasting the two formats.
4. Code an HTML document that contains a "clickable" image.
5. Locate a free "Under Construction" image from the Web and include it on a Web page. In addition to **SRC**, make sure to use the **ALT**, **HEIGHT**, and **WIDTH** attributes of the image tag.
6. Experiment with scaling an image. How small can you scale an image before it becomes fuzzy? Does this depend on the image quality that you started with? How large can you expand an image? What happens to the quality of the image as it gets larger?

chapter 22

INTERNET FILE TRANSFERS

In this chapter we discuss the following command:

Unix Command	DOS Command	Description
ftp	FTP	transfer files from one computer to another

22.1 Introduction

There will be many different occasions you may need to transfer files from one computer to another. For example,

❑ you work on a computer at home and need to transfer a file to a machine at your business office.

❑ you and a collaborator need to exchange files.

❑ you want to download software such as a helper, plug-in, or freeware application from another computer.

❑ you scan in some images on one system and need to move them to another computer for permanent display.

❑ you develop software on one machine and need to move it to another system.

File transfer is an application that allows you to move files between two computers on the same network. For example, you can copy files between two computers that are on the Internet. The two most important facilities file transfer provides are the abilities

1. to copy a file from another computer to your computer.
2. to send a file from your computer to another computer.

The goals of this chapter are to acquaint you with the basics of file transfer and the Unix file transfer command, namely **ftp**. We also discuss *anonymous file transfer* and how to locate files to transfer.

22.2 File Transfer

We begin with a high-level description of file transfer. In order for you to transfer files between two machines you need to be able to log in to both machines.[1]

---

1. In the special case of *anonymous ftp*, you need a personal account on only one of the machines.

Figure 22.1 illustrates the idea of the process of file transfer. Assume computers A and B both reside on the Internet or some other common network. Furthermore, assume that **file1** is local to machine A and **file2** is local to machine B. This is shown in the figure by including the file name inside the computer "box."

In the first part of Figure 22.1 we depict the process of sending **file1** from computer A to computer B. A file transfer connection to computer B is opened from computer A. During this step, the user logs into computer B from computer A. Next, **file1** is sent over the network to computer B using the "send" option of file transfer. This process is known as *uploading* a file from computer A to computer B. The figure shows **file1** on its way to computer B. When the transfer is complete, a copy of **file1** will exist on both machines.

In the other direction, file transfer can be used to bring **file2** over to computer A from computer B. This process is known as *downloading* a file from computer B to computer A. Again, computer A needs to establish a file transfer connection with computer B. Next, **file2** is retrieved over the network from computer B using the "get" option of file transfer. The second part of the figure shows **file2** on its way to computer A. Notice the direction of the arrows showing **file2** being transferred from computer B to computer A. When the transfer is complete, a copy of **file2** will exist on both machines.

Note that when transferring files between machines (especially personal computers), it is good practice to run virus-detection software on the files before using them. This helps safeguard against your computer getting infected. However, it is not a guarantee that there will be no problems.

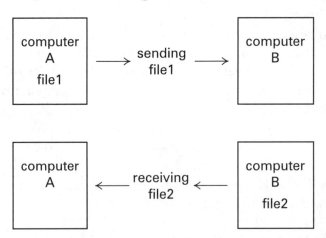

Figure 22.1—Schematic of File Transfer

There are other ways of copying a file from one computer to another, but usually file transfer is the fastest and most convenient method. If the file to be transferred is not too large, it may be possible to email the file to an account on the second machine. In some circumstances, emailing a file is not practical, especially when it may be requested many times, as is often the case with *freeware* (software that is available at no cost). Another possibility is to copy a file onto a diskette and then use the diskette to install the file on a different machine. For computers separated by hundreds or thousands of miles, "walknet" is not a satisfactory solution.

In the next section, we examine the specifics of the Unix **ftp** command for transferring files between two systems.

Exercises

1. Have you ever transferred files between two computers? If so, describe the command you used and your experience.
2. Give three examples of when you or someone you know needed to transfer files between different computers.

22.3 ftp Command

The name **ftp** is an abbreviation for "file transfer protocol." The command is named after the protocol that is used to implement it. **Ftp** is a text-based file transfer client. There are also graphic-based **ftp** clients that provide a point-and-click interface. Their functionality is essentially the same as that of Unix **ftp**. To launch the Unix file transfer client you enter the command

```
%ftp
```

On most Unix systems, you will be greeted by the following prompt

```
ftp>
```

This prompt indicates the **ftp** command is running and waiting for your input. Note that the prompt consists of four symbols. At this point the best thing to do is enter **?** or **help** in order to receive documentation about **ftp**. In Figure 22.2 we display the **ftp** documentation from our system. The **help** information is a listing of available commands. From the list of over 50 options, there are a handful that are very important and regularly used. Most of the others are very specific and you will rarely use them. We will cover the most important options of **ftp**. You can look up information about any of the options by entering

```
ftp>help command
```

341

where **command** is the name of the command you would like documentation about.

```
Commands may be abbreviated. Commands are:
!             cr          macdef      proxy        send
$             delete      mdelete     sendport     status
account       debug       mdir        put          struct
append        dir         mget        pwd          sunique
ascii         disconnect  mkdir       quit         tenex
bell          form        mls         quote        trace
binary        get         mode        recv         type
bye           glob        mput        remotehelp   user
case          hash        map         rename       verbose
cd            help        ntrans      reset        ?
cdup          lcd         open        rmdir
close         ls          prompt      runique
```

Figure 22.2—**ftp** Commands

The first command you will use when transferring files is the **open** command. This will allow you to open a connection to another machine. Typing

```
ftp>help open
```

results in the following display:

```
open             connect to remote tftp
```

As you can see, **ftp**'s help facility is a bit cryptic. The idea is to open a connection to the machine you want to exchange files with. For example, suppose you wanted to obtain a file from the host **bambam.nebraska.edu**. To establish this connection, you would enter

```
ftp>open bambam.nebraska.edu
```

If the connection is opened successfully, you will see a response such as

```
Connected to bambam.nebraska.edu.
220 drake FTP server (SunOS 5.6) ready.
Name (mymachine.school.edu:userid):
```

where **mymachine.school.edu:userid** is the name of your machine followed by your userid. This message is a login prompt, and you can now log in to the remote machine as you would normally log in to any machine—you simply enter your userid and password for the remote machine. If there is a problem opening the connection, it is likely that you mistyped the name of the remote host or that perhaps the host is down. If the problem persists, you may need to consult with a Unix guru.

There are two fundamental **ftp** commands: one that allows you to download a file to your computer and the other that allows you to send a file over to the remote computer. We next explain both of these in detail.

The command to bring a file over to your computer is **get**. The command **recv** (an abbreviation for "receive") has the same effect as **get**. Once you open the connection to a remote machine, you can use the **ls** and **cd** commands to list files and change directories, respectively, on the remote machine. To bring over the file **important.text**, simply **cd** to the directory where the file resides and perform an **ls** to verify that the file is where you thought it was. Then enter the command

```
ftp>get important.text
```

If the transfer is successful, you will see a message such as

```
200 PORT command successful.
150 ASCII data connection for important.text
(130.154.188.11,34200) (376 bytes).
226 ASCII Transfer complete.
local: important.text remote: important.text
388 bytes received in 0.024 seconds (16.02 Kbytes/s)
```

Notice the last line of this message includes the size of the file and the rate of transfer of the data. The rate of transfer is expressed in terms of *Kbytes/s*. A Kbyte or *kilobyte* is 1,000 bytes,[2] and "s" represents seconds. So, in this case the transfer rate was 16,020 bytes per second.

If the transfer is not successful, you will get an error message. This usually means you mistyped the name of the file you were trying to retrieve, or that the file is not located where you thought it was. In the transfer above, note that the local (new) copy of the file is also called **important.text**. To have the file brought over with the file name **new.text**, you can enter the command

```
ftp>get important.text new.text
```

In this case, a copy of the remote file **important.text** will be placed in the current directory on your local machine in a file having the name **new.text**. Be careful not to overwrite an existing local file.

The command to upload a copy of a local file onto a remote machine is **put**. The **send** command has the same effect. Initially, it is a good idea to **cd** to the

---

2. Technically, 2^{10} or 1,024 bytes.

local directory where the file that you want to send resides. As before, you next need to establish a connection with a remote host. Once this is done, you can **cd** to the directory where you would like to place the copy of the file. Suppose you want to deposit a copy of the file **goldfinger**. Simply enter the command

```
ftp>put goldfinger
```

If successful, you will see a message such as

```
200 PORT command successful.
150 ASCII data connection
for goldfinger (130.154.188.11,34206).
226 Transfer complete.
local: goldfinger remote: goldfinger
376 bytes sent in 0.0042 seconds (87.03 Kbytes/s)
```

If the transfer is not successful, you will get an error message. This usually means you mistyped the name of the file you were trying to send, or that the file was not in your current working directory.

Note: When sending or retrieving files using **ftp** it is important to exercise caution. It is very easy to overwrite an existing file without any warning. For example, getting the remote file **pets** will overwrite an existing local copy of **pets**, and sending the local file **animals** will overwrite the existing remote copy of the file **animals**.

The **mget** and **mput** abbreviations stand for "multiple get" and "multiple put," respectively. These options allow you to retrieve multiple files at once or send multiple files at once. They are very useful when you need to transfer a large number of files. If you do not want to be asked whether you want to transfer each file, you can turn **prompt** off by entering

```
ftp>prompt
```

When using **mget** and **mput**, be careful not to overwrite existing files having the same name as the files you are transferring.

There are several other commands that are helpful for you to know while using **ftp**. We now run through several of them. The **lcd** command stands for "local change directory." This command will allow you to change directories on your local machine. Remember, while using **ftp**, the **cd** command is used to change directories on the remote machine. Normally, before launching **ftp** it is a good idea to change to your local directory where you will be transferring from or receiving to. However, if these are two separate directories, the **lcd** command will come in handy.

The **status** command displays the current information regarding your **ftp** session. A sample output from the **status** command is shown in Figure 22.3. A great deal of the **status** information is self-explanatory, and what is not can easily be checked out through the **ftp help** facility. One general remark is in order, though. Notice that there are lots of **on** and **off** messages displayed in Figure 22.3. Many of the options to **ftp** function in a toggle manner, like switches. That is, they are either **on** or **off**. You can switch between the two options by executing the corresponding command. For example, in the figure we see that "hash mark printing" has a **status** of **off**. To turn hash mark printing **on**, you simply enter

```
ftp>hash
```

Thus, the command names act as switches. If the feature is **on**, typing the corresponding command switches the feature **off**, and vice versa. When transferring large files, you may want to set **hash** to **on**. The **hash** feature prints a hash mark, **#**, on the screen after each segment (a buffer full) of the file is transferred. This can serve as a reassurance to you that the file is still being transferred properly. Otherwise, your terminal may sit idle for half an hour while you are wondering if something went wrong.

```
Connected to drake.armstrong.edu.
No proxy connection.
Mode: stream; Type: ascii; Form: non-print; Structure: file
Verbose: off; Bell: off; Prompting: on; Globbing: on
Store unique: off; Receive unique: off
Case: off; CR stripping: on
Ntrans: off
Nmap: off
Hash mark printing: off; Use of PORT cmds: on
```

Figure 22.3—**status** of an **ftp** Session

Another important feature of **ftp** is the **binary** option. You should turn this option **on** by entering

```
ftp>binary
```

if you are going to transfer a *binary* file—for our purposes, a file that does not consist of plain text. For example, a compressed data file or an image file should be transferred with the **binary** option **on**.

Once you have completed your **ftp** session, you can end it by typing

```
ftp>bye
```

The **quit** command can also be used for this purpose. It is a good idea to check the permissions on files that you bring over using **ftp**. Sometimes files are brought over as world readable, whereas you may prefer that they be only user readable.

The **ftp** command has many other features. From time to time you will need to invoke some of these. You can use the **help** command to learn about the items you need. The following list summarizes the **ftp** commands we have covered.

❑ **binary**—toggle the transfer mode for binary files.
❑ **bye** or **quit**—terminate the session and exit the file transfer program.
❑ **cd**—change directory on the remote machine.
❑ **get** or **recv**—download a file.
❑ **hash**—turn on hash mark printing.
❑ **help** or **?**—provide a list of commands or help on a specific command.
❑ **lcd**—change directory on the local machine.
❑ **ls**—list the files in the current directory.
❑ **mget**—download multiple files in a single step.
❑ **mput**—upload multiple files in a single step.
❑ **open**—open a connection to a remote machine.
❑ **prompt**—toggle the query mode.
❑ **put** or **send**—upload a copy of a file.
❑ **status**—check the settings of your **ftp** session.

To learn more about the **ftp** command, you can enter

```
%man ftp
```

Exercises

1. Enter the **ftp** command. Open a connection to a remote machine, if possible, and if not, open a connection to your own local machine. Use the **status** command to print out the status of your **ftp** session. Explain what each item in the **status** display means.
2. Describe the syntax of the **mget** and **mput** commands. Give examples of when it would be practical to use these commands.
3. Using **ftp**, transfer at least three different-sized files between two machines. Explain and compare the transfer rates you observed. If the rates were different, describe why.

22.4 Anonymous File Transfer

On some systems, files are made available to anyone who wants to retrieve them (for example, freeware, public documents, research papers, and so on). If a file needs to be widely distributed, it may not be feasible to assign accounts and passwords to everyone interested in receiving a copy of the file. In response to this problem, *anonymous file transfer* was established. Users log in with **anonymous** as their account name and then provide a password. The standard practice is to use your complete email address as a password because this helps the administrator at the file transfer site monitor file transfer usage. On other systems, a password called **guest** is expected. The system will usually let you know what password to enter. You should never use your real account password when logging in anonymously, since the information you submit is not secure.

After logging in using anonymous file transfer, you will be restricted to accessing specific directories. Usually, accessible directories are in an area named something like **public**. Within those directories you will often be confined to just downloading files. In many cases, such directories contain a help file, called something like **README**, where additional information can be found.

Figure 22.4 illustrates an anonymous file transfer session. It is easy to distinguish between user entries and **ftp**'s replies, since most of the messages coming from **ftp** are prefaced by a number. In this case we opened a connection to **cs.unh.edu**. Notice we entered the userid **anonymous**, and that our password was not echoed on the screen. In this case, we were prompted to send our complete email address as a password. After logging in, we checked to see what files were available. There was one file available called **welcome.msg** containing a welcome message. Once we were finished with our work, we exited **ftp** by typing the **bye** command. A goodbye message and a summary of our activity was then printed.

```
pirates% ftp
ftp>open cs.unh.edu
Connected to cs.unh.edu.
220 cs.unh.edu FTP server (Version wu-2.6.0(6) Wed Oct 20
15:30:52 EDT 1999) ready.
Name (cs.unh.edu:greenlaw): anonymous
331 Guest login ok, send your complete e-mail address as
password.
Password:

230-All logins, commands, and transfers may be logged.
230-Please disconnect now if you find this unacceptable.
230-Hello!
230-This FTP server (ftp.cs.unh.edu) is maintained by the
```

```
230-Computer Science Department, University of New
Hampshire.
230-Contact ftpadmin@cs.unh.edu with technical problems or
for more info.
230-You are user #1 of a maximum 20 possible.
230-It is Mon Jun  5 17:59:26 2000 in Durham, New
Hampshire.
230-
230 Guest login ok, access restrictions apply.

ftp> ls
200 PORT command successful.
150 Opening ASCII mode data connection for file list.
welcome.msg
226 Transfer complete.
13 bytes received in 0.013 seconds (0.97 Kbytes/s)


...


ftp>bye
221-Total traffic for this session was 1078 bytes in 2
transfers.
221-Thank you for using the FTP service on cs.unh.edu.
221 Goodbye.
```

Figure 22.4—Anonymous File Transfer Session

We should note that in general, file transfer can also be launched from within a browser window by entering the URL **ftp://hostname**.

Exercises

1. List the host names of two different anonymous **ftp** sites. Log in to one of them. Print out a directory listing of the directory you were initially placed in. Transfer over a file and print out the transfer statistics.
2. Why would a researcher want to maintain an anonymous **ftp** site?
3. Conduct some research about **ftp** on the Web. Is the **ftp** command considered a security risk? Explain your findings.

4. Try to launch **ftp** through your browser. Explain the results.
5. Research the meaning of the numbers that prefix **ftp**'s responses (see Figure 22.4). Explain their meanings.

22.5 Finding Files to Transfer

Now that you know how to transfer files using **ftp**, the obvious question to ask is how do you find files that you are interested in transferring. Unless you know exactly where a file is located on the Internet, it will be very difficult to find it since files can be archived at file transfer sites scattered throughout the world. *Archie*, derived from "file archive," is a service that maintains databases containing listings of files from various file transfer sites. Performing a query to find a specific file involves either sending email to an Archie site or connecting to an Archie server via **telnet**. Archie will respond and indicate the location(s) of the file you want, provided the file is listed in one of its databases. To locate an Archie server, you can connect to any of the major search engines and enter the query "Archie." One location of an Archie server is

> `www.thegroup.net/AA.html`

You will find a form at this site where you can submit a search request. Other Archie servers have similar interfaces.

Exercises

1. Report the URLs for two sites that have Archie servers available.
2. Research Archie on the Web and write a one-page paper describing your findings.

PROGRAMMING

PROGRAM DEVELOPMENT USING UNIX

In this chapter we introduce the following commands:

Unix Command	DOS Command	Description
CC	—	compile a C++ program
cc	—	compile a C program
ci	—	check in a file under RCS
co	—	check out a file under RCS
gcc	—	compile a C program using the GNU C compiler
gdb	—	use the GNU program debugger for C, C++, and Modula-2
g++	—	compile a C++ program using the GNU C++ compiler
make	—	maintain, update, and regenerate programs and files based on user-defined dependencies
rcs	—	use the revision control system
script	—	make a copy of a terminal session

23.1 Introduction

One major reason for the success of the Unix operating system is that it provides an excellent program development environment. There are many different tools integrated together to meet the programming needs of an individual programmer or a development team. In this chapter we are going to provide you with a glimpse into the available software. We will focus on the C programming language, although many other languages, such as Ada, C++, Modula, and Lisp, are available on most Unix platforms.

In particular, you will learn about

❑ the C programming language.
❑ coding, compiling, debugging, and executing a program.
❑ scripting a program.
❑ developing and maintaining a set of programs.

23.2 The C Programming Language

In this section we provide a short introduction to the C programming language, or C for short. This is the programming language in which nearly all of the Unix operating system is written. C is useful for its expressiveness and capabilities. Because of this, nearly all networking software is written in C. For example, the protocols that drive the Internet are written in C. C is not an easy language to learn for a beginning programmer. In fact, C is not usually the first language that people are taught. Having provided you with these cautions, we will now take a look at a couple of C programs. Our goal is not to teach you how to program in C, but rather to try to give you a feel for what C programs are like.

The first program we want to consider is the classic introductory C program for printing the phrase "hello, world!" This program, called **first.c**, is shown in Figure 23.1. All C programs should be stored in files with a **c** extension. Blank lines and extra spaces may be included in a C program to improve the program's readability. Such extra white space does not affect the meaning of the program. We now explain each line of the program in turn.

```
/* The canonical first C program. */

#include <stdio.h>
main()

{
printf("hello, world!\n");
}
```

Figure 23.1—The C Program **first.c**

The first line of the program

```
/* The canonical first C program. */
```

is a comment. Comments in C are enclosed between /* and */ pairs; they do not affect the execution of the program. It is a good convention to comment your programs. At the top of a program, it is customary to include a description of the program and its purpose. Throughout the program, it is standard practice to describe more complex statements or to explain the logic of the program.

The second line of the program

```
#include <stdio.h>
```

instructs C to include the file **stdio.h** from its library. This file contains basic information that allows your program to perform standard input and output operations. The file **stdio.h** comes with all C installations. The file extension **h** is used for C files that are called *include* files. Such files are included at the beginning of C programs using the syntax shown in Figure 23.1; they contain program initializations and *declarations* as well as standard library routines.

The third line of the program is

```
main()
```

This defines a function called **main**. The empty parentheses following **main** indicate that the function has no arguments. This line is followed by the body of the program

```
{
printf("hello, world!\n");
}
```

The body of a C program always is enclosed between curly braces. In this case, the body consists of the single line

```
printf("hello, world!\n");
```

This line consists of a function call to the routine **printf** that is defined in **stdio.h**. The **printf** function is the basic function for printing output in C. We will not go into the details of the syntax for **printf**, which can be found in any standard C reference, except to point out that in this case **printf** is instructed to print the expression "hello, world!" followed by a new line character. Notice that the line with the call to the **printf** function ends with a semicolon (;). C syntax requires all statements to end with a semicolon.

Obviously, if all we could do with C is write toy programs, the language would not be very useful. In fact, C is a general-purpose language that can be used to code nearly any algorithmic procedure. We consider one more simple C program that is used to find *prime* numbers up to a certain specified value. This program illustrates a number of additional features of C. Before describing the program, we need a few preliminaries.

A *divisor* is a number that divides another number evenly. For example, 5 is a divisor of 25 but 5 is not a divisor of 27. Recall that a prime number is a number that has only 1 and itself as divisors. So, the first few prime numbers are 2, 3, 5, 7, and 11. The **mod** function (or *remainder* function) returns the remainder of a division. For example, 27 mod 5 = 2, 17 mod 4 = 1, and 12 mod 6 = 0.

The C program shown in Figure 23.2 prints to the screen all prime numbers less than the value N. (The program is based on Eratosthenes Sieve.) The idea used to test if a number is prime is simply to check if any smaller number divides it. If no smaller number divides it, then the number is prime; otherwise, it is not prime. For example, to test if 7 is prime, we could try to divide 7 by 2, 3, 4, 5, and 6. Since no smaller number (except 1) divides 7, we can conclude that 7 is prime. In fact, we only need to check numbers that are less than or equal to $\lfloor 7/2 \rfloor$.[1] The notation $\lfloor x \rfloor$ means round down the value of the number x. It would suffice to check if 2 or 3 divided 7 in order to determine whether or not 7 is prime.

```c
/* Program for printing out the prime numbers less than N. */

#include <stdio.h>
#define N 1000

main()
{
    int i, flag, j;
    printf("This is a prime number lister up to %d. \n", N);
    for (i = 2; i <= N; ++i) {
        flag = 1;
        for (j = 2; j <= (i/2); ++j) {
            flag = i % j;
            if ( flag == 0 ) break;
        }
        if ( flag == 1) printf("%d\n", i);
    }
}
```

Figure 23.2—The C Program **prime.c**

The program **prime.c** shown in Figure 23.2 is not the most efficient program for locating prime numbers. However, it is useful for illustration purposes. We now explain the new concepts introduced by this program.

---

1. We really only need to check values that are less than or equal to the square root of 7.

The first thing to notice is the third nonblank line of the program

```
#define N 1000
```

This expression assigns the constant **N** the value of 1,000. If we need to change the value of **N** throughout the program, all we need to do is edit this one line. Declarations such as this one often occur in include files having an extension of **h**.

The next line of interest in the program is

```
int i, flag, j;
```

This line defines the three variables—**i**, **flag**, and **j**—to be integers. All variables used in a C program must be declared. It is customary to group such declarations at the beginning of the program.

The following line

```
printf("This is a prime number lister up to %d. \n", N);
```

has the effect of printing the message

```
This is a prime number lister up to 1000.
```

on the screen. The **%d** in the code provides formatting information for the value **N**.

This line is followed by the first of two **for** loops in the program. The general syntax of a C **for** loop is

```
for (expression1; expression2; expression3)
statement;
```

In C code, **expression1** is typically an initialization, **expression2** is a condition, and **expression3** is a form of incrementing. The placeholder **statement** (called the *body* of the **for** loop) can be any single C statement, or if enclosed in curly braces, any number of C statements. The initial part of the first **for** loop in the **prime.c** program

```
for (i = 2; i <= N; ++i)
```

says to initialize **i** to a value of 2. Then while **i** is less than or equal to the value **N**, execute the body of the **for** loop. After the body of the **for** loop has been executed, the statement in **expression3** is performed. In this case, **expression3** is the statement

```
++i
```

This is C syntax for increment the value **i**. Here, this means add 1 to the value **i**.

The next line of the program is

```
flag = 1;
```

This sets the value of the variable **flag** to 1. Following this assignment statement is another **for** loop.

```
for (j = 2; j <= (i/2); ++j)
```

This **for** loop is nested inside the first **for** loop. This loop behaves similarly to the first one. The only thing worth noting is the expression

```
j <= i/2
```

This means that the **for** loop is executed only if **j** is less than or equal to **i** divided by 2. Since **i** and 2 are integers, the value of this division is truncated by C. For example, $5/2 = 2$ as does $4/2 = 2$.

The next line of code in the program is

```
flag = i % j;
```

The **%** sign is the mod operator. This statement says assign **flag** the value of **i** mod **j**.

The next line of code in the program is

```
if ( flag == 0 ) break;
```

This is an example of a C **if** statement. It means if the value of **flag** is equal to 0, then exit the **for** loop. The reason for exiting the **for** loop in this case is that the number **i** cannot be prime. That is, the last value of **j** divides **i** evenly. Notice that a double equals sign (`==`) is used to check if the value **flag** is equal to 0. A single equals sign (`=`) is used for assignment, whereas a double equals sign is used to compare two values. Be careful not to confuse these two operators, as your program will have a very different meaning in most cases.

The next line of code in the program is

```
if ( flag == 1) printf("%d\n", i);
```

This is another **if** statement. It means if the value of **flag** is equal to 1, then print the value of **i**. The reason for printing **i** in this case is because **i** is in fact a prime number. Why is this? The inner **for** loop checks to see if any number less than **i/2** divides **i**. If no such number exists, then **flag** always has the value 1. The value of **flag** is set to 0 only if a divisor for **flag** is found. Only numbers for which the value of **flag** is 1 are printed. The outer **for** loop is used to cycle through all of the numbers less than or equal to **N**.

The program **prime.c** demonstrates how to use C **if** statements, **for** loops, assignment statements, and basic arithmetic operations. C is a very powerful language and includes many other features as well. The interested reader can learn more about the C programming language by pursuing the references given at the end of this book.

We have provided an introduction to the C programming language by looking at a couple of programs. However, we have not explained the coding and debugging process, nor how to run a C program on a Unix system. These are the topics of the next couple of sections. Once we have covered these issues, we ask you to write a few programs of your own.

Exercises

1. Can you find any online help about the C programming language? Describe your findings.
2. Conduct some research on the C programming language. Why is the language called C? Write a one-page paper explaining how C got its name.

23.3 Coding, Compiling, Debugging, and Executing a Program

In this section we cover the classic code, compile, debug, and execute program development cycle. All programmers work by performing these four operations.

To create a C program, you simply invoke your favorite editor and then type in the code. It is usually a good idea to work out the logic of a program with paper and pencil first. As noted earlier, your program should be saved in a file with an extension of **c**. For starters, you may want to enter the program shown in Figure 23.1. As with any programming language, you need to take care in entering your program into the computer. It is critical that you type in all the special symbols such as /*, */, {, #, and } in the correct places and correct order. Any mistake will result in a nonworking program.

Suppose that you have typed in the program in Figure 23.1 and saved it in the file **first.c**. It is a good idea to proofread your code to make sure you did not make any mistakes. Once you believe that everything is correct, you can *compile* your program. A *compiler* is a program that processes programs to check them for syntax errors. If a program has correct syntax, the compiler will generate an *object* or *executable* file that you can run. The process of using a compiler is called *compilation*. We say that you are *compiling* your program when you perform a compilation. It is always a good idea to check your program over very carefully before compiling. This practice will help you to become a better programmer.

To compile the program **first.c** using the C compiler, you simply enter the command

```
%cc first.c
```

from the directory containing the file **first.c**. The **cc** stands for "C compiler." The GNU C compiler is invoked by typing

```
%gcc first.c
```

The **gcc** stands for "GNU C compiler." (We should point out that **CC** and **g++** are the corresponding commands to invoke the C++ compilers. C++ is the object-oriented version of the C programming language.) If your program is error (or bug) free, you will be returned to the Unix prompt. If there is an error, the compiler will report it to you. If the program compiles correctly, an object file will be produced. By default, the executable file for a compiled program is placed in a file called **a.out**. To execute (or run) the program, you simply enter the command

```
%a.out
```

or

```
%./a.out
```

if the current working directory is not in your path. Note that the protections must be such that the file can be executed. For example, after compiling **first.c**, we can run it resulting in the output

```
hello, world!
```

To place the object file in the file **first.o**, you can use the **o** flag to the **cc** command. For example, you could enter the command

```
%cc -o first.o first.c
```

You can now run the program by typing

```
%first.o
```

or

```
%./first.o
```

Note that the protections must be such that the file can be executed. It is customary to save executable files into files having an **o** extension. The **o** stands for "object." These are binary files.

If you are writing a complex program, it is fairly unlikely that you will get it to compile successfully the first time. An error discovered by the compiler is called a *compile-time error*. Furthermore, even if you achieve a successful compile, there may still be some *run-time errors* remaining in the program. These are mistakes that you only discover once you run the program. That is, a syntactically correct program may not behave the way you expected it to semantically.

If your program has an error, you will need to fix the bug by editing the code. You will need to save the program again, and then recompile it. Once you have done this, you will need to run the program again to test it out. You may need to repeat this cycle several times. With large programs, this development cycle may need to be repeated thousands of times. Extremely complex programs have a never-ending coding cycle, since there are always some bugs remaining in them.

We now consider a compile-time error to illustrate the type of message you may expect to see from the C compiler. Suppose we accidentally omitted the { from the program **first.c** shown in Figure 23.1. Compiling by entering the command

```
%cc first.c
```

results in the following error messages:

```
first.c:7: parse error before 'printf'
first.c:7: warning: data definition has no type or storage class
```

There are parts of this message that are cryptic and hard to understand. In general, this is the case with error messages from the C compiler. However, there is some very important information in the error message that can help us to fix the bug in our program. One important clue to where the error is located is given by the line number. In this case we are told there is an error in line 7 of the file **first.c**. Furthermore, the error occurs before the call to the **printf** routine. In this case the C compiler has found exactly where our mistake is located. An experienced C programmer would look at this code and immediately notice that the opening { was missing. Editing the file **first.c** by adding the { character back in before the **printf** statement, saving, recompiling, and running the program again will result in the desired output. It can be instructive to introduce artificial bugs into correct programs in order to see how the compiler responds.

If your program is tens of thousands of lines long and has no syntax errors, but has a run-time error, it can be very difficult to locate the run-time error. Unix provides a debugger that allows you to walk through the execution of a C program step by step. The debugger provides all sorts of useful information about the program. In addition, it allows you to check the values that variables have been assigned. The Unix C debugger is invoked by the command

```
%gdb
```

The **gdb** stands for "GNU debugger." We will not get into the details of **gdb** here but instead simply make you aware of this useful debugging tool. To learn more about **gdb**, you can enter the command

```
%man gdb
```

or pursue the references provided at the end of this book.

Exercises

1. Create a directory called C and save the program shown in Figure 23.1 in a file called **first.c** in this directory. Copy the file to one called **myname.c**. Modify the program so that it prints your name. Print out your program. Delete the opening " in the **printf** statement and recompile your program. Print the error message you receive. Perform the same task but delete the latter ". Did you get the same error message?

2. Write a C program to print numbers that are not prime. Such numbers are called *composite* numbers. Print out the composite numbers less than 100. How many were there?

3. Write a C program to print all numbers less than 1,000 that are divisible by both 2 and 13. What are the numbers and how many did you find? Also, print out three of the error messages you received during the debugging phase.

23.4 Scripting a Program

In the last section we described how to code, compile, debug, and execute a C program. There will be times you want to record the running of a program or the contents of a terminal session. For example, suppose you write a program for a class and need to turn in sample output from a run of your program. The Unix **script** command is ideal for performing such a task. You simply enter the command

```
%script
```

when are you ready to begin recording. From this point on, everything that you type at the terminal and all the output that is displayed on your screen will be recorded in the file called **typescript**. This is the default file used by the system to do the recording. You can specify a file name as an argument to the **script** command and have all of the output written to this file instead of the **typescript** file. For example, the command

```
%script record
```

causes all the output from the **script** command to be placed in a file called **record**.

When you are done recording, you simply type **Control-D** or the word **exit**. At this point, the file **typescript** or the file you specified as an alternative will contain everything that was displayed on your screen up until the **Control-D**. The

script command will write a time stamp both at the beginning and at the end of your file. For example, at the beginning of the file you will see a message such as

```
Script started on Mon Aug 7 15:57:26 2000
```

and at the end of the file you will see another message such as

```
Script done on Mon Aug 7 15:57:40 2000
```

You can view the script file in the standard manner, for example, using the **more** command. If you need a hard copy, you can send the file to a printer.

As an example, suppose you wanted to create a script that shows the program for printing the "hello, world!" message, a successful compilation of the program, and a successful run of the program. This could be accomplished by typing the following commands:

1. **%script record**
2. **%more first.c**
3. **%cc first.c**
4. **%a.out** (or **./a.out**)
5. **Control-D**

In Figure 23.3 we depict the output of the file **record** created by carrying out these steps. Notice that it took only 14 seconds to generate this recording. The first line in the file indicates when the script was started. The command

```
%more first.c
```

is used to display the program. Following the display of the program, we see the command

```
%cc first.c
```

that is used to compile the program. The program compiled without errors and Unix returned with the prompt symbol. At this prompt, we entered the command

```
%a.out
```

in order to run the program. The program was run and its output displayed as

```
hello, world!
```

We were then returned to the Unix prompt. Having completed all of the recording that we needed, we then typed **Control-D**. This finished the scripting session. Note that Unix inserted the word **exit** when we typed **Control-D**. The **script** command also time stamped the date and time when the script was completed. The file **record** was written with all of the scripting information contained in it.

```
Script started on Mon Aug 7 15:57:26 2000
%more first.c
/* The canonical first C program. */

#include <stdio.h>
main()

{
printf("hello, world!\n");
}
%cc first.c
%a.out
hello, world!
%exit

Script done on Mon Aug 7 15:57:40 2000
```

Figure 23.3—The Script File **record** Illustrating the Program **first.c**,
Compilation of the Program, and a Run of the Program

We have provided one sample use of the **script** command. You will find it useful in other circumstances for recording information appearing on your terminal. It is usually a good idea to test everything out to make sure it runs correctly before beginning your scripting session.

Exercises

1. Write a C program that prints out your email address. Create a scripting session that displays the program, shows a successful compile of the program, and a successful run of the program.
2. Describe two other practical uses for the **script** command.
3. Write a C program that prints all prime numbers less than 100. Use the **script** command to record a run of the program. Store the output of the sample run in a file called **test**. Is there a way to run the program again and have the new output concatenated to the end of the file **test**? (*Hint:* Take a look at the **man page** for the **script** command.)

23.5 Developing and Maintaining a Set of Programs

We have described the basics of the C programming language and its usage. In particular, you should now be able to code, compile, edit, and run basic C programs. The tools we have described so far, though, are not adequate for working on a set of programs. If you are working on a group project, you will need additional tools to make sure that the files different members of the group are using remain consistent. In this section we introduce you to several Unix commands that are useful for developing and maintaining a set of files. The goal here is not to teach you all of the details of the tools, but rather to explain what tools exist. In this way, you are informed as to what is available. You can pursue each item in greater detail through the references or via their corresponding **man pages**.

23.5.1 make Command

The first utility we discuss is called **make**. This command is useful for maintaining a group of files. If you write a large program, typically it will be divided into many pieces, and therefore actually consist of many different files. The **make** utility allows you to specify various dependencies among the files so that they can be compiled and linked together in the correct order. If properly set up, the dependencies instruct **make** to perform the minimum amount of work necessary to rebuild the central program. Such efficient recompilations are very important because they can save programmers time.

To use **make**, you create a file called **makefile** that contains a list of the relationships among the files involved in your project. We show an example of a simple **makefile** in Figure 23.4. This **makefile** specifies that the object file **program** depends on the files **file1.o** and **file2.o**. These in turn depend on their corresponding C programs and the include file called **include.h**. The object files are all generated by the C compiler **cc**. The dependencies specify, for example, that if **include.h** changes, then **file1.c**, **file.2**, and **program** need to be recompiled and relinked. Or, for example, if only **file1.c** changes, then **file2.c** does not need to be recompiled to regenerate **program**. Note that a **tab** character is used in every other line of text in this example.

```
program:  file1.o file2.o
          cc -o program file1.o file2.o

file1.o: include.h file1.c
          cc file1.c

file2.o: include.h file2.c
          cc file2.c
```

Figure 23.4—A Sample **makefile**

In order to use **make** effectively, you will need to learn its peculiar syntax. Once you have created a **makefile**, you can process it by typing

`%make`

This command will recompile the necessary files and relink as necessary. Part of the reason why **make** is so useful is that it only recompiles what is absolutely necessary. We can illustrate this point by the following scenario. Suppose you are working on a project involving 100 files. Suppose that all files were compiled and linked together. Now suppose that only a single file, which does not directly impact any of the other files, needs to be modified. With an appropriately—designed **makefile**, only this one file will need to be recompiled rather than having to recompile the entire 100 files. Recompiling a single file versus 100 files can result in a huge time savings.

We should note that the **touch** command described in Section 9.6.3 is sometimes used to update the time stamp on a file in order to force **make** to recompile the file.

In order to learn more about **make**, you should enter the command

`%man make`

23.5.2 Software Revision Control System—RCS

Imagine that you are working on a project with five other programmers: Daisy, Duffy, Francine, Harry, and Nell. Suppose that you are all sharing a common directory, where all of your programming code resides. Furthermore, suppose there are 100 different files that you are sharing. Without any systematic and automated software *revision control system (RCS)* in place, it is very easy to see how the files could become inconsistent and valuable changes lost. For example, suppose Duffy (the weakest programmer of the group) decides to work on a file called **critical.c** and forgets to inform everyone that he is doing this. Meanwhile, Nell (the strongest programmer of the group) puts 10 days of solid work into **critical.c**. After completing her work, Nell moves the file **critical.c** back to the public directory where everything is stored. Unaware of Nell's work because of unread email, Duffy puts back his version of **critical.c**, thereby wiping out all of Nell's work. In the meantime, Daisy and Harry get mixed up and overwrite Francine's work, and so on. An RCS is designed to help users maintain consistency of their files so that such problems can be avoided.

The simple scenario just described illustrates what can (and does) go wrong when a group of users try to share code without any software to help (protect) them. Unix provides the **rcs** command, which helps you set up a revision-control software system. The key to such a system is to require users to *check out* files and to *check in* files. If Nell has a file checked out, then no one else can check out that file. When her changes are finished, Nell can check in the file. Only one user at a time can check out a given file. By enforcing a check in and check out policy such as this, RCS can help users maintain the consistency of their files. The system will prevent users from clobbering each other's work. Such a system is also useful for preserving a *snapshot* of a given project at any point in time. In practice, these snapshots are useful as backups and for restoring a system.

The Unix command for checking out a file is

```
%co file
```

where **file** is the name of the file to be checked out. The **co** stands for "check out." The Unix command for checking in a file is

```
%ci file
```

where **file** is the name of the file to be checked in. The **ci** stands for "check in."

RCS time stamps files with dates written inside the files themselves, creates version numbers for the files, and maintains the integrity of the files. For example, RCS makes sure that a file can only be checked in by the person who checked it out.

RCS is an excellent tool for helping with program development. In particular, it functions well for maintaining a group of files that are being worked on by multiple people. It is a good idea to read the **man pages** for the **rcs**, **co**, and **ci** commands in order to learn more about their details.

Exercises

1. Write a one-page paper explaining the **make** command to a beginning C programmer.
2. Write a one-page paper explaining the **rcs** command to a beginning C programmer. Be sure to include a description of why such a system is needed.
3. Create a **makefile** to compile a single C program. Produce a script session that displays your file, a run of the **makefile**, and a run of your program.
4. Examine the **man pages** for **rcs**, **co**, and **ci**. Report three interesting facts about each command.

23.6 Summary

In this chapter we have provided an introduction to the C programming language and to many of the important Unix programming development tools. We looked at commands for compiling, debugging, making, maintaining, and scripting programs. If you intend to do a significant amount of programming with Unix, you will want to investigate the **man pages** associated with the commands described here. In addition, you will want to pursue the references provided at the end of this book.

SUMMARY OF UNIX COMMANDS

In this appendix we provide a list of the Unix commands described in this book, along with a brief description of each command. Each command is indexed in the book's general index. More details about each command can be found in the body of the text.

Unix Command	Description
alias	define another name for a command
apropos	search the online manual for a keyword
CC	compile a C++ program
cal	display a calendar
cc	compile a C program
cd	change to another directory
chmod	change the protection of a file or a directory
chsh	change your login shell
ci	check in a file under RCS
clear	clear the screen
co	check out a file under RCS
compress	compact the storage space used for a file
cp	copy a file
date	display the current date and time
diff	find the difference between two files
du	estimate file space usage
dvips	convert a dvi file to a PostScript file
echo	display a line of text
emacs	invoke the **emacs** text editor
exit	close your current session on your computer account

Unix Command	Description
fg	activate the most recently stopped job
file	determine the type of a file
find	locate a file
finger	locate information about a user
fortune	print a random epigram
gcc	compile a C program using the GNU C compiler
gdb	use the GNU program debugger for C, C++, and Modula-2
ghostview	preview a PostScript file
g++	compile a C++ program using the GNU C++ compiler
grep	find a pattern in a file
gzip	compact the storage space used for a file
gunzip	decode a file that has been compressed via the **gzip** command
head	display the first part of a file
history	print a listing of recently executed commands
ispell	run the interactive spelling checker
jobs	obtain a listing of suspended jobs
kill	terminate a Unix process
latex	process a file using LaTeX
last	display a record of the logins and logouts to a computer or a computer account
lock	temporarily suspend your terminal
login	start work on your computer account
logout	close your current session on your computer account
lpq	check the print queue
lpr	print a file
lprm	remove a job from the print queue
ls	list the files in a directory
man	access the online help facility

Unix Command	Description
mail	run the Unix email program
make	maintain, update, and regenerate programs and files based on user-defined dependencies
mkdir	create a directory
more	display a file one screenful at a time
mv	rename a file
passwd	change the password of your computer account
pine	run the **pine** mail program
ping	check the status of another computer
printenv	print information about your current working environment
ps	check the status of processes
pwd	print working directory
quota	display disk space and limits
rcs	use the revision control system
rm	delete a file
rmdir	delete a directory
script	make a copy of a terminal session
set	display shell variables; turn on a shell variable
setenv	display environment variables; change the value of an environment variable
shar	create a shell archive
sort	sort the lines of text files
spell	spell check a file
tail	display the last part of a file
tar	create a tape archive
touch	change the time stamp on a file
umask	set file creation mask
unalias	remove an alias for a command
uncompress	decode a file that has been compressed via the **compress** command

Unix Command	Description
unset	turn off a shell variable
unshar	unpack a shell archive
uptime	display runtime statistics about the computer system
uudecode	decode a uuencoded file
uuencode	encode a binary file
vi	invoke the **vi** editor
w	display runtime statistics about the computer system and determine who is logged onto the system and what commands they are executing
wc	count the lines, words, and characters in a file
whatis	display a brief description of a command
whereis	search for source, binary, and **man page** files for a Unix command
which	determine where a command is located
whoami	print effective userid
xdvi	preview a **dvi** file

MAPPING FROM UNIX TO DOS COMMANDS

In this appendix we provide a mapping from Unix commands to DOS commands. The Unix commands are listed in alphabetical order. We list only Unix commands for which there is a close DOS equivalent. Of course, not all of the commands match up precisely.

Unix Command	DOS Command	Description
apropos	HELP	search the online manual for a keyword
cat	TYPE	concatenate and display files
cd	CD	change to another directory
chmod	ATTRIB	change the protections on a file or directory
clear	CLS	clear the screen
compress	COMPACT	compact the storage space used for a file
cp	COPY	copy a file
date	DATE	display the current date and time
echo	ECHO	display a line of text
emacs	EDIT	edit a file
exit	EXIT	close your current session on your computer account
find	FIND	locate a file
file	FTYPE	determine file type
grep	FIND	search for a pattern in a file
gzip	COMPACT	compact the storage space used for a file

Unix Command	DOS Command	Description
gunzip	EXPAND	expand a file that has been compressed
history	DOSKEY	print a list of recently executed commands
kill	PAUSE	terminate a process
login	LOGIN	start work on your computer account
logout	EXIT	close your current session on your computer account
lpr	PRINT	print a file
ls	DIR	list the files in a directory
man	HELP	access the online help facility
mkdir	MKDIR	create a directory
more	MORE	display a file one screenful at a time
mv	RENAME	rename a file
pico	EDIT	edit a file
pwd	CHDIR	print the name of the current working directory
rm	DEL	delete a file
rmdir	RMDIR	delete a directory
set	SET	turn on a shell variable
setenv	PATH	set your path
shar	BACKUP	create a shell archive
sort	SORT	sort the lines of a text file
tar	BACKUP	create a tape archive
uncompress	EXPAND	expand a file that has been compressed
unshar	EXPAND	unpack a shell archive
vi	EDIT	edit a text file

Unix Command	DOS Command	Description
whatis	HELP	display a brief description of a command
whereis	FIND	search for a file
which	FIND	determine where a command is located

MAPPING FROM DOS TO UNIX COMMANDS

In this appendix we provide a mapping from DOS commands to Unix commands. The DOS commands are listed in alphabetical order. We list only DOS commands for which there is a close Unix equivalent. Of course, not all of the commands match up precisely.

DOS Command	Unix Command	Description
ATTRIB	chmod	change the protections on a file or directory
BACKUP	shar	create a shell archive
BACKUP	tar	create a tape archive
CD	cd	change to another directory
CHDIR	pwd	print the name of the current working directory
CLS	clear	clear the screen
COMPACT	compress	compact the storage space used for a file
COMPACT	gzip	compact the storage space used for a file
COPY	cp	copy a file
DATE	date	display the current date and time
DEL	rm	delete a file
DIR	ls	list the files in a directory
DOSKEY	history	print a list of recently executed commands
ECHO	echo	display a line of text
EDIT	emacs	edit a file

DOS Command	Unix Command	Description
EDIT	pico	edit a file
EDIT	vi	edit a file
EXIT	exit	close your current session on your computer account
EXIT	logout	close your current session on your computer account
EXPAND	gunzip	expand a file that has been compressed
EXPAND	uncompress	expand a file that has been compressed
EXPAND	unshar	unpack a shell archive
FIND	find	locate a file
FIND	grep	search for a pattern in a file
FIND	whereis	search for a file
FIND	which	determine where a command is located
FINDSTR	grep	search for a pattern in a file
FTYPE	file	determine the file type
HELP	apropos	search the online manual for a keyword
HELP	man	access the online help facility
HELP	whatis	display a brief description of a command
LOGIN	login	start work on your computer account
MD	mkdir	create a directory
MKDIR	mkdir	create a directory
MORE	more	display a file one screenful at a time

DOS Command	Unix Command	Description
MOVE	**mv**	rename a file
PATH	**setenv**	set your path
PAUSE	**kill**	terminate a process
PRINT	**lpr**	print a file
PROMPT	**set**	change the prompt
REN	**mv**	rename a file
RENAME	**mv**	rename a file
RESTORE	**tar**	restore files that were backed up
RD	**rmdir**	delete a directory
RMDIR	**rmdir**	delete a directory
SET	**set**	turn on a shell variable
SORT	**sort**	sort the lines of a text file
TYPE	**cat**	concatenate and display files
XCOPY	**cp**	copy files and directory trees

SUMMARY OF PICO COMMANDS

In this appendix we provide a summary of **pico** commands, along with a brief description of each command. Most commands are described in detail in the body of the text.

Recall that the notation **C-A** means hold down the **Control** key and type the **A** key. It is not necessary to type capital **A**, as **pico** is not case sensitive.

Pico Command	Description
C-A	move cursor to beginning of line
C-B	move cursor backward one space
C-C	report current cursor position on the screen
C-E	move cursor to the end of line
C-F	move cursor forward one space
C-G	display **pico** help
C-J	justify text in current paragraph
C-K	cut text
C-N	move cursor to next line
C-O	save file
C-P	move cursor to previous line
C-R	insert file
C-T	invoke the spelling checker
C-U	paste text
C-V	move forward a screen
C-W	search for a pattern of text
C-X	exit **pico** without saving the file
C-Y	move backward a screen
C-Z	suspend **pico**

SUMMARY OF PINE COMMANDS

In this appendix we provide a summary of **pine** commands, along with a brief description of each command. For each of **pine**'s main screens we list the most important commands. Most commands are described in detail in the body of the text.

MAIN MENU SCREEN

Pine Command	Description
?	obtain help
C	compose and send/post a message
I	view messages in the current folder
L	select a folder or newsgroup
A	update the address book
S	configure **pine** options
Q	exit the **pine** program

HELP SCREEN

Pine Command	Description
?	obtain help
C	compose and send/post a message
I	view messages in the current folder
L	select a folder or newsgroup
A	update the address book
S	configure **pine** options
Q	exit the **pine** program

COMPOSE MESSAGE SCREEN From the To Field

Pine Command	Description
C-C	cancel the message
C-D	delete a character
C-G	get help
C-J	attach a file
C-K	cut a line of text
C-O	postpone message composition
C-R	display the rich header
C-T	go to the address book
C-U	paste the cut lines of text
C-V	move to the next page or the end of a single-page message
C-X	send the message
C-Y	move to the previous page or the top of a single-page message

MESSAGE INDEX SCREEN

Pine Command	Description
?	obtain help
C	compose and send/post a message
I	view messages in the current folder
L	select a folder or newsgroup
A	update the address book
S	configure **pine** options
Q	exit the **pine** program

FOLDER LIST SCREEN

Pine Command	Description
C-C	cancel the message
C-D	delete a character

C-G	get help
C-J	attach a file
C-K	cut a line of text
C-O	postpone message composition
C-R	display the rich header
C-T	go to the address book
C-U	paste the cut lines of text
C-V	move to the next page or the end of a single-page message
C-X	send the message
C-Y	move to the previous page or the top of a single-page message

ADDRESS BOOK SCREEN

Pine Command	Description
C-C	cancel the message
C-D	delete a character
C-G	get help
C-J	attach a file
C-K	cut a line of text
C-O	postpone message composition
C-R	display the rich header
C-T	go to the address book
C-U	paste the cut lines of text
C-V	move to the next page or the end of a single-page message
C-X	send the message
C-Y	move to the previous page or the top of a single-page message

SETUP SCREEN

Pine Command	Description
C-C	cancel the message
C-D	delete a character
C-G	get help
C-J	attach a file
C-K	cut a line of text
C-O	postpone message composition
C-R	display the rich header
C-T	go to the address book
C-U	paste the cut lines of text
C-V	move to the next page or the end of a single-page message
C-X	send the message
C-Y	move to the previous page or the top of a single-page message

SUMMARY OF EMACS COMMANDS

In this appendix we provide a list of the most important **emacs** commands described in this book, along with a brief description of each command. More details about each command can be found in the body of the text. The commands are grouped according to how they were presented in the text.

Online Help, Exiting

Emacs Command	Description
C-h t	bring up the **emacs** tutorial
C-h ?	bring up the **emacs** help facility
C-g	cancel a command
C-x C-c	exit **emacs**

Saving Files, Deleting a Character

Emacs Command	Description
Backspace	delete the character to the left of the cursor
Delete	delete the character above the cursor
C-x C-c	exit **emacs**
C-x C-s	save a file
C-x C-w	write out the current buffer

Cursor Movement

Emacs Command	Description
C-a	move to the beginning of a line
C-b	move backward one character

C-e	move to the end of a line
C-f	move forward one character
C-l	redisplay the window, moving the text around the cursor to the center of the screen
C-n	move to the next line
C-p	move to the previous line
C-v	move forward one screen
M-a	move backward to the beginning of a sentence
M-b	move backward one word
M-e	move forward to the end of the sentence
M-f	move forward one word
M-v	move backward one screen

Cutting and Pasting Text

Emacs Command	Description
C-@	set a marker
C-k	cut some text to the kill buffer
C-w	wipe out some text to the kill buffer
C-x u	undo the last edit
C-y	paste the text from the kill buffer
M-d	delete a word to the kill buffer

Search and Query Replace

Emacs Command	Description
C-r	reverse search
C-s	forward search
M->	move to the bottom of a buffer
M-<	move to the top of a buffer
M-%	query replace

Miscellaneous

Emacs Command	Description
C-x C-f	load a file into a buffer
C-x i	insert a file
C-o	switch to the other window
C-x 1	display only the active window on the screen
C-x 2	divide the active window into two windows
C-u n ZZ	execute command ZZ n times

SUMMARY OF VI COMMANDS

In this appendix we provide a list of the most important **vi** commands described in this book, along with a brief description of each command. More details about each command can be found in the body of the text. The commands are grouped according to how they were presented in the text.

Switching Modes

Vi Command	Description
A	switch to **input mode** and be positioned to insert text at the end of the current line
a	switch to **input mode** and be positioned to insert text after the current cursor position
I	switch to **input mode** and be positioned to insert text at the beginning of the current line
i	switch to **input mode** and be positioned to insert text before the current cursor position
O	switch to **input mode**, open a new line above the current line, and be positioned to insert text at the beginning of the newly inserted line
o	switch to **input mode**, open a new line below the current line, and be positioned to insert text at the beginning of the newly inserted line
Escape	switch to **command mode**

Online Help, Exiting

Vi Command	Description
:help	obtain online help information about **vi**
:q	exit **vi**; if you have modified the editing buffer, the editor will not exit
:q!	exit **vi** regardless of whether the last changes have been saved

Saving Files, Deleting a Character

Vi Command	Description
backspace	in **command mode**, delete the character in front of the cursor and move the cursor one character to the left
delete	in **command mode**, delete the character above the cursor
:w	write out the contents of the editing buffer
:w!	write out the contents of the editing buffer even if this means overwriting another file

Cursor Movement

Vi Command	Description
^B	move backward one screen
^D	move forward half a screen
^F	move forward one screen
^U	move backward half a screen
b	move backward to the first character of the previous word
e	move forward to the last character of the next word
h	move backward one character
j	move down to the next line

k	move up to the previous line
l	move forward one character
w	move forward to the first character of the next word
0	move to the beginning of the current line
-	move backward to the beginning of the previous line
+	move forward to the beginning of the next line
$	move to the end of the current line

Deleting and Putting Text

Vi Command	Description
d cursor move	delete from the current cursor location to the location specified by the cursor movement command; the deleted text is placed in the delete buffer
dd	delete the current line of text; the deleted text is placed in the delete buffer
*n*command	repeat the **command** *n* times
p	put the text from the delete buffer into the editing buffer
:set number	turn on line numbering

Search and Replace

Vi Command	Description
?	reverse search
/	forward search
1G	move to the top of a buffer
G	move to the bottom of a buffer
:%s/oldpattern/newpattern/c	search and replace with confirmation

Miscellaneous

Vi Command	Description
^W p	switch to the other window
:new file	split the window and load **file** into the new buffer
:r file	insert **file** into the editing buffer
:split	divide the active window into two windows
*n*ZZ	execute command **ZZ** *n* times

FORMATTING A DOCUMENT IN LATEX

appendix H

In this chapter we introduce the following commands:

Unix Command	DOS Command	Description
dvips	—	convert a dvi file to a PostScript file
ghostview	—	preview a PostScript file
latex	—	process a file using LATEX
xdvi	—	preview a dvi file

H.1 Introduction

LATEX is a document preparation system that is particularly good for formatting computer science material and mathematical documents. Many books and technical papers are formatted using LATEX. This powerful formatting system is easy to use and capable of helping you generate nearly any type of document layout that you would like. In this appendix, our goal is to provide you with an introduction to LATEX so that you can begin to format your work in LATEX. In particular, we cover

- ❏ basic LATEX commands.
- ❏ the process of compiling and printing a LATEX document.
- ❏ how to generate a letter using LATEX.
- ❏ important LATEX environments.
- ❏ formatting mathematical items in LATEX.
- ❏ producing your résumé in LATEX.

For a more in-depth study of LATEX, you can pursue the references provided in this book.

H.2 A Letter Produced with LATEX

The best way to begin learning LATEX is to examine a sample document. A *LATEX document* is just a file containing LATEX code or a hard copy that was produced using LATEX. In Figure H.1 we depict the LATEX code for producing a letter to ABC Airlines. The output actually produced by this LATEX code is shown in Figure H.2. It is a good idea to compare the two figures. By doing this, you can learn a great deal about LATEX formatting commands. In what follows we describe the basic elements contained in the LATEX code for this letter. As we do so, we will also describe a number of important general issues regarding LATEX.

```
\documentclass{letter}

\begin{document}

\address{Sean Davenport\\
2 Abercorn Street\\
Savannah, Georgia 31419\\
e-mail: sean@hotmailer.com}

\signature{Sean Davenport}

\begin{letter}{Consumer Affairs\\
ABC Airlines Inc.\\
Hartsfield International Airport\\
P.O. Box 50\\
Atlanta, GA 30320}

\opening{Dear ABC Airlines Representative,}

This letter is to inform you of a series of baggage
handling problems I have recently had with ABC Airlines.

\begin{enumerate}
\item
In February 2000 I was returning from Los Angeles through
Atlanta to Savannah. My bags were {\em lost}.
\item
In March 2000 I was traveling from Savannah through Atlanta
to Boston. My bags were {\bf lost}.
\item
In May 2000 I returned from Paris through Atlanta to
Savannah. My bags were {\large lost}.
\end{enumerate}
```

```
\closing{Sincerely,}

\end{letter}
\end{document}
```

Figure H.1—LATEX Code for a Standard Letter—
The Output Produced by This Code Is Shown in Figure H.2

Sean Davenport
2 Abercorn Street
Savannah, Georgia 31419
e-mail: sean@hotmailer.com

Consumer Affairs
ABC Airlines Inc.
Hartsfield International Airport
P.O. Box 50
Atlanta, GA 30320

Dear ABC Airlines Representative,

This letter is to inform you of a series of baggage
handling problems I have recently had with ABC Airlines.

1. In February 2000 I was returning from Los Angeles
   through Atlanta to Savannah. My bags were *lost*.

2. In March 2000 I was traveling from Savannah through
   Atlanta to Boston. My bags were **lost**.

3. In May 2000 I returned from Paris through Atlanta to
   Savannah. My bags were lost.

                    Sincerely,

                    Sean Davenport

Figure H.2—A Standard Letter Produced Using LATEX—
The Code for the Letter Is Provided in Figure H.1

We begin our walk through the LATEX code shown in Figure H.1 by first observing that nearly all LATEX commands fit one of the following two syntax models:

- ❑ **\command**
- ❑ **\begin{command}**
  text to be formatted
  \end{command}

That is, commands begin with a \ (backslash) character and are often bracketed by curly braces ({ and }). Sometimes the argument to a command is placed between curly braces. A command having the syntax of the first of these descriptions is

```
\item
```

and a command fitting the latter of these descriptions is

```
\begin{enumerate}
```

```
...
```

```
\end{enumerate}
```

In general, LATEX commands often come in opening and closing pairs.

All LATEX documents begin with the

```
\documentclass{...}
```

command. The **documentclass** informs LATEX what type of information you are formatting. In this case the **documentclass** is **letter**. LATEX has special information coded into it associated with each **documentclass**. The **letter documentclass**, for example, has special commands for **address**, **signature**, **opening**, and **closing**— the various parts of a standard letter. Notice that LATEX positions these elements in specific parts of the output. That is, the position of these elements in the output is not related to their position in the actual file containing the LATEX code. The formatting system takes care of providing the standard layout for a letter; you simply specify the ingredients of the letter.

LATEX provides a variety of **documentclass**es. The ones most commonly used are **article** and **letter**. Others such as **book, report**, and **thesis** exist, as well as many additional styles. We will focus on the **letter** and **article documentclass**es in this book.

After specifying a **documentclass**, you need to begin your LATEX document with the

```
\begin{document}
```

and end it with a corresponding

```
\end{document}
```

command. In the letter shown in Figure H.1, the next element appearing is the return address. This is entered inside the **address** command. The double backslash (\\) is used to denote a line break. Following the return address is the **signature** command. This command inserts its argument at the appropriate place for a signature in a letter and leaves room for you to actually sign the letter, as illustrated in Figure H.2.

The next part of a letter starts with the

```
\begin{letter}
```

command. Notice the corresponding

```
\end{letter}
```

which is required at the end of the body of the letter. The address the letter is being sent to is specified next, with each part of the address on a separate line. This address is followed by the **opening** of the letter. Any text that you type into a LᴬTEX document and separate from other text by a blank line is treated as a paragraph. Paragraphs are formatted in the standard manner. LᴬTEX ignores white space, so extra blank spaces have no significance. They can be used to improve readability in a file without affecting the appearance of the output.

After the first paragraph of the letter, the **enumerate** environment generates a numbered list. It begins with the

```
\begin{enumerate}
```

command and ends with the corresponding

```
\end{enumerate}
```

command. Each item in the list to be numbered is prefaced by the

```
\item
```

command. LᴬTEX numbers the items consecutively. This makes it convenient to move things around and have LᴬTEX automatically renumber correctly. Within the **item**s shown in Figure H.1, we have used three additional formatting commands. They are

❑ **{\em text to be formatted}**

The text to be formatted appearing within the curly braces appears emphasized.

❑ **{\bf text to be formatted}**

The text to be formatted appearing within the curly braces appears in boldface.

❑ **{\large text to be formatted}**
The text to be formatted appearing within the curly braces appears in a large font.

The last part of the letter consists of the **closing** command.

You should now have a good understanding of how to code a simple letter using L^AT_EX. Once you have produced the letter using your favorite editor and working from our template, you still need to be able to process the letter using L^AT_EX. We now describe how to perform this task.

Most Unix systems have a version of L^AT_EX running on them. To use L^AT_EX, you simply enter the command

```
%latex
```

You will get a response such as

```
This is TeX, Version 3.14159 (C version 6.1)
**
```

The ****** is the L^AT_EX prompt.[1] You can now enter the name of the file you wish to process. The file in Figure H.1 is called **abc.tex**. In general, all L^AT_EX files should have a **tex** extension. When you type the name of a file to L^AT_EX and press **Enter**, L^AT_EX will compile the file. It checks to make sure that all the L^AT_EX code is correct. If there is a problem with the code, L^AT_EX will complain and you will need to edit the file to remove the error(s). If your file compiles correctly, L^AT_EX will generate several files for you. These files have the same initial name component as your original file, but a different file extension. The extensions and the contents of these files are as follows:

❑ **log**—A file where you can find a description of the output generated by L^AT_EX created in processing your file.

❑ **aux**—An auxiliary file that contains L^AT_EX-specific information.

❑ **dvi**—A file generated in L^AT_EX output format, which you can convert to PostScript and print.

There are times L^AT_EX will produce additional files as well. For example, if you are working on a book, you might see a **toc** file containing the table of contents. For our purposes, the other types of files L^AT_EX produces are not important. We should note that it is a good idea to delete these auxiliary files after running L^AT_EX. Otherwise, you may find yourself running low on disk space.

After successfully compiling the file **abc.tex** using L^AT_EX, you will see a file called **abc.dvi** in your directory. This file can be converted to a PostScript file using the **dvips** command. For example, typing

---

1. The L^AT_EX system is based on the more general T_EX system. L^AT_EX code is processed by the T_EX system. It is easier to learn how to use L^AT_EX, so we describe it rather than T_EX.

```
%dvips -f abc.dvi -o abc.ps
```

will create the PostScript file **abc.ps**. You can send this file to a PostScript printer in the standard fashion. It is worth noting that **xdvi** is the standard **dvi** previewer for Unix systems, and **ghostview** is the standard PostScript previewer for Unix systems. To preview the **dvi** file **abc.dvi**, simply enter the command

```
%xdvi abc.dvi
```

To preview the PostScript file **abc.ps**, simply enter the command

```
%ghostview abc.ps
```

You can save lots of paper by using the previewer to get your output correct before generating a (final) hard copy.

In summary, the process of a creating the document **abc.tex** using LATEX involves the following basic steps:

1. Create the file **abc.tex** with your favorite editor and format it using the appropriate LATEX commands.
2. Compile the document using **latex**.
3. Debug the document as necessary. This will involve re-editing and recompiling some number of times.
4. Convert the file **abc.dvi** to a PostScript file called **abc.ps**.
5. Preview the file and re-edit as necessary. Return to Step 2 as needed.
6. Send the file **abc.ps** to a PostScript printer.

Exercises

1. Generate a three-paragraph letter to your best friend. Include all of the LATEX elements illustrated in Figure H.1.
2. What happens to your LATEX output if you put an **enumerate** environment inside another **enumerate** environment?
3. Begin selectively deleting items from the LATEX code shown in Figure H.1. What is the least amount of code you can have and still get the "letter" to compile without any LATEX errors?
4. Read the **man page** for the **dvips** command. Report two interesting facts.
5. Write a paragraph describing how to use the **xdvi** previewer. Is there a **man page** on your system for **xdvi**?
6. Write a paragraph describing how to use the **ghostview** previewer. Is there a **man page** on your system for **ghostview**?

H.3   Important LaTeX Environments

In the sample letter shown in Figure H.1, we introduced you to the **enumerate** environment. This environment is used to number items in a list. LaTeX provides several other useful environments as well. We describe the **center**, **description**, **itemize**, and **quote** environments here. In the exercises we ask you to investigate a few additional environments.

The **center** environment is used to center text. To center a heading such as "Big Fish," you could use the following LaTeX code:

```
\begin{center}
Big Fish
\end{center}
```

The result of this code is

Big Fish

By using the line break command, you can center a group of lines all at once.

LaTeX provides the **description** environment as a convenient way of formatting a list of items, each of which has a short, associated description. The syntax for the **description** environment is similar to that of the **enumerate** environment. The LaTeX code in Figure H.3 provides some sample code involving the **description** environment. The result of this code is shown in Figure H.4.

```
\begin{description}
\item[deer fly]
A fast fly with a painful bite.
\item[horse fly]
A super fast fly with a stinging bite.
\item[mosquito]
A troublesome insect that drains your blood.
\item[sand gnat]
A small biting bug that swarms humans.
\end{description}
```

Figure H.3—LaTeX Code for the **Description** Environment—
The Output Produced by This Code Is Shown in Figure H.4

Note that the items being described in the **description** environment are displayed in boldface. Additionally, note how a blank line is placed between successive items in the list produced by LaTeX. If you have a short list of items, you may decide to format it with the **description** environment.

> **deer fly** A fast fly with a painful bite.
> **horse fly** A super fast fly with a stinging bite.
> **mosquito** A troublesome insect that drains your blood.
> **sand gnat** A small biting bug that swarms humans.

Figure H.4—A Description Produced Using LATEX—
The Code for the Description Is Provided in Figure H.3

The **itemize** environment is like the **enumerate** environment except it generates a list where items are marked by bullets (•s), not numbers. The spacing of the items in the list is similar to that of **enumerate**, as is the command syntax.

The **quote** environment is useful if you want to set off a quote from the rest of the text. The text to be quoted is bracketed by

> `\begin{quote}`

and

> `\end{quote}`

pairs. Here is an example of the output produced by the **quote** environment.

> It is not the critic who counts, not the man who points out how the strong man stumbled, or where the doer of deeds could have done them better. The credit belongs to the man who is actually in the arena; whose face is marred by dust and sweat and blood; who strives valiantly, who errs and comes up short again and again; who knows the great enthusiasms, the great devotions, and spends himself in a worthy cause; who, at the best, knows in the end the triumph of high achievement; and who at the worst, at least fails while daring greatly, so that his place shall never be with those cold and timid souls who know neither victory nor defeat. —Teddy Roosevelt

The commands described in this section can serve to format a wide range of text. It is a good idea to experiment with them and to try using them in combination.

Exercises

1. Write a LATEX document that centers the following two lines:
   For never was a story of more woe,
   Than that of Juliet and her Romeo.
2. Produce a list describing the following items: American, Brie, Blue, Gouda, Mozzarella, Parmesan, and Swiss. Include a one-line remark pertaining to each item and format the list using the **description** environment.

3. Produce a bulleted list of your favorite 10 CDs.
4. What is the effect of nesting several **itemize** environments?
5. Produce a nested bulleted list with three items at the outer level and three items within each inner level.
6. Can you nest the **itemize** and **enumerate** environments? Can you think of an application where, if you could nest them, it would come in handy?
7. What are the differences between the **quote** and **quotation** environments?
8. Provide a sample use of the **verse** environment.
9. Is there a **list** environment in LaTeX? If so, describe it.

H.4 Formatting Mathematical Items

LaTeX is the document formatter of choice for a vast number of computer scientists and mathematicians because of the high-quality output it generates and because of its capabilities for formatting mathematics. In this section we touch on some of those capabilities by examining how to format some well-known mathematical formulas.

In order to format mathematics in LaTeX, you must be in **math mode**. The two common ways to include items in **math mode** is between matching dollar signs ($) or between an opening \[and ending \]. An opening dollar sign puts you in **math mode** and a closing dollar sign takes you out of **math mode**. The square bracketing with preceding backslashes puts you in **display math mode**. **Math mode** is used for formatting mathematics within a paragraph and **display math mode** is used for highlighting and centering mathematics by itself.

Suppose we wanted to discuss the well-known formula for the area of a circle. That is, the formula $A = \pi r^2$. We can express this formula inside a paragraph (like this one) using **math mode**. The following LaTeX code can be used to generate the formula:

```
$A = \pi r^2$
```

The same formula would appear in **display math mode** as follows:

$$A = \pi r^2$$

Observe how the formula is set off from the rest of the text and centered. Letters in **math mode** appear in italic font to indicate they are mathematical symbols, and not just standard characters. The caret (^) is used to generate superscripts and the underscore character (_) is used to generate subscripts. For example, H_2O can be produced by

```
$H_20$
```

To produce a multicharacter subscript or superscript, you need to enclose the characters in curly braces.

Notice that in **math mode** the command

```
\pi
```

is used to generate the Greek letter π. By capitalizing the **p**, we can generate a capital Π. Other Greek letters can be obtained similarly, for example, α (α) and β (β).

One of Newton's laws states that force (F) equals mass (M) times acceleration (A). We can format Newton's law using **display math mode**, resulting in the following appearance

$$F = M A$$

The Pythagorean theorem states that the sum of squares of the sides of a right triangle is equal to the square of its hypotenuse. If we use a and b to represent the lengths of the two sides, and c to represent the length of the hypotenuse; then we can express this famous formula as

$$c^2 = a^2 + b^2$$

whose corresponding LaTeX code is

```
\[ c^2 = a^2 + b^2 \]
```

Producing fractions in LaTeX is easy when you use the **frac** command. For example, to generate $\frac{1}{2}$, you can write

```
$\frac{1}{2}$
```

We can generate much more complex expressions and equations such as

$$B(\theta) = \begin{matrix} & a & b & c & d & e & f & g & h \\ 1 & 1 & 1 & 0 & 0 & 0 & 0 & 0 & 0 \\ 2 & 0 & 0 & 1 & 0 & 1 & 0 & 1 & 0 \\ 3 & 0 & 0 & 0 & 1 & 0 & 1 & 1 & 0 \\ 4 & 0 & 0 & 1 & 1 & 1 & 1 & 0 & 0 \end{matrix} . \tag{H.1}$$

as well, but now we are going beyond the scope of this chapter. It should be clear that LaTeX can be used to format nearly any mathematical expression you encounter.

Exercises

1. Write LATEX code to display the following items:
   a. $sin^2\theta + cos^2\theta = 1$
   b. $1+2+3+4+5 = 15$
   c. $1+2+3+4+5 \neq 115$
   d. $10 > 7\frac{3}{4}$
   e. $\frac{1}{2} + \frac{3}{4} = m$

2. Generate the chemical formulas for silicon dioxide and methane in **math mode**.

3. Write LATEX code to display the following items:
   a. $(101)_2 = (5)_{10}$
   b. $(101)_3 = (1010)_2$
   c. $2^{2^2} = 2^4 = 4 \cdot 4 = 4 \times 4 = 8 \cdot 2 = \sum_{i=1}^{16} 1 = 100-84 = \frac{32}{2} = 16$
   d. Produce LATEX code for generating Equation H.1. (*Hint:* Use the **array** and **equation** environments.)

H.5 Producing Your Résumé in LATEX

You have learned a great deal about Unix in this book and also a few things about LATEX. Because the quality of output generated by LATEX is superior to that of other formatters, you will likely decide to format your résumé in LATEX. In this section we present a sample résumé and go over a few additional LATEX commands in the process. You can use the résumé template we present as a starting point for converting your own résumé into LATEX.

Figure H.5 depicts the LATEX code that produced the résumé shown in Figure H.6. The résumé was produced using the **article documentclass**. It is a good idea to compare Figures H.5 and H.6 to see the effect of the various LATEX elements. In what follows, we cover the new material that this example presents.

```
\documentclass{article}

\begin{document}
\begin{center}
{\bf Killface the Cat}\\
In the Woods\\
Savannah, Georgia\\
telephone: (555) 867-5309\\
email: killface@hotmail.com
\end{center}
```

```
{\sf Objective}\\
A contributing position within an organization
that emphasizes eating cat food (preferably salmon
flavored).\\

{\sf Education}\\[-.3in]
\begin{tabbing}
PhD \hspace*{.1in} \= Meowing \hspace*{.2in} \= Massachu-
setts Institute of Technology \= 1995\\
PhD \> Clawing \> California Institute of Technology \>
1993\\
MS \> Shedding \> Oxford University \> 1991\\
BA \> Art \> Pomona College \> 1987
\end{tabbing}

{\sf Experience}\\
Netscape Navigator, HTML, Internet, PC applications\\

{\sf References}\\
Dottie, Julie, Morris, Celeste Noble

\end{document}
```

Figure H.5—LATEX Code for a Résumé—The Output Produced by This Code Is Shown in Figure H.6

Notice that the **center** environment is used to center Killface's address, which consists of multiple lines. The double backslash (\\) line break command is used to separate the various lines in her address. The next thing to notice is that for headings on her résumé Killface uses a sans serif font specified with the **\sf** command. Another interesting thing to notice is that the \\ takes an optional argument. This argument is specified directly after the \\ in square brackets ([ ]). Following the Education heading, the **tabbing** environment is used. This creates some extra unneeded space that is removed by specifying -**.3in** as an optional argument to \\. This command means move the output up .3 inches from where it would have been. The effect is to close up the space left by the **tabbing** environment. If the minus sign (-) were omitted, .3 inches of vertical space would be inserted.

Killface the Cat
In the Woods
Savannah, Georgia
telephone: (555) 867-5309
email: killface@hotmail.com

Objective

A contributing position within an organization that emphasizes eating cat food (preferably salmon flavored).

Education

PhD	Meowing	Massachusetts Institute of Technology	1995
PhD	Clawing	California Institute of Technology	1993
MS	Shedding	Oxford University	1991
BA	Art	Pomona College	1987

Experience

Netscape Navigator, HTML, Internet, PC applications

References

Dottie, Julie, Morris, Celeste Noble

Figure H.6—A Resume Produced Using LaTeX—The Code for the Résumé Is Provided in Figure H.5

The **tabbing** environment allows you to set tabs. Tabs are specified using the \= command, and are moved to using the \> command. Each line in the **tabbing** environment ends with a \\. The command **\hspace*** is used to insert some horizontal space. After PhD, we moved over .1 inches, for example. In Figure H.5 three tabs were set in the **tabbing** environment. They were used to line up the field, institution, and year categories. The tabs you specify are valid only within the **tabbing** environment where you set them. The **tabbing** environment is very versatile and is useful for formatting any text that appears in columns or requires special horizontal spacing.

The LaTeX template for Killface's résumé should give you a good starting point for formatting your own résumé. Do not forget to include your Unix experience in it.

Exercises

1. Produce your résumé in LATEX.
2. Produce a friend's résumé in LATEX (if possible, for someone who aleady had an existing résumé in Word). Compare and contrast the two résumés. Which do you prefer and why?

H.6 Summary

We have touched on the very basics of LATEX here. LATEX is an extremely powerful document-preparation system. There are environments for **figures** and **tables**, and commands for producing virtually every mathematical symbol. You may pursue these other useful facets of LATEX through the references.

ACRONYMS

This appendix contains a list of acronyms that are used in the text. The acronym and its meaning are presented. The list is sorted based on the acronym itself. Page numbers on which the acronym is used can be traced via the index.

ASCII—American Standard Code for Information Interchange

ARPA—Advanced Research Projects Agency

ARPANET—Advanced Research Projects Agency Network

AT&T—American Telephone & Telegraph

BITNET—Because It's Time Network

BBN—Bolt, Beranek, and Newman

BSD—Berkeley Software Distribution

CDE—Common Desktop Environment

CERN—French acronym for the European Laboratory for Particle Physics (Conseil Européen pour la Recherche Nucléaire)

CGI—Common Gateway Interface

CIS—Computer and Information Services

CPU—central processing unit

CSNET—Computer Science Network

DNS—domain name system

FIFO—first-in, first-out

GIF—Graphic Interchange Format

GMT—Greenwich Mean Time

GNU—GNU's Not Unix

GUI—graphical user interface

HTML—Hypertext Markup Language

HTTP—Hypertext Transfer Protocol

IE—Internet Explorer

IP—Internet Protocol

IRC—Internet Relay Chat

ISP—Internet service provider

JPG—Joint Photographic Expert Group

LAN—local area network

MIME—Multipurpose Internet Mail Extensions

MIT—Massachusetts Institute of Technology

MUD—multiuser dungeon

NSF—National Science Foundation

NSFNET—National Science Foundation Network

PC—personal computer

PID—processor identification

RCS—Revision Control System

TCP—Transmission Control Protocol

TCP/IP—Transmission Control Protocol/Internet Protocol

TTY—teletype (used to refer to any terminal)

UCB—University of California at Berkeley

UDE—Unix Desktop Environment

URL—Uniform Resource Locator

USENET—User Network

UUCP—Unix to Unix Copy

VIM—Vi IMproved

WWW—World Wide Web

WYSIWYG—what you see is what you get

account name   A name that identifies you to a computer, also called a userid.

adjacent nodes   Two nodes in a tree that have an edge between them.

algorithm   A well-defined sequence of steps.

alias   An easy-to-remember name associated with a Unix command. The alias is saved by the operating system, and you can use it to refer to the command.

anonymous file transfer   A mechanism that allows any user to transfer a file from a system.

argument   An item that follows a command and is passed to the subroutine that executes the command.

assembly language   A programming language whose instructions are specific to a given type of computer hardware and are difficult for human beings to understand.

authenticate   To verify to the computer that you are who you say you are.

blind carbon copy   A copy of an email message that is sent to another user but without displaying an address for that user in the email message's header.

Bourne shell   The original Unix command interpreter developed by Steven Bourne at Bell Labs.

browser   A software application that provides an interface between users and the Internet. Netscape's Navigator and Microsoft's Internet Explorer are two popular browsers. Browsers are also called "Web clients."

BSD Unix   The Berkeley Software Distribution of the Unix operating system.

children   The children of a node in a tree are the nodes that are adjacent to it and below it.

clickable text   A hyperlink that consists solely of text.

client   A customer in the client-server model.

client-server model   The scheme in which many clients make requests to a small number of servers. The servers respond to clients' requests.

command line   The location on the screen where the Unix prompt is displayed and commands are entered to the Unix operating system.

C-shell   The Unix command interpreter developed by William Joy for BSD Unix.

current working directory   The directory you are in at the present moment.

default password   The initial password you are assigned to grant you access to an online item (for example, your computer account). Default passwords should be changed during your first access. The word default applies in other settings, usually with similar meaning.

dequeueing   The process of removing a job from a print queue.

domain name space   A distributed naming scheme that allows for the assignment of unique names to computers on the Internet.

DOS   The text-based disk operating system developed by Microsoft.

download   The process of moving data from one computer (usually a remote computer) to another computer (usually a local machine).

email   Messages that are sent electronically over a network. The shorthand "email" stands for "electronic mail."

email address   An address of the form **userid@hostname.subdomain.domain** that identifies a specific user's electronic mailbox.

email client   A program designed for managing, reading, composing, and sending email. Synonyms are *mailer, email application,* and *email program.*

emoticons   Symbols made up of keyboard characters designed to express emotion. They are used most commonly in text-only communication such as email. A "smiley" :-) is an example of an emoticon.

executable code   The code that a computer actually runs; it is expressed in a low-level language (binary) that is very difficult for people to understand.

file extension   The part of a file name occurring after the last period.

flag   An option to a command that specifies an alternate meaning for the command.

freeware   Software that you can use at no charge. The author usually retains the copyright on the software, but frequently freeware is unregistered. You usually are not provided with the source code.

frequently asked questions (FAQs)   Questions that many computer users ask. Because the answers to such questions are important to many people, they are usually collected and posted either to a mailing list or to a newsgroup or displayed on a Web page.

graphical user interface (GUI)   A mouse-driven and graphically-oriented computer interface. This is in contrast to a keyboard-driven interface.

help facility   Online documentation that accompanies a software package.

high-level programming language   A programming language that is algorithmic in nature, can be implemented on a variety of different computer systems, and has a syntax that is intuitive and mathematical. Examples of such languages are Ada, APL, BASIC, C, C++, FORTRAN, Java, Lisp, and Pascal.

home directory   The initial file space you are placed in when logging into a Unix system.

home page   The Web page that is loaded when a browser is first activated. Also, the first page in a set of related Web pages.

hyperlink   Text and/or graphics on a Web page that will cause the browser to retrieve and render another Web page or graphic when the hyperlink is selected.

input   Data produced by some source and handed off to another entity for processing.

Internet   A global system of networked computers including their users and data.

Internet address   Numerical computer names that uniquely identify each computer on the Internet. Each address consists of four bytes, where each byte represents a decimal number from 0 to 255. The address is often represented by four decimal numbers separated by dots.

Internet Explorer   The name of Microsoft's Web browser.

Internet Protocol (IP)   One of the primary protocols in the TCP/IP suite. IP specifies how data is routed from computer to computer on the Internet.

Java   An object-oriented programming language that was developed by Sun Microsystems. It is widely used to create dynamic Web pages.

JavaScript   A scripting language that is embedded directly within HTML and is useful for adding some dynamic features to Web pages.

kernel   The inner core of the Unix operating system code.

Linux   A very popular version of free Unix that was created by merging the work of Richard Stallman's GNU project and Linus Torvalds' Unix kernel.

mailbox   A file that holds a user's email messages.

mailer   A program that is used to compose, manipulate, and send email. Synonyms are email application, email client, and email program.

mailing list   A group of users with a shared interest whose email addresses are kept in an electronic list that can be used to send email to each member on the list.

man pages Unix online documentation that comes from the Unix Reference Manual.

netiquette Informal rules of network etiquette.

Netscape Refers to Netscape Communication's Web browser.

operating system A complex computer program that serves as an interface between a computer's hardware and a computer user.

output Processed data that is generated by some entity for display on a device.

parent The parent of a node is the node that is above it and adjacent to it in the tree.

password A secret code that is used to authenticate you to a computer when you log in.

password file The place where information is stored about local user accounts on Unix systems.

path A sequence of adjacent nodes in a tree.

pathname A file or directory name that consists of directory names and possibly a file name separated by /s.

plaintext A message in its original form; that is, not encoded.

portable Describes software that is easy to install on many different computer systems.

print queue The list of jobs to be printed by a printer.

prompt A symbol the computer displays to a user to indicate the computer is ready for input.

public domain software Free software whose source code often is available. There may be guidelines as to how you are "allowed" to modify the original source code.

recursive The property where an object is defined in terms of itself.

root The node at the top of a tree. The root is the only node in a tree without a parent.

root directory The directory at the top level of the Unix file-system hierarchy.

semantics Pertaining to the meaning associated with commands or statements in a given computer language; the interpretation of the syntax of a computer language.

server A resource provider in the client-server model.

shareware Software that you can download and test out for a brief trial period. If you decide to use the software, you pay a small fee. Many times the fee is collected on an honor-system basis.

shell The interactive program, which is part of the Unix operating system, that executes your commands as you enter them. The shell also has its own interpreted programming language.

signature file A file that contains an email signature. A person's signature file is usually appended to all email messages they send.

smiley A happy face, written as :-).

snail mail Regular postal mail; also referred to as "s-mail."

source code Refers to the high-level programming language code for a given program.

spam Inappropriate or junk email.

standard error A diagnostic data stream that is automatically opened and associated with a Unix program. By default, standard output goes to the terminal screen.

standard input An input data stream that is automatically opened and associated with a Unix program. By default, standard input comes from the keyboard.

standard IO A term referring to both Unix standard input and output.

standard output An output data stream that is automatically opened and associated with a Unix program. By default, standard output goes to the terminal screen.

stream A logical path over which data flows.

subdirectory If **A** and **B** are directories in a file space represented by a tree **T**, then **B** is a subdirectory of **A**, if there is a path from **A** to **B** going down **T**.

syntax Pertaining to rules or structure that describe the form of statements in a computer language or operating system.

System V Unix The Unix system that evolved out of AT&T.

time sharing The process of having multiple users served by the same computer resource by allowing each user to have access to the resource in turn.

Transmission Control Protocol (TCP) One of the primary protocols in the TCP/IP suite. TCP defines a set of rules for how computers on the Internet can communicate.

Transmission Control Protocol/Internet Protocol (TCP/IP) The protocol suite that determines how computers connect, send, and receive information on the Internet.

tree A hierarchical, loopless structure composed of nodes and edges; the Unix file system is usually depicted graphically via such an object.

triage   A strategy designed to process the most important items first; for example, dealing with priority email messages first and less important messages second.

Unix   A widely used operating system, particularly in academic, research, and development environments. The system was developed by Ken Thompson, Dennis Ritchie, and several others at Bell Labs in 1969.

Unix Reference Manual   Documentation describing the Unix operating system.

upload   The process of moving data from one computer (usually a local computer) to another computer (usually a remote machine).

usage   An explanation of how a command works and is used in practice. Either a syntactic or semantic description of a command.

userid   A name that identifies you to a computer. Also called a "user name" or "account name."

user portable   A computer system or program where a computer user can move easily from one computer installation to a different one running the same system, and have little or no trouble adjusting to the new system.

vacation program   A program that can be set up to automatically reply to each email message you receive. Such a program is usually installed when you are going to be away for a week or more.

Web   See *World Wide Web*.

Web page or **page**   A file that can be read over the World Wide Web.

Web presentation   A collection of associated and hyperlinked Web pages that usually has some underlying theme.

Web server   A computer that satisfies requests for Web pages.

Web site   An entity on the Internet that publishes Web pages. A Web site typically has a computer serving Web pages, whereas a Web presentation is the actual Web pages themselves.

Windows   An operating system with a graphical user interface developed by Microsoft.

World Wide Web or **Web**   An application that uses the Internet to transport hypertext/multimedia documents. It is also referred to as "WWW."

We used the references listed below as well as many online help facilities and the Unix and Linux operating systems in writing this book. Many of the references listed contain additional material not covered in this book, so they are a good place to begin further exploration of more advanced topics.

Some of our references are Web presentations. Each citation for a Web presentation provides its title (as capitalized by the author), the date the material was last revised, the date the material was accessed on the Web by us, and a URL. Sometimes we just include the URL for the "main page" of a presentation, although we may have read through many other pages on the site.

Armstrong, James, Jr. *A History of UNIX.* 18 July 2000. December 2000. <http://www.ehlis.com/adam/solaris/history.html>

Goossens, Michel, Frank Mittelbach, and Alexander Samarin. *The Latex Companion.* Reading, M.A.: Addison-Wesley, 1994.

Greenlaw, Raymond and Ellen Hepp. *In-Line/On-Line: Fundamentals of the Internet and the World Wide Web.* 2d ed. New York: McGraw-Hill, 2001.

Greenlaw, Raymond and Ellen Hepp. *Introduction to the Internet for Engineers.* New York: McGraw-Hill, 1999.

Hafner, Katie and Matthew Lyon. *Where Wizards Stay Up Late: The Origins of the Internet.* New York: Simon and Schuster, 1996.

Hahn, Harley. *Harley Hahn's Student Guide to Unix.* 2d ed. New York: McGraw-Hill, 1996.

The Internet Society. *History of the Internet.* 22 February 2001. December 1997. <http://www.isoc.org/internet-history/#Introduction>

Kernighan, Brian and Dennis Ritchie. *The C Programming Language.* 2d ed. Upper Saddle River, New Jersey: Prentice Hall, 1988.

Kristula, Dave. *The History of the Internet.* March 1997. December 1997. <http://www.davesite.com/webstation/net-history.shtml>

Lamport, Leslie. *A Document Preparation System: Latex User's Guide and Reference Manual.* Reading, M.A.: Addison-Wesley, 1986.

Lemay, Laura. *Teach Yourself Web Publishing with HTML 3.2 in a Week.* Indianapolis: Sams Publishing, 1996.

Montgomery, John. *An Introduction to Unix.* 27 March 1998. 2000. <http://www.unix-wizards.com/unix.html>

Musciano, Chuck and Bill Kennedy. *HTML: The Definitive Guide.* Sebastopol, C.A.: O'Reilly and Associates, 1996.

The Open Group. *History & Timeline.* 1998. 2000. <http://www.unix-systems.org/what_is_unix/history_timeline.html>

Peterson, Jim and Avi Silberschatz. *Operating System Concepts.* Reading, M.A.: Addison Wesley, 1983.

Public Broadcasting System. *Life on the Internet: Net Timeline.* 1997. <http://www.pbs.org/internet/timeline>

Reichard, Kevin and Eric Foster-Johnson. *UNIX in Plain English.* 3rd ed. Indianapolis: M & T Books, 1999.

Ritchie, Dennis M. *Early Unix history and evolution.* 29 September 2000. December 2000. <http://cm.bell-labs.com/cm/cs/who/dmr/hist.html>

Ross, Seth T. *A Quick History of UNIX.* 6 September 1999. 2000. <http://www.albion.com/security/intro-2.html>

Severance, Charles. *A Brief History of Unix.* 31 May 1995. 2000. <http://www.hsrl.rutgers.edu/ug/unix_history.html>

Siever, Ellen. *Linux in a Nutshell.* 2d ed. Sebastopol, C.A.: O'Reilly and Associates, 1999.

Tanenbaum, Andrew. *Computer Networks.* 3rd ed. Upper Saddle River, New Jersey: Prentice Hall, 1996.

Wang, Paul. *An Introduction to Unix with X and the Internet.* Pacific Grove, C.A.: PWS Publishing Company, 1997.

Yeager, Nancy and Robert McGrath. *Web Server Technology: The Advanced Guide for World Wide Web Information Providers.* San Mateo, C.A.: Morgan Kaufmann Publishers, 1996.

Zakon, Robert. *Hobbes' Internet Timeline - the definitive Internet history.* 19 November 2000. December 2000. <http://www.zakon.org/robert/internet/timeline>

PREPARING
THE WAY OF
THE LORD